Praise for *On Value and Values*

"*On Value and Values* by Doug Smith is a radiant, intelligent, wonderfully readable book. It is part adventure story in the spirit of Robert Pirsig's *Zen and the Art of Motorcycle Maintenance*, part guidebook for American leaders like *In Search of Excellence* by Tom Peters and Robert Waterman. This impressive book will challenge everyone who reads it and give them a blueprint for changing their lives. Virtually every part of American life has become a marketplace, with the pursuit of prosperity driving out an appreciation of principle. Smith explains how our understanding about the relationship between these elementary concepts has been turned inside out. As a compelling alternative, he shows how the pursuit of personal values we hold dear allows us to increase all kinds of value in our lives."

—Lincoln Caplan, Editor and President,
Legal Affairs magazine

"In the grand tradition of Aristotle's *Politics,* Alexis de Tocqueville's *Democracy in America,* and Robert Putman's *Bowling Alone,* Doug Smith's book *On Value and Values* is a passionately written, ethically informed, and carefully researched social commentary. Like his illustrious predecessors, Smith demands that we think differently about what community means in our own times. Yet unlike most writers concerned with building community, Smith is unburdened by nostalgia or sentimentality—this book looks forward to a challenging tomorrow, not backwards at a lost yesterday. Based on deep thought and on an equally deep practical knowledge of how modern organizations really work, Doug Smith teaches us why we may hope for a bright future and what we need to do in order to get there. I will recommend this book to my students—as I recommend it to everyone seeking to conjoin material success and ethical values in the 21st century."

—Professor Josiah Ober,
Department of Classics and Center for Human Values,
Princeton University

On Value and Values

Thinking Differently About We in an Age of Me

Douglas K. Smith

FT Prentice Hall

FINANCIAL TIMES

An Imprint of PEARSON EDUCATION

Upper Saddle River, NJ • New York • London • San Francisco • Toronto • Sydney
Tokyo • Singapore • Hong Kong • Cape Town • Madrid
Paris • Milan • Munich • Amsterdam

www.ft-ph.com

Library of Congress Cataloging-in-Publication Data

Smith, Douglas K.
   On value and values : thinking differently about we in an age of me / by Douglas K. Smith
      p. cm
   Includes bibliographical references and index.
   ISBN 0-13-146125-7
      1. Values. 2. Value. I. Title.
BJ1031.S63 2004
121'.8--dc22   2003064360

Editor-in-Chief *Tim Moore*
Developmental Editor: *Russ Hall*
Editorial/Production Supervision: *Donna Cullen-Dolce*
Cover Design Director: *Jerry Votta*
Cover Design: *Nina Scuderi*
Interior Design: *Gail Cocker-Bogusz*
Manufacturing Buyer: *Maura Zaldivar*
Marketing Manager: *John Pierce*
Editorial Assistant: *Richard Winkler*

 © 2004 Pearson Education, Inc.
Publishing as Financial Times Prentice Hall
Upper Saddle River, New Jersey 07458

Financial Times Prentice Hall offers excellent discounts on this book when ordered in
quantity for bulk purchases or special sales. For more information, please contact: U.S.
Corporate and Government Sales, 1-800-382-3419, corpsales@pearsontechgroup.com.
For sales outside of the U.S., please contact: International Sales, 1-317-581-3793,
international@pearsontechgroup.com.

Printed in the United States of America

1st Printing

ISBN 0-13-146125-7

Pearson Education Ltd.
Pearson Education Australia Pty, Limited
Pearson Education Singapore, Pte. Ltd.
Pearson Education North Asia Ltd.
Pearson Education Canada, Ltd.
Pearson Educación de Mexico, S.A. de C.V.
Pearson Education—Japan
Pearson Education Malaysia, Pte. Ltd

for jane
with love

In an increasingly competitive world, it is quality
of thinking that gives an edge—an idea that opens new
doors, a technique that solves a problem, or an insight
that simply helps make sense of it all.

We work with leading authors in the various arenas
of business and finance to bring cutting-edge thinking
and best learning practice to a global market.

It is our goal to create world-class print publications
and electronic products that give readers
knowledge and understanding which can then be
applied, whether studying or at work.

To find out more about our business
products, you can visit us at www.ft-ph.com

FINANCIAL TIMES PRENTICE HALL BOOKS

For more information, please go to www.ft-ph.com

Business and Society

Douglas K. Smith
> *On Value and Values: Thinking Differently About We in an Age of Me*

Business and Technology

Sarv Devaraj and Rajiv Kohli
> *The IT Payoff: Measuring the Business Value of Information Technology Investments*

Nicholas D. Evans
> *Business Innovation and Disruptive Technology: Harnessing the Power of Breakthrough Technology…for Competitive Advantage*

Nicholas D. Evans
> *Consumer Gadgets: 50 Ways to Have Fun and Simplify Your Life with Today's Technology…and Tomorrow's*

Faisal Hoque
> *The Alignment Effect: How to Get Real Business Value Out of Technology*

Economics

David Dranove
> *What's Your Life Worth? Health Care Rationing…Who Lives? Who Dies? Who Decides?*

John C. Edmunds
> *Brave New Wealthy World: Winning the Struggle for World Prosperity*

Jonathan Wight
> *Saving Adam Smith: A Tale of Wealth, Transformation, and Virtue*

Entrepreneurship

Oren Fuerst and Uri Geiger
> *From Concept to Wall Street: A Complete Guide to Entrepreneurship and Venture Capital*

David Gladstone and Laura Gladstone
> *Venture Capital Handbook: An Entrepreneur's Guide to Raising Venture Capital, Revised and Updated*

Thomas K. McKnight
> *Will It Fly? How to Know if Your New Business Idea Has Wings… Before You Take the Leap*

Erica Orloff and Kathy Levinson, Ph.D.
> *The 60-Second Commute: A Guide to Your 24/7 Home Office Life*

Jeff Saperstein and Daniel Rouach
> *Creating Regional Wealth in the Innovation Economy: Models, Perspectives, and Best Practices*

Stephen Spinelli, Jr., Robert M. Rosenberg, and Sue Birley
> *Franchising: Pathway to Wealth Creation*

Executive Skills

Cyndi Maxey and Jill Bremer
It's Your Move: Dealing Yourself the Best Cards in Life and Work

Finance

Aswath Damodaran
The Dark Side of Valuation: Valuing Old Tech, New Tech, and New Economy Companies

Kenneth R. Ferris and Barbara S. Pécherot Petitt
Valuation: Avoiding the Winner's Curse

International Business

Peter Marber
Money Changes Everything: How Global Prosperity Is Reshaping Our Needs, Values, and Lifestyles

Fernando Robles, Françoise Simon, and Jerry Haar
Winning Strategies for the New Latin Markets

Investments

Zvi Bodie and Michael J. Clowes
Worry-Free Investing: A Safe Approach to Achieving Your Lifetime Goals

Aswath Damodaran
Investment Fables: Exposing the Myths of "Can't Miss" Investment Strategies

Harry Domash
Fire Your Stock Analyst! Analyzing Stocks on Your Own

David Gladstone and Laura Gladstone
Venture Capital Investing: The Complete Handbook for Investing in Businesses for Outstanding Profits

D. Quinn Mills
Buy, Lie, and Sell High: How Investors Lost Out on Enron and the Internet Bubble

D. Quinn Mills
Wheel, Deal, and Steal: Deceptive Accounting, Deceitful CEOs, and Ineffective Reforms

John Nofsinger and Kenneth Kim
Infectious Greed: Restoring Confidence in America's Companies

John R. Nofsinger
Investment Blunders (of the Rich and Famous)…And What You Can Learn from Them

John R. Nofsinger
Investment Madness: How Psychology Affects Your Investing…And What to Do About It

H. David Sherman, S. David Young, and Harris Collingwood
Profits You Can Trust: Spotting & Surviving Accounting Landmines

Leadership

Jim Despain and Jane Bodman Converse
And Dignity for All: Unlocking Greatness through Values-Based Leadership

Marshall Goldsmith, Vijay Govindarajan, Beverly Kaye, and Albert A. Vicere
The Many Facets of Leadership

Marshall Goldsmith, Cathy Greenberg, Alastair Robertson, and Maya Hu-Chan
Global Leadership: The Next Generation

Management

Rob Austin and Lee Devin
Artful Making: What Managers Need to Know About How Artists Work

J. Stewart Black and Hal B. Gregersen
Leading Strategic Change: Breaking Through the Brain Barrier

William C. Byham, Audrey B. Smith, and Matthew J. Paese
Grow Your Own Leaders: How to Identify, Develop, and Retain Leadership Talent

David M. Carter and Darren Rovell
On the Ball: What You Can Learn About Business from Sports Leaders

Subir Chowdhury
Organization 21C: Someday All Organizations Will Lead this Way

Ross Dawson
*Living Networks: Leading Your Company, Customers, and Partners
in the Hyper-connected Economy*

Charles J. Fombrun and Cees B.M. Van Riel
Fame and Fortune: How Successful Companies Build Winning Reputations

Amir Hartman
Ruthless Execution: What Business Leaders Do When Their Companies Hit the Wall

Harvey A. Hornstein
*The Haves and the Have Nots: The Abuse of Power and Privilege in the Workplace…
and How to Control It*

Kevin Kennedy and Mary Moore
Going the Distance: Why Some Companies Dominate and Others Fail

Roy H. Lubit
Coping with Toxic Managers, Subordinates…and Other Difficult People

Robin Miller
The Online Rules of Successful Companies: The Fool-Proof Guide to Building Profits

Fergus O'Connell
The Competitive Advantage of Common Sense: Using the Power You Already Have

Tom Osenton
The Death of Demand: The Search for Growth in a Saturated Global Economy

W. Alan Randolph and Barry Z. Posner
*Checkered Flag Projects: 10 Rules for Creating and Managing Projects that Win,
Second Edition*

Stephen P. Robbins
Decide & Conquer: Make Winning Decisions to Take Control of Your Life

Stephen P. Robbins
The Truth About Managing People…And Nothing but the Truth

Ronald Snee and Roger Hoerl
  Leading Six Sigma: A Step-by-Step Guide Based on Experience with GE and Other Six Sigma Companies
Susan E. Squires, Cynthia J. Smith, Lorna McDougall, and William R. Yeack
  Inside Arthur Andersen: Shifting Values, Unexpected Consequences
Jerry Weissman
  Presenting to Win: The Art of Telling Your Story

Marketing

David Arnold
  The Mirage of Global Markets: How Globalizing Companies Can Succeed as Markets Localize
Michael Basch
  CustomerCulture: How FedEx and Other Great Companies Put the Customer First Every Day
Jonathan Cagan and Craig M. Vogel
  Creating Breakthrough Products: Innovation from Product Planning to Program Approval
Al Lieberman, with Patricia Esgate
  The Entertainment Marketing Revolution: Bringing the Moguls, the Media, and the Magic to the World
Tom Osenton
  Customer Share Marketing: How the World's Great Marketers Unlock Profits from Customer Loyalty
Bernd H. Schmitt, David L. Rogers, and Karen Vrotsos
  There's No Business That's Not Show Business: Marketing in Today's Experience Culture
Yoram J. Wind and Vijay Mahajan, with Robert Gunther
  Convergence Marketing: Strategies for Reaching the New Hybrid Consumer

Personal Finance

Steve Weisman
  A Guide to Elder Planning: Everything You Need to Know to Protect Yourself Legally and Financially

Public Relations

Gerald R. Baron
  Now Is Too Late: Survival in an Era of Instant News
Deirdre Breakenridge and Thomas J. DeLoughry
  The New PR Toolkit: Strategies for Successful Media Relations

Strategy

Edward W. Davis and Robert E. Spekmam
  The Extended Enterprise: Gaining Competitive Advantage through Collaborative Supply Chains
Joel M. Shulman, With Thomas T. Stallkamp
  Getting Bigger by Growing Smaller: A New Growth Model for Corporate America

Contents

Acknowledgments   xiii

Preface   xv

Chapter 1   On Value and Values   1

Chapter 2   A World of Purposes, not Places   19

Chapter 3   The Split   35

Chapter 4   Explaining Values   51

Chapter 5   Shared Paths   65

Chapter 6   Consumers and Employees   77

Chapter 7   Investors   93

Chapter 8   Ideas and Purposes, 1   107

Chapter 9   Ideas and Purposes, 2   125

Chapter 10   Civil Society   141

Chapter 11   Community   159

Chapter 12   Democracy   173

Chapter 13   Governance and Problem Solving   187

Chapter 14   The Greatest Good and the Common Good   207

Chapter 15   Capital and Caring   219

Chapter 16   So What?   235

Chapter 17   Illustrative Suggestions   251

                Index   277

Acknowledgments

Tim Moore and Russ Hall contributed mightily to this book. Charlie Baum, Donna Cullen-Dolce, Steve Dichter, Jon Fullerton, Henning Gutmann, Susan Webber, Anita Kiewra, Mike Loftin, Brook Manville, Josh Ober, Mark Singer, and Alena Smith helped. I am grateful to thousands of people with whom I've worked in scores of organizations. I would also like to thank many who have taught me so much about blending value and values in good lives—especially Aki, Amy, Ann, Ann, Alan, Alena, Art, Bea, Bill, Bob, Bob, Bob, Brad, Brian, Brian, Brook, Cam, Carole, Chad, Charlie, Chip, Chris, Christine, Dale, Dave, David, Dennis, Diana, Dick, Don, Don, Don, Dwight, Eben, Ellen, Ellen, Faith, Felix, Gene, Georgia, Geraldine, Hazel, Howard, Iris, Izzy, Jack, Jack, Jan, Jane, Jared, Jay, Jay, Jean, Jeffrey, Jenna, Jennifer, Jennifer, Jenny, Jerilyn, Jim, John, John, Jon, Jonathan, Joy, Judy, Julien, Katrina, Katz, Kim, Kurt, Larry, Laurie, Leo, Logan, Lupi, Lynn, Mac, Marcia, Margaret, Mark, Mark, Marsha, Marty, Mary, Mike, Nancy, Natalie, Paula, Peggy, Peter, Phia, Phil, Posey, Rebecca, Rhonda, Rick, Rudite, Ruth, Sally, Sandy, Sarah, Shinichi, Steve, Steve, Susan, Ted, Terry, Tinky, Tom, Tricia, Vicky, Vivian, and Yoon Jung.

PREFACE

As this book reaches readers in the spring of 2004, people the world over, and especially Americans, turn attention to the quadrennial presidential election in the globe's most powerful and influential market democracy. The twin towers of that democracy—individual political liberty and self-interested market economics—took root in 18th and 19th centuries bearing little resemblance to our 21st century. In 1776, the United States formed in revolt against a royal "we" whose oppressions of individual liberty and the pursuit of happiness were intolerable. Today, an opposite condition prevails. Hundreds of millions of people in market democracies across the globe are more absorbed with concerns about "me" than any "we," royal or otherwise.

Today, political liberties are consumed in self-interested market economics. This year's presidential contest plays out in markets. A profound 18th century innovation—building a nation in which all are created equal—is today vulnerable to 21st century market, economic, and technological forces that have catapulted concern for value, money, and winning above concerns for political liberties, social equalities, religious faith, environmental stewardship, technological access, medical fairness, and the rule of law. Those other values have not evaporated or disappeared. They pervade and trouble our lives. But, with the exception of religious faith, they have retreated in the face of extreme fundamentalism centered on value and individualism.

Beyond friends and family, we have lost a center of gravity joining value with values. If we look hard enough, we see why: the fragmenting of traditional "we's" in which people share fates because of the places they live together. The split between value and values is a corollary of "I's" who have spun out of orbit from "we's." Those of us who live in markets, networks, nations, and organizations no longer belong to place-based traditional "we's." Therefore, we must learn to think differently about "we" in this age of "me" if we are to have any chance of putting "me" back into "we's" that are *real*.

This book is a guide for our efforts. Chapters 1 through 3 describe the world in which so many of us live: a world of markets, networks, nations, organizations, friends and family. I call this a *world of purposes* and contrast it to the *world of places* our parents and grandparents inhabited. Billions of people on the planet continue to live—and to share fates—because of places. But not us. What we share with others—fates, ideas, roles, relationships—depends more on the purposes we bring to markets, networks, and organizations than the places we reside. Chapters 1 through 3 draw this world of purposes to help you figure out how and why purpose and place shape the values you share with others.

The characteristic ethical challenge in our world of purposes is rejoining value and values. Chapters 1 through 3 recount how concerns for value (money and wealth) have split off and subordinated concerns for other values. Strongly shared and predictable beliefs and behaviors—shared values of all sorts—arise among people who share relationships, roles, status, ideas, and, especially, fates. In a world of places, these sources of shared values reinforced one another to produce highly predictable beliefs and behaviors that were sometimes excellent, sometimes atrocious, sometimes indifferent. Our new world of markets, networks, nations, organizations, friends and families has transformed the operation and effects of the sources of shared values. Our shared relationships differ, our shared roles differ, our shared ideas differ. We share fates with other people in friends, family, and organizations, not places. Chapters 4 through 9 describe how humanity's sources of shared values—relationships, roles, ideas, fates—have morphed in markets, networks, and organizations to foster powerful forces with which we must contend if we are to build shared values.

Chapters 10 through 15 recount our contemporary experience of the twin towers of market democracies—political liberty and self-interested economics—as well as a series of corollary values. What we believe and how we behave with regard to liberty and civil society (Chapter 10), community (Chapter 11), democracy (Chapter 12), problem solving and governance (Chapter 13), the common good and the greatest good (Chapter 14), and capitalism and caring (Chapter 15) play out in markets, networks, nations, and organizations, and among friends and families, instead of places. We encounter our most fertile experiences of such values in organizations that, in turn, have become the most crucial and real "we" beyond friends and family. Chapters 10 through 15 help us see that, by using organizations to think differently about "we," all of us can act to restore value to the house of values in our world of purposes.

Chapter 16 lays out a five-part strategy for blending value and values in how we live our lives. It delineates a framework for ethical action through which we can reconnect making a good living to leading a good life. Chapter 17 describes a number of specific suggestions for taking action within the ethical framework of Chapter 16.

That we must find the courage to act is, I think, what Thomas Jefferson would have called self-evident and Adam Smith prudent. The twin towers of 21st century market democracies rise from the works authored by these two men in 1776. That year *The Declaration of Independence* and *The Wealth of Nations* launched humanity on a journey toward "I's" and "we's" who could fulfill the best in our natures. That path is now gravely threatened. An extreme individualism equating happiness with value alone now trumps choices and policies made in markets of all kinds, political and otherwise. "We" are in retreat because so many place-based "we's" in which we once experienced shared fates have become the imaginary "we's" of small towns, neighborhoods, and communities in which we don't. *Value and "I"* can never migrate back into a sustainable blend with *values and "we"* unless "we's" are real instead of imagined. Those of us who live in a world of purposes must think differently about the real "we's" of our lives—especially our organizations—and purposefully blend value and values in those "we's" in ways that will not shame or condemn our children.

Jefferson and Smith, along with so many others, left us a legacy of celebrated, excellent values. We must act to preserve and extend those values. The twin towers of political liberty and self-interested market economics are *our* responsibility. Oddly, though certainly, our legacy depends on rediscovering how "we's"—real "we's"—give life to the freedom and happiness of "I's" if we are to save the "I" from self-destruction. We must work *together*, learn *together* and pray *together* in real "we's" so that peace and prosperity spread to all the world, and our children inherit a bountiful and good future to pass on to their children. We must act. But, first we must see who and when we are a real we capable of shared purpose and shared action because the twin towers of freedom and happiness—and the fate of the planet—now belong to us.

1 On Value and Values

For many years now, I have heard people speak about value and values disjointedly, as though the singular, value, and the plural, values, are alienated from one another. *Value* arises in conversations about economics, finance, shopping, investment, business, and markets. People worry about getting value for money or shareholder value or market value. They use value to describe business or economic prospects. Value connotes a pointed estimation of current or anticipated worth never too distant from monetary equivalence. There is no value that is not a dollar value.

The plural values, meanwhile, crops up when people talk about beliefs and behaviors regarding how human beings do or do not get along with one another and with gods, spirits, and nature. Values are nouns, but nouns concerned with verbs of attitude and action. Values sort into several categories. People refer to social values and political values; and, to family and religious, and environmental values. Values are estimations not of worth but of worthwhileness. Unlike value, talk of values ignores money; it opines on timeless appraisals instead of transient ones. There is a deep, backward- and forward-looking quality to values. If value is what makes us wealthy, values, we assume and regularly assert, are what make us human.

Conversations about value seem more hard-nosed and action-able than those about values. And why not? We live in an age of pro-digious value creation. In degree, kind, and number, the material

1

well-being of hundreds of millions of people exceeds any the most inventive and insightful of our ancestors imagined. Economic reversals to one side, we do an amazingly fine job of generating value. Our most effective and enduring social formations—markets, networks, and organizations—are both causes and effects of our confidence in value.

Discussions of values, particularly other people's values, sound more like lamentations than celebrations. We wring our hands. We worry. We remind ourselves that values matter. We exhort ourselves to be better. Meanwhile, we awake each day to some headline, movie, music, advertisement, or poll that makes us flinch. Unlike our attitude toward value, we remain profoundly uncertain about how to deepen, enrich, and syndicate values beyond exhortation.

Mostly, we keep talking. Occasionally, of course, I have heard conversations about values blend with discussions about value. Nearly always, people connect value and values once I raise the pattern with them. Still, I am unaware of other, similar semantic habits. There are words—deer, armor, shrimp, furniture—whose plural and singular are identically spelled. Notwithstanding the orthographic oddity, though, a single deer is routinely considered one of a larger, plural group of deer.

It seems that, having slipped into separate conversational streams, value and values have each evolved this way. As with deer or armor, we use adjectives to distinguish one form of *values* from another, one kind of *value* from another kind. There are social values, political values, family values, and religious values. We also speak about economic value, shareholder value, market value, investment value, customer value, and so on. But value itself has lost its perch among values. Unlike deer, the singular value is not spoken of as a subset of the plural values.

Value and values have diverged. We behave as if value were a different species than values, like deer versus shrimp. This split may be only a curiosity, something William Safire or his successor as celebrity semanticist might review in a Sunday column. But I don't think so. To me, it is our Minotaur—that long ago half-man, half-bull progeny of venality, passion, and cleverness, of the pursuit of value without reference to values.

Instead of half-bull, half-man, however, our freak is half-dollar, half-human. Our Labyrinth is a new world of purposes: the unprecedented constellations of markets, networks, organizations, friends, and families in which a growing number of us live as consumers, employees, investors, networkers, family members, and friends. If you live in *this* world, then, likely as not, you worry about the deep chasm separating value and values.

You venerate democracy, but know that too few eligible voters go to the polls in most state, local, and federal elections (perhaps, at times, including yourself). You plead with your children about the importance of education; and watch as learning deteriorates from market battles more concerned with adults and money than students and learning. You know that environmental damage goes mostly unaccounted for by organizations and markets. But it often seems the organizations best positioned to find sustainable approaches are the least concerned or the most extreme. You fear the geopolitical struggle now pitting terrorists and despots against market democracies. But you worry that a materialistic culture obsessed with value may offer insufficient promise to people seeking alternatives to fundamentalism and tyranny.

You want more meaning in your life; you want to make a difference. But you already have so little time beyond what you spend at work, at home, and with friends. You think spiritual concerns should have a higher profile in people's lives. But not the profile on display in a Catholic Church beset by priestly pedophilia, an Islam hijacked by terrorists and princes, a sometimes racist Protestantism fueled by white flight or black hate, or a belligerent Israel that can appear to have forgotten the lessons of the Holocaust. You understand that financial security requires risk taking in capital markets. But you awake each day to greed, self-dealing, and gimmicky gamesmanship among companies and the auditors, accountants, and lawyers who enforce the rules. You are filled with glee when your side wins—at sports, at work, in politics. You feel like shouting "Yessss!!" But you worry that, Vince Lombardi's famous dictate to the contrary, perhaps winning is *not* the only thing.

The world has turned mean and dangerous. It seems to lack a center of gravity. When you ask why, your answer all too often concerns values. If so, you need to find some way to bridge the divide separating value from values. *You* must do so; no one is going to do it for you. Here's a way to start: *reconnect value and values in the markets, networks, organizations, families, and friends within which you actually live your life. Do so as employees in organizations, as consumers and investors in markets, and as networkers in networks.*

Put aside places we call the United States and England—or Ohio, Atlanta, and Tokyo. You do not *live* the *active* part of your life in such places anymore. Yes, they matter. Citizens of nations like the United States, Japan, and France have rights and opportunities that are the envy of hundreds of millions of people around the globe. But few of us *live* life as citizens of the United States. Instead, tens of millions of us *live* as friends and families, and as consumers, employees, investors, and networkers in markets, organizations, and networks. It is in markets, organizations, and networks, and among family and friends that you spend your time, pursue your most pressing purposes, and find meaning in your life. If you want to connect your life to the lives of others on a foundation that blends value and values—*if you want to live good lives and make a difference*—then act *within* the organizations, markets, and networks within which you actually conduct your life today. Restore value and values to the center of gravity of *those* social formations, and do so in a manner to inspire and not shame your children.

· ·

This book frames ethical challenges we face in our efforts to lead good lives as consumers, networkers, investors, employees, family members, and friends. Ethical questions are as old as human time. People in every age have confronted the task of leading a good life. Thousands of philosophers, theologians, leaders, and teachers have proposed answers worth consulting. As we make our way forward, I do not suggest ignoring any of them. I contend, however, that our most pressing dilemma—how to reintegrate value and values—is unprecedented. Not because it is a new question. *Rather, our dilemma is unparalleled because the future of humanity now rests on how hundreds of millions of us blend value and values in markets, networks, and organizations, and among friends and families, as opposed to places.*

THE VOCABULARY OF VALUE AND VALUES

Certain words and phrases are key to understanding the concepts being shared throughout the book. For convenience, a short list, along with an explanation of each term, is provided here:

Shared Values: Actual beliefs, behaviors, attitudes, and speech regarding social, political, economic, family, religious, technological, environmental, and other matters. Shared values are strong when predictable (regardless of whether any of us might consider them good or bad).

Shared Paths: Relationships formed among a consistent number of people who are known to one another by name and who persistently interact over some open-ended time frame.

Shared Roles and Status: Functional roles (e.g., consumer) and status positions (e.g., boss) that people mutually recognize and actually adopt in their day-to-day lives. As used throughout this book, "employee" is a shared role that includes paid work as well as volunteers who contribute meaningful time to formal and informal organizations in which they participate

Shared Ideas: Ideas about which people share some understanding, even if it is a misunderstanding.

Shared Fates: The inescapable, tangible, and everyday sense that one's interests and purposes depend on other people. This is a felt sense of shared fates as opposed to an abstract one. In the abstract, we all share fates with six billion people on Earth. In an everyday, felt sense, we do not.

Thick We's: People who inescapably share fates with one another. Thick we's inevitably must balance self-interest with their common good. They must implement their common good together because they share fates.

Thin We's: People who have similar interests, but do not share fates with one another. Thin we's have no need to implement a common good together.

Collectivities of I's: Groups identified as market or network segments because of similar interests, motivations, demographics, or other criteria. Collectivities of I's are thin we's.

Common Good: The shared purposes and shared values of a thick we. In an organization, for example, the common good is often described in a statement of vision or mission. Thick we's are responsible for implementing their common good together. "We" is the highest common denominator in the common good of a thick we.

Greater Good: Any number of interests or purposes that might define or measure happiness in large social formations, such as markets, networks, and nations. Calculation of the greatest good for the greatest number requires a single, lowest common denominator (e.g., money).

Social Formations: Contexts that bring people into contact with one another. Family and friends are small social formations. Markets, networks, and nations are large ones.

Mid-level Social Formation: A social formation in which people who are not necessarily friends or family share fates with one another.

World of Places: Any world in which the power of place forges strong shared values. In world of places, place-based social formations, such as towns or villages, are thick we's.

World of Purposes: A world in which place has lost its power to blend and shape strong shared values. A world of purposes has six social formations: markets, networks, nations, organizations, friends, and family. Organizations are the crucial mid-level social formation and thick we in a world of purposes.   ∎

. . . .

This dramatic shift in context demands that we think differently about "we." One starting point comes from the philosopher Avishai Margalit. In his book *The Ethics of Memory*, Margalit distinguishes thick we's from thin we's. Thin we's, he writes, have a single bond: humanity. Thick we's comprise sturdier stuff: shared national, religious, and ethnic culture enriched by family and friendship. Thick relationships are constructed around caring and hatred; they produce more interesting ethics than thin ones. In a world shaped meaningfully by place, thick relationships arise among people who *inescapably and self-consciously share fates* because of the places they live together. *Billions of people still live in such places, including many millions in the developed world.* But hundreds of millions of us no longer live together in places. Instead, we live in a world shaped more by our purposes than the places we reside. Yet, our ethics matter not only to ourselves but also to those who continue to live in a world of places because—as cheerleaders and critics of globalization and religious fundamentalism have noted—*we* have the whip hand of the planet's most powerful forces.

Our we's emerge in markets, networks, and organizations— social formations that have reconstituted what is thick, what is thin, and when and why we inescapably share fates. We are no longer merely fellow humans to millions of people who are otherwise strangers. Instead, our relationships are thickened by being employees, customers, or investors—by sharing well-understood roles that sustain predictable beliefs and behaviors. When any of us, for example, order a sweater over the phone or go to the mall or a movie, our interactions as customers with the employees serving us reflect shared values thicker than the slender thread of common humanity. Meanwhile, residing in the same place—the same town, city, or neighborhood—is less certain to thicken relationships than it once was. Our relationships are thicker with those with whom we work together in organizations than live together in towns. We are more likely to have thick relationships with people at work and thin ones with neighbors down the block or around the corner.

It makes for a differently ordered human experience. As individuals and groups, we live in markets, organizations, networks, and among families and friends. *Our markets, networks, and organizations are wholly intertwined.* This is not theory. We do not live in theoretical markets, theoretical networks, and theoretical organizations. We do not shop in theoretical malls, log onto a theoretical Net, or go to work in a theoretical organization. We live in real markets, networks and organizations—and we live in them together. Only oddly so when contrasted with humanity's long experience in a world of places. We are interdependent and isolated simultaneously. We share lives with millions of people with whom we have more than thin relationships but less than thick ones.

We know this. Yet, we must ask if we appreciate and accept our responsibilities as ethical actors within *this world*. We know, for example, that no boundaries of land or water—or legal jurisdiction— seal off the values of Europeans or Asians from those of Australians, Africans, or Americans North or South. We know that place cannot distance us from the beliefs, behaviors, attitudes, and speech of others, including terrorists, fundamentalists, and tyrants. Tomorrow morning, you will pick up your newspaper or turn on the radio and learn about a person or group whose activities can reach into *your* life and shake it up for good or ill. Some accounts are dramatic. They create what Margalit calls flash bulb memories: the terrorist attacks of September 11th, 2001, public school killings, accidents at nuclear facilities. Others fade, such as Japan's persistent failure to revitalize its economy, the chemical industry's success in avoiding costly anti-terrorist preparation, the aging fleet of commercial aircraft, and the break up of one conglomerate or the emergence of another. Unlike flash bulb recollections, we tend to forget such stories. *But we cannot escape the anxieties they foster*. Those linger in our souls. We have no *place* to hide from them. We cannot escape because, in our world, all news is local.

We know value reigns in markets, networks, and organizations. But we have not come to grips with what to do about it—in part, because we rightly cherish the value bestowed on us. We should be fair to ourselves. This new reality has exploded upon us. We can find harbingers in political, economic, technological, and other developments that are centuries old. But hundreds of millions of us have only just transitioned into this new world over the past two or three decades. It has happened that fast.

This suddenness suggests we have much to gain by rethinking our past as well as our future. We must be careful, however, with the lessons drawn and the time we take to draw them. Our new reality is profoundly different. It decimates practices that guided our forebears who pursued ethical lives in a world where place mattered. Much of our public philosophy, for example, assumes that good lives flourish in democracies *constructed primarily on local governments*. Yet, that hallowed dogma fails to fit or explain how we actually live our lives today.

We don't practice the many interdependent values of democracy—free speech and assembly, dissent and consent, responsibility for implementing decisions—in local places. Yes, we can vote. But voting is a single thread of democracy. In the absence of accompanying political and social values, voting is as much a specialized currency for consumption in political markets for governmental control as an expression of self-governance. We consume services provided by governmental organizations, and we have the important right to express consumer satisfaction or dissatisfaction. *But in our new world, the purposes and fates we self-consciously share with other people rest more on the many political values—democratic and otherwise—practiced in organizations than on voting in town, or other elections.*

In our world, purposes, more than places, shape values. Our purposes—earning a living, raising a family, enjoying friends, finding meaning, leading a good life—condition the people with whom we most thickly share our lives and fates. We interact more purposefully with people in markets, networks, and organizations than places. For millions of us, place has atrophied as a *force* conditioning values. We justly celebrate values linked to shared ideas, such as small towns, villages, city neighborhoods, and so forth. But the ideas have more vitality than the places. We are more likely to experience small town values in advertisements and movies than in towns or neighborhoods.

Meanwhile, the value and values on display in markets, networks, and organizations do not square with what is conveyed by the shared ideas of small town or neighborhood. Experience skews towards value. Markets, of course, are tuned to value by history and design. According to inherited understanding, the production of value *is* their function. But there is neither a divine nor scientific— *nor economic*—mandate that we perpetuate this narrow view. We can evolve. We can expand our vision and experience of blending value and values in markets, networks, and organizations without jeopardizing value itself. *Doing so is the characteristic ethical challenge of our new age of humankind.* We must take on this challenge, however, in the real markets, real networks, and real organizations in which we live more than in the cities, towns, and neighborhoods in which we reside.

. . . .

In my work over more than a quarter century across a wide range of markets, networks, and organizations, *I have observed one hundred percent of the time that people who thrive find a path through a paradox*. On the one hand, no organization succeeds by fearfully clinging to how things have been done in the past. *You cannot build a new world in old world ways.* On the other hand, effective change demands some vital link to the past. *In every single organization that has migrated to a new era, the people of that organization found their best future in **some** part of their best past.*

The lessons drawn for this book come from my work with organizations facing change in the sectors and industries listed in Table 1.1.

TABLE 1.1   Industries Facing Changes

Industries	
Accounting/Auditing	Food and Beverage
Agricultural Machinery	Government
Adult Literacy	Health Care
Aviation	Information Services
Banking	Insurance
Biotechnology	Journalism
Cable Television	Kitchen Technology
Clothing	Land Use Planning
Community Development	Law
Computers	Outsourcing
Consulting	Packaging
Corporate Training/Education	Pharmaceuticals
Crafts and Hobbies	Professional Sports
Credit Cards	Public Policy
Direct Mail	Publishing
Disaster Relief	Retail
eCommerce	Software
Education, K-12 and University	Telecommunications
Energy	Transportation
Entertainment	Travel
Fabric Finishing & Dying	Utilities

We should heed the lessons of successful change in organizations. We can find our best future in our best past without embalming ourselves in that past. Many values stand out from the best part of our past:

- Family values that center on parents who put children above self and children who honor mother and father;
- Social values such as tolerance, benevolence, and integrity;
- Political values of participation, voice, liberty, dignity, rights, responsibilities, and consent;
- Religious values arising from faith in something greater than self;
- Environmental values of respect and concern for our precious blue planet;
- Economic values such as the division of labor and the power of markets to grow and spread material well-being;
- Legal values that elevate the rule of principle over the rule of personality;
- Medical values that promote prevention as well as cures; and
- Technological values that go beyond innovation to include access for all through standardization.

Our best future, like our best past, hinges on restoring a blend of value and values to our lives in markets, networks, and organizations, and among friends and families. Nothing best about the past ever came from enthroning value over values. Quite the contrary. People who promote value without values hollow out and sicken individual and group souls. One need only consult the tragic centuries of slavery and slavery's aftermath to feel this lesson. Or, colonialism. Or, fascism. The same applies to any value category. When power concentrates in a single variable, the worst steps forward in those with power as well as many of those they rule.

Down the trail of the single exalted value lies unhappiness—a pattern in fact as well as fiction. We recoil, for example, from the scene in the movie *Patton* when its eponymous protagonist slaps a soldier considered a malingerer under the General's single, unyielding standard of military honor. In Jane Austen's novels, on the other hand, we are reassured when characters inclined to singularity—pride, prejudice, persuasion—grow in happiness through moderating blends of prudence, propriety, and benevolence. This same pattern explains our wondrous ability to appreciate an infinite spectrum from good bad guys to bad good guys.

Few of us, in fact, are good good guys or bad bad guys—pure saint or pure sinner. Most of us have our saintly or sinful moments in a life that blends goodness and badness along the road of making do. Ours is, I think, a both/and reality. Those who worship one value above others, by contrast, imprison themselves in either/or world-views. They are fundamentalists, even if their brands of fundamentalism vary.

In *The Ethics of Memory*, Margalit identifies fundamentalists by their insistence on particular historical facts that trace to biblical stories or national constitutions. I prefer to know them by their answers. Fundamentalists, dangerous and otherwise, demand adherence to what Virginia Postrel calls *the one best way*. Postrel writes differently about we. In *The Future and Its Enemies,* she contrasts we's who are stasists from we's who are dynamists and notes that this distinction increasingly explains coalitions better than more familiar labels like liberal or conservative. In her view, stasists are reactionaries because they reject dynamic both/and approaches in favor of answers hewing to one best way. Stasists fear ambiguity. Consciously or not, they are "my way or the highway" kind of folks.

Fundamentalists insist that either their single answer must be pursued or horrific consequences will follow. Inevitably, the either/or choices engender layer upon layer of contradictions—an encrustation that, usually rather late in the game, becomes apparent to people imperiled by the single answer. Throughout the 1990s, for example, shareholder value fundamentalists promoted a new capitalism linking stock prices to revenues instead of profits. They rewarded executives for pumping up stocks without concern for the sustainable value or values of their companies. Rather late in the game, tens of millions of investors and employees woke up to discover they had been conned.

Markets, networks, and organizations are peculiarly vulnerable to dangerous fundamentalism. The divorce of value and values weakens confidence. It exposes us to simplemindedness. We can no longer rely on the force of place to thicken relationships and strengthen values—to provide a center of gravity to stabilize roles, relationships, and purposes shared by thick we's who inescapably share fates. Instead, we pursue a rainbow of differentiated purposes in markets, networks, and organizations, and among friends and family.   Absent the crucible of place, our lives become fragmented and complex. Dynamism upends stability. Thick we's are more difficult to locate and sustain. Markets, networks, and organizations divide us from one another and from ourselves. As individuals, we must work hard to make sense of the many purposes in our lives if we are to lead integrated and ethical lives instead of scattered ones. It is no accident that stress is the disease of our age.

A single answer to life's many purposes is a seductive substitute for the blending effects of place that previously subjected value to a broader family of values shared by people who lived together. Today, fundamentalists—whether religious, economic, political, technological, or environmental—can reach tens, even hundreds, of millions of people with their single answers and their consequences. There is no bulwark of place to keep out fundamentalism, which explains why so many of us are anxious.

There is tremendous good news in our new world. Unlike people bottled up in cultures of place, we have extraordinary opportunities to fulfill individual aspirations and dreams. We are not vulnerable to the whims of invading, unwanted rulers who have life and death powers. Moreover, unlike most people who continue to live in places, *we* have the option of migrating out of our world of markets, networks, and organizations. We can go back to nature or pick up and move to any number of worlds of places still dotting the globe. Occasionally, we hear about someone who has—like John Walker Lindh, the American who joined the Afghan Taliban. That choice, however, is rare. *Hundreds of millions of us prefer the world we live in.*

Let us then take responsibility for it. Let us stop migrating *psychologically* to shared ideas, such as small town and neighborhood, or slick single answers, such as shareholder value and unalloyed individualism. Let's rid ourselves of illusions that there exists some *place*—even our homes—that insulates us from the rest of our world. Let's acknowledge that only our blended and balanced purposes—our commitment to both value and values—can protect and empower us in the markets, networks, and organizations in which we live our lives.

. . . .

We *can* bring the best parts of our past forward into our best future. But only if we see how thoroughly our world differs from the past. That it does, I think, is self-evident. It is obvious that we spend more time and energy in organizations than in towns, cities, or neighborhoods. It is obvious that our most critical purposes are fulfilled in markets, networks, organizations, friends and families. It is obvious that politics is a business, sports is a business, media is a business, and health care is a business. It is obvious that the family is under siege, the planet is at risk, and technology has transfigured existence. There is much that is obvious. More often than not, however, we step back, bewildered by the obvious, instead of asking, "So what do we do about it?".

This book asks "So what?" It also asks who are the *we's* who must act. It offers explanations and makes recommendations. The first three chapters describe the situation in which so many of us find ourselves: a world of markets, organizations, networks, families, and friends that estranges value from values. Chapters 4 through 9 revisit age-old sources of shared values—shared relationships, shared roles, and shared ideas—and how they have morphed in the cauldron of markets, organizations, and networks. In contrast to a world of places, for example, our relationships, roles, and ideas skip chaotically as we shift from home to work to mall to roads to Net. There is less *continuity and congruence* across our activities—a phenomenon that explains why values shared in markets often conflict with those shared at home and those at home clash with those at work.

Chapters 10 through 15 concentrate on organizations. In previous ages (and in places still having potency *as* places), towns, manors, fiefs, and other place-based communities were *the mid-level social formations* linking individual and family to more encompassing wholes, such as nations or empires. In our world, organizations, not towns, are the mid-level social formations. Today, the largest wholes are markets, nations, and networks; friends and family remain the smallest formations. It is in organizations, however, and not in places, that we most meaningfully share fates with other people beyond friends and family.

The split between value and values traces across our new social formations. We look to markets for value while, among friends and family, our preference is for values. Networks are chameleon-like because we use them to connect with others. If we use networks to connect in markets, our pointed purpose is value; if friends and family, values. It is in organizations that we find the richest brew of value and values among we's thickened by factors other than family or friendship. Organizations (including nonprofit, for-profit, and governmental organizations) compete in markets and networks. Organizations must attend to value. But organizations *are* organizations because they number human beings whose relationships, shared purposes, and shared fates are thick, not thin. *Neither value nor values can be ignored in organizations*.

Today, value and values face off in a win/lose struggle in too many organizations, whether large or small, formal or informal, incorporated or not. Whether the contest is over profits or budgets or both, habit favors value over values; or, in many nonprofits, the reverse. Too rarely do value and values blend together as the *equivalent* concerns of a thick we who share fates. It is too much either/or, too little both/and.

Organizations are our great, neglected crucible—our most unique and different thick we. In sorting out how best to conduct ourselves in markets and networks, we tend to underestimate *our* mid-level societies. Public policy debates concentrate on markets versus governments or on individuals and families. When this happens, we ignore the mid-level social formations most instrumental to our shared futures and shared values: organizations. In our new world, for example, no reform or policy ever happens in the absence of thick we's who share fates in organizations. *Ever.* Yet, we often analyze, propose, and act as if no social formation was interposed between individual and market or, more illogically, that only family and town separate individuals from larger formations of markets, nations, and governments. This focus on individualism and place obscures our vision. Chapters 10 through 15 review how impossible it is to carry forward the best parts of our past regarding concerns such as liberty, community, democracy, utility, and the good life into our future if proposals fail to account for more than markets, governments, value, and individualism.

We *do* live in a world without precedent. We *do* confront deep and profound change. So what should we do about it? Chapter 17 offers a series of specific suggestions headlined in Table 1.2. Some focus on organizations and some on markets and networks. I ask you to read them for their merit. Some are novel, while others are not. You may or may not agree with them; you will consider some loony and others simply wrong. But, even when you disagree, I ask you to consult them as illustrations of a different way of thinking about we and of acting ethically in a world now so different.

Notwithstanding any particular recommendation, my core proposition calls for a shift in perspective about the world we inhabit and why and who *we* are. Chapter 16 offers a five-part strategy for leading good lives in our new world of purposes. This opening chapter previews the central questions and themes of this book; Chapter 16 reviews them by asking, "So What?" Both Chapter 1 and Chapter 16 are overviews readers might consult to quickly learn what this book is about.

TABLE 1.2   Illustrative Suggestions

	Suggestions
1	The Ethical Scorecard
2	Annual Report to People of the Enterprise
3	Brand Values Committee of Board of Directors/Trustees
4	Corporate Purchasing on Behalf of Employees and Their Families
5	Jury Trials of Fact Inside Organizations
6	Employee Based Participation in Selection and Guidance of Lobbyists
7	Customer and Employee Membership on Board of Directors/Trustees
8	Minimum Values Standards in Qualifying Vendors
9	Forward Auditing
10	Employee Participation in Organization Charity
11	From Organizational Newsletter to Free Press
12	Dynamic Deductibility: Creating an Efficient Capital Market for Nonprofits
13	Private Capital Leagues for Nonprofits
14	Establishing a Third Legislative House: Lobbyists
15	Census Tracking: Counting Organizational Membership in Addition to Jobs
16	Founding a "Problem Solvers" Party
17	Require Government Organizations to Have and Report Against Vision, Strategy, and Values
18	Selective Knowledge Testing of Voters for Information Only
19	TV Show: "Brand Values"
20	TV/Web Show: "Brand Trials"
21	TV/Radio Show: "Civil Disagreement"
22	TV/Web Show: "What Works"
23	Reality Show: "Congress of Organizations"
24	Abolish Political Party Affiliations for State and Local Judges
25	360 Degree Feedback on Local Officials Just-in-time to Vote
26	Opt-in State and Local Purchasing Efforts
27	New Media: Trusted Infomediaries

This book asks us to wake up to how differently we lead our lives so that we can bring the best ideas and practices from our past into our future. Acting ethically is never easy. It has never been a small thing to act ethically in places. Nor is it trivial to lead good lives in markets, networks, or organizations, or among families and friends. Courage and hard choices lie ahead. Still, taking on the challenge to live good lives in our new world of purposes—and especially in organizations—is, I think, more pragmatic than attempting to breathe new life into dead places. We *already* share fates with other people in organizations; that mass migration has *already* happened.

Organizations are the crucibles shaping what matters to our lives as consumers, networkers, investors, friends, and families.Our future, then, depends on broadening our vision regarding how and why, and on what basis, organizations succeed in markets, nations, and networks. Yes, accomplishing any shift means taking risks to challenge orthodoxy. But—note well—such obstacles also confronted people of earlier ages who sought to make place-based social formations more conducive to good lives.

We can craft a better future out of self-evident forces by practicing the both/and spirit of martial arts—a spirit that teaches us to use the forces at work instead of ignoring or opposing them. We need to use what is obvious to make our lives and the lives of our children better. We need to recognize powerful forces that surround and infuse us, and act to guide those forces to reintegrate value and values in the thick we's of our lives. We need—each and every one of us, individually and together—to find ways to reconnect making a good living with leading a good life in markets, networks, organizations, and among families and friends. In a world shaped by purposes instead of places, it is time to make it our purpose to restore value to the house of values. It is time to think differently about we—and to act.

2 A World of Purposes, not Places

Our world is different. It is a world shaped by the purposes we pursue in markets, organizations, and networks, and among family and friends. It is certainly a world long in the making; we can trace it back centuries. But it has only recently sprung on us full force. In the latter part of the 20th century, hundreds of millions transitioned from lives conditioned by place to ones forged by purposes in markets, networks, and organizations. *Billions of people, of course, still live in places.* I think, in fact, the planet divides along this experiential line. *This book, however, is primarily concerned with living in a world of purposes, not places.* It asks that we who live in a world of purposes reframe concerns about ethics, justice, fairness, and the good life in order to reintegrate value and values in markets, networks, and organizations. It does so with concern for children and young adults who now despair over finding some way to participate in a world where value is at war with values. If we are to teach our children well, the lessons should focus on markets, networks, organizations, friends, and families, not Boston or Kyoto, New Jersey or Monaco, the United States or Australia.

I sometimes call this new world Cybernia. But the label is unimportant. You may or may not like Cybernia. You may be sick of everything cyber. My editor, for one, detests the word. One reader suggested Cyberia. You may have a much better name. Names aside, what is critical is the *coldeyed recognition* that this world of purposes differs profoundly from prior human experience. Not completely, of course. I am not suggesting an either/or-ish, on/off switch from all about place to nothing about place. We continue, for example, to reside in places. We have houses, apartments, condominiums, dorm rooms, and mobile homes. We even have McMansions, the tongue-in-cheek tag given to the look-alike homes of millionaires. Yet, relative to meaningful terms in our past, we are, comparatively speaking, homeless—although without the dire consequences long associated with that condition. For millions of us, *place is a lifestyle choice* that, like so much else, is produced and delivered through markets, networks, and organizations.

Nor am I suggesting that people who still live in a world of places are purposeless. They have plenty of purposes. But the culture and values *of places* weave through their purposes. Place significantly conditions relationships, roles, resources, and ideas. Place is more than a statistic. It matters. Place shapes who is a stranger and who is not.

Historically, place spawned linguistic differentiation. Mastery of place enhanced Darwinian fitness. People spoke with other people, worked with other people, and worshipped, traded, played, married, and lived and died with other people who inhabited the same *place*. People affiliated through blood, and through faith, class, ethnicity, status and role—just as we do. But they did so within boundaries of place.

Were life and the values of life entirely constrained by place? *Of course not.* A widening river of ideas, individuals, and innovations eroded the boundaries of place. Whether religious (e.g., monotheism), military (e.g., various empires), commercial (e.g., trade in gold or spices), or technological (e.g., the printing press), developments chipped away barriers and linked people up with one another. People who lived in places felt the effects. A profound force was at work: the movement toward larger and larger we's, we's stamped by shared ideas inked into shared identities. In Western history, the likes of Alexander, various Roman leaders, the Catholic Church, and European powers constructed large-scale we's to hold sway over stretches of the globe. Nor was this impulse confined to Europeans. As my co-author and I catalogue in *Sources of the African Past*, vast expanses of West Africa combined into an Islamic we in the 18th and 19th centuries. Buddhism, Taoism, Confucianism, and sectarianism did the same in Asia.

Yet, however much enlarging we's connected people through ideas, laws, commerce, religion, military power, and so forth, the *day-to-day* reality of life—and the values sustained by that reality—remained substantially forged within the *places people lived together*. Yes, again, there were plenty of people who broke through barriers of place to lead cosmopolitan lives. And, from the history of cities, we learn about the good and bad effects on values when place gets diluted by population size and other forces. Still, most of humanity continued to work, marry, play, worship, trade, fight, live, and die within cultures and communities of places. The *force* of place remained strong. The shared fates sorting people into thick we's were grounded in place. The social formations that mattered most—tribe, family, town, neighborhood, job, church, school, nation—were associated with and rooted in place.

Place-diminishing technologies are as old as the breaking of horses and the discovery of the wheel. They include clocks, printing presses, sailing ships, and roads. By the 19th century, the technological pace picked up with railroads, telegraphs, and radio. But it was the latter part of the 20th century that witnessed a critical shift in inertial forces, the inflection point beyond which place lost power over hundreds of millions of people. With automobiles, airplanes, telephones, televisions, computers, faxes, photocopies, and the Internet, place atrophied as a *force*. Even the place we call home retains only the shakiest of holds on our lives as families.

Among those of us who live in a world of purposes, there is no place that is an unknown place. As the Ford Motor Company commercial of the early 21st century put it, "No boundaries." We have penetrated every place on the planet. Yes, there are billions of people whose lives are still mostly conditioned by the places they live, *including many millions in developed nations*. There are people who remain lodged for good or ill in exotic areas in the Amazon rain forest or the far reaches of Alaska or Mongolia. But none of them live in *our* world. Their places are known to us but not suffused with our culture. Life in such places is not lived among franchises, strip malls, highways, airports, elections, product launches, advertising campaigns, talk radio, professional sports, reality TV, sound bites, stock exchanges, ATMs, hard currencies, email, music videos, brands, celebrities, and networking. Their lives—and their values—are shaped by the places they live.

Technology did not do this *to* us. Rather, technology melded with ideas and innovations in markets, organizations, and networks to enable *people* to transform the world from a world of places to a world of purposes—from a world in which the unfortunate fate of being placeless becomes that of being purposeless. Today, Darwinian fitness runs to men and women who master markets, networks, and organizations. They are the likely biological winners. Linguistic variation no longer arises from place. In North America, for example, place-based languages actively spoken have shrunk *tenfold* over the past century. Our new languages are C++, Java, COBOL, HTML, and XML—and the rapidly morphing jargon of medicine, law, management, science, finance, and youth culture. Residing in different places does not make us strangers to one another. Our shared experiences in markets, network, and organizations make us less strange to one another than ever before.

. . . .

We know the world has shrunk. Whatever the descriptor—global village, wired world, Planet Hollywood—the prevailing message is about interdependency. One popularly shared idea claims that no more than six degrees of separation exist between each of us and everyone else. Those you know directly are separated from you by one degree. According to the theory, *you* know someone who knows someone who knows someone who knows someone who knows someone who knows *me*. You and I are separated by no more than six steps, and possibly fewer.

This theory is explained by networks. Imagine you have reasonably current relationships with 300 people. If your world were *entirely* subsumed in a single place, all those people would have relationships with one another. If, for example, you and I lived with 298 others in a place cut off from other places, it is likely the 300 of us would directly know one another. There would be one degree of separation.

Say, however, that you represented our place in dealings with another place of 300. If so, then I would be separated at most by only three degrees from people in that other place because (1) you would know them directly (two degrees for me), or (2) the people you knew would know the others (three degrees for me). This illustrates jumping a network. It only takes one person with a separate network to connect all people in those networks by two or three degrees. In our world of markets, networks, and organizations, *every person we know has other networks*. We all jump networks. It is easy, then, to grasp the phenomenon of six degrees of separation because the numbers get very big very fast. If, for example, you have reasonably current relationships with 300, each of whom jump 10 different networks, then you are separated by, at most, three degrees from the total number of people in those networks. Say each network averages 300 unique, nonoverlapping people. You are separated by *three degrees* from 300 x 10 x 300, or *900,000* people. If all of them also jump 10 networks with 300 each, you are separated by only *five degrees* from *2.7 billion* people.

In *The Tipping Point*, Malcolm Gladwell uses six degrees of separation to explain fads and other social phenomena. He notes that *some* people know many more than 300 others and jump many more than ten networks. He calls them connectors. Yet, whether or not you are a connector, the math remains startling. In our world of markets, networks, organizations, friends, and families, there are millions of people with whom you are likely to share small-world stories.

This thickens our accidental relationships. When we successfully play "do you know" with strangers, the identified chain of acquaintances familiarizes us with one another. We feel less estranged because we can trace common relationships. The attributes and explanations—"went to the same college," "plays the piano," "also worked in that start-up," "is a lawyer"—provide shared references that add dimensions to our relationships beyond the bare fact of our common humanity. We discover a *psychological* proximity within which to navigate and get to know each other.

There is a flip side to six degrees of separation, one that helps explain concurrent shifts in *how well* we know one another and why. I call it six degrees of integration. It suggests a thinning corollary to the thickening of relationships with tens of thousands of strangers. It can help you analyze the extent to which your life is conditioned by place versus purposes in markets, networks, organizations, and among friends and families.

In a hermetically sealed world, such as the place of 300 people described above, everyone is separated from everyone else by one degree. We all know each other. And, I think, we know each other *very well*—that is, along many dimensions. Table 2.1 lays out a template of activities and purposes: social, religious, work, commerce, governance, education, sport, hobby, and charity. The more of these characterizing any relationship, the more likely the people in that relationship have strong shared values. Relationships among people with six degrees of integration probably have more predictably shared values than, say, relationships of only two degrees. This is not a perfect indicator, mind you. Just odds.

TABLE 2.1 Purpose Versus Place

Name	Work	Social	Religion	Sport	Hobby	Commerce	Education	Charity	Governing	PLACE

Instructions for Relationships/Purposes/Place Form:

1. List the names of people with whom you have a current relationship.
2. Indicate the purposes or activities in your relationship. For example, if you work with someone, check off work. If you socialize, check that. Check as many as apply.
3. Check any purpose or activity that is a *meaningful* part of your relationship. For example, you might have a current relationship with someone you went to college with...check "education." I am looking for what's real. For example, use something like "often" or "several times" to decide whether you socialize with another person. If you have participated meaningfully with another person in a charity event, even if only once, you ought to check it.
4. After you have completed the purposes and activities, indicate the smallest place within which you and the other person both reside. For example, if you live in Boston and the person lives in a different section of Boston, you would indicate C for same city. If on the other hand, the person lives in Springfield, Massachusetts, then you would enter S for same state, and if the person lives in Cleveland, Ohio, N for same nation.

NH: Same neighborhood
T: Same town
C: Same city
S: Same state
N: Same nation
W: Same world

By strong, predictable shared values, I do not mean perfect agreement. *Nor do I mean good values, bad values, or anything in between.* Rather, as described further in Chapter 4, I mean predictable in the sense of (1) behavior and belief likely to be repeated and (2) some shared understanding of why. In a relationship with, say, three or more degrees of integration, the odds increase that people involved count on previous beliefs and behaviors to persist. Values are predictable and understandable in that sense—whether for good or ill. In our hermetically sealed place of 300 people, for example, the vast majority of relationships would easily have three or more degrees of integration. Indeed, I think that, over time, all would have six or more. The emergent picture would be very thick (see Table 2.2).

TABLE 2.2 Hypothetical 300 Person Place

Name	Work	Social	Religion	Sport	Hobby	Commerce	Education	Charity	Governing	PLACE
1	√	√	√	√			√		√	Village
2	√	√	√			√	√		√	Village
3		√	√	√			√			Village
4	√	√	√			√			√	Village
5	√	√	√	√	√	√			√	Village
6		√	√		√	√			√	Village
7		√	√		√	√	√			Village
8	√	√	√	√	√		√		√	Village
9	√	√		√	√		√			Village
10	√	√		√			√		√	Village
11	√	√		√			√		√	Village
12	√	√			√	√			√	Village
...										Village
...	√	√	√		√	√	√		√	Village
296	√		√	√	√	√	√			Village
297	√	√		√	√	√	√			Village
298	√				√	√	√			Village
299		√	√						√	Village

The template in Table 2.1 has a tenth column: smallest same place. In thinking about people with whom you have reasonably current relationships, use this column to identify the *smallest* same place in which you both reside. My friend Charlie, for example, lives in Oregon. I live in New York. Our smallest same place is a nation. In contrast, the smallest same place for the 300 in the made-up village is the village. To the extent you live in a world of purposes instead of places, the degrees of integration in your relationships are likely to reflect factors in the first nine columns more than the tenth. Charlie and I met each other because of work and have interacted for a variety of purposes over many years. Our friendship has five degrees of integration, but none because of place. As you ponder what characterizes *your* relationships, you may find that purposes and activities explain more than smallest same place. If so, it is likely that your template will be thinner than the very dense Table 2.2.

The greater the number of people on the planet with whom you are separated by six degrees, the more likely it is that your template will look thinner than Table 2.2. It is more likely that you will simultaneously have thicker relationships with many more people (six degrees of separation) and thinner ones too (less than six degrees of integration). Such a picture would suggest that your life—and your values are better explained by purposes in markets, networks, and organizations than places. You, of course, need to reach your own conclusions. This book, though, is written for people who *do* live, entirely or mostly, in a world of purposes instead of places. I use we, our, and your accordingly. In laying out the simultaneous thickening and thinning of relationships in a world of purposes, I am not discussing good or evil. The thickening implied by six degrees of separation holds the promise of shared values with millions more people than could be sustained in a world of places. I think we can trace predictable behaviors and beliefs regarding tolerance, diversity, and problem solving to the expanding psychological familiarity we have with so many people who would otherwise be strangers to us in a world of places. Meanwhile, the thinning of our relationships suggests challenges (weakening of marriage and family) as well as opportunities (increased individual freedom).

Through thick and thin, though, we live in a world of markets, organizations, networks, family, and friends. Our lives are not dictated by place or by the culture or values of places surrounding our dwellings: The towns, neighborhoods, cities, nations, ethnic groups, and religions coincident with place. We choose where, how, and with whom to share our lives—and for how long. Community is an anachronism in this new world *if* we insist on locating it in places. Citizenship becomes no more than a nostalgically shared idea if we make the same mistake. In our placeless world, our dominant shared role *vis-à-vis* government is *consumer*, not citizen. We experience the self-governance historically linked to the role of citizen in organizations, not places. If we find the meaning of community, we do so in organizations and among friends, not places.

We—you, me, others we know—conduct life in *markets* in which we shop, sell, invest, seek employment, and vote; *organizations* where we work, learn, affiliate, play, and pray; and *networks* across which we communicate, travel, play, and connect with other people and with markets and organizations. We *live* in a culture of markets, organizations, and networks, not a culture of place. *If we seek to live more ethical lives, lives that blend value and values, then we must do so in markets, networks, and organizations.* We cannot safely assume that our new and different circumstances respond constructively to practices dependent on the force of place. That option is closed. Seeking to breathe new life into place-based community and place-based citizenship is a stillborn proposition.

In our world of purposes, each market is an empire, each organization a town, each network a Roman road. But, unlike we's stretching across the centuries, we are neither subjects nor citizens whose lives, liberties, and pursuits of happiness play out within a *single* empire, a *single* town, or a *single* Roman road. We participate in *hundreds* of markets, *dozens* of networks, and *handfuls* of organizations. Our homes remain precious, though not because the surrounding neighborhoods or towns circumscribe what anthropologists call a thick description of our lives. Rather, our homes matter because they, along with work, school, malls, television, the Internet, cars, and phones comprise critical nodes of our crisscrossed existence.

"Where do you live?" is interesting. But "What do you do?" is more telling. Go ahead. Answer it. What you do shapes more of who you are than where you live. You spend far more *purpose-filled time and effort* in the organization where you work, volunteer, or learn than in the neighborhood or town in which you reside. You connect to the world electronically, psychologically, and purposefully, not territorially. You devote more of your life to shopping, earning, learning, playing, praying, and investing than voting, governing, or communing with your neighbors.

When you work or learn, you do so in organizations, markets, and networks. When you consume or invest, you do so in markets, organizations, and networks. When you play, the equipment, products, services, and locations are provided by markets, organizations, and networks. You likely eat many of your meals in organizations away from home. The food you consume, whether at a restaurant or at home, arrives on your plate through markets, networks, and organizations. When you worship, you do so in an organization that competes for your soul in markets for spiritual fulfillment. When you vote, you do so in markets for political leadership and government control.

Our markets, organizations, and networks are what network experts call many-to-many phenomena. The flows of goods, services, ideas, and information move from many originating points to many destination points. Markets, organizations, and networks interlace our lives, making it impossible to pinpoint a single context in which we live the whole of existence. We do not live in a *single* market or *single* organization. Rather, we participate simultaneously in many. There are thousands of markets, organizations, and networks affecting our lives. Their influences range from the benign to the profound. Our kids come home with new hairdos or tattoos. We wake up one day to discover that a home computer is a necessity. Or that unethical behavior in the executive suite of some company we never heard of has wiped out the financial security of tens of thousands

Markets, organizations, and networks do not contend with one another for total control of our lives. *Their objectives are partial, not total.* Indeed, Microsoft, a company with seemingly boundless aspirations, may be the exception that proves this rule: markets, organizations, and networks are limited and fragmenting in purpose and effect. They want only a *share*. They compete for share of mind, share of time, share of wallet, share of voice, share of vote, and share of spirit. None seeks to control your entire mind, entire body, entire wallet, or entire time. They look to profit from your participation, loyalty, and habits in parts instead of wholes.

Organizations such as the Gap, L.L. Bean, Old Navy, Ann Taylor, Levi's, the Limited, Wal-Mart, and Banana Republic seek to clothe you. Ford, Toyota, Saab, Chevrolet, Volkswagen, Hyundai, Kia, and Mercedes want to transport you. Broadcast, cable, satellite, and other networks want to inform and entertain you. The long distance companies want to help you communicate. Periodically, the Republican and Democratic Parties want your vote. Your company wants your talent, ideas, and effort—but only a share of your time. The

American Red Cross, the Salvation Army, Doctors Without Borders, Planned Parenthood, the Sierra Club, and hundreds of thousands of other nonprofit organizations want your philanthropic dollar or charitable hour. Your children, at least until they are teenagers, want your quality time. The pattern is kaleidoscopic instead of checkerboard. Our lives are layered by context upon context. We live in multiple markets, multiple organizations, and multiple networks. Our world is a crazy quilt; it is not simple.

Little of this, I think, is sinister. *But it is different. We* are different. We seek each other's business and conversation, chat and company. We seek profits, achievement, leisure, love, and spirit. We seek values and meaning. There are invisible hands aplenty in our new world of purposes. But we will not integrate value and values if we insist on conspiracy theories. There is no man or woman behind the curtain in this Oz. There are only tens of millions of us going about our fragmented lives as consumers, employees, investors, family members, and friends within a morass of markets, organizations, and networks.

Earlier, when I mentioned the market for spiritual commitment, you might have winced. We are not comfortable joining ideas like market and spirituality, because we find it hard to liberate market from its commercial heritage. Yet, combining these ideas only extends one of humanity's best traditions: relating spiritual voice to prevailing contexts of earthly power. Our earthly power plays out in markets, networks, and organizations. Throughout history, the visible and invisible church (or synagogue, temple, or mosque) reconciled religion to the politics, culture, and economics of places. To juxtapose spiritual life and earthly power, for example, the great 4th century Catholic theologian St. Augustine penned *The City of God*.

Today, religion, politics, economics, technology, medicine, law, family, and other values play out in markets, organizations, and networks. If we cannot speak about the *markets* of God, the *networks* of God, and the *organizations* of God, then we cannot reasonably hope for spiritual fulfillment. In our world, religious organizations prosper when they self-consciously condition activities in a framework of markets and networks for spiritual fulfillment. Any pragmatic and hopeful solution to the child abuse crisis in the Catholic Church, for example, will emerge from considering the Catholic Church as an *organization* (with, for example, hiring and retention policies and procedures) competing in a *market* (whose customers, for example, demand an experience to match the brand promise of Catholicism). Yes, discussions among Catholics should echo ancient terms of faith. That is part of their best past. If the Church is not responsive to the social formations in our world of purposes, however, all affected will be left with no more than a media event.

The same lesson applies to nonreligious values. In part, value and values have split because our inherited comprehension of markets and organizations is heavy with connotations of value alone. Meanwhile, terms such as community and citizen are loaded with conditions of place having little continued vitality. To reintegrate value and values, we need to blend them in markets, organizations, and networks, not places. We will find it easier to do so if we think of markets, organizations, and networks as more than economic or technological formations, and if we imagine *meanings* for community and citizen disconnected from the barriers of place.

Common sense can guide us. We have accommodated before to enlarged meanings for market, organization, and network. Today, we use market to describe activities that would have astonished our great-grandparents. Marriage and relationship counseling, hospice services, nutrition and diet, well being, eco-tourism, bottled water, adoption, stress management, physical fitness, consulting, and charity— these describe *markets* that either did not exist or were entirely localized activities until quite recently.

We live in markets: good, bad, and ugly. We participate in the markets just listed. We also know about markets for drugs, child pornography, and hatred. *The Sopranos* depicts how hard it is to live ethically in markets and organizations that are inherently unethical. So does *The Insider*, the movie about a whistleblower who questioned the adamant opposition of the tobacco industry to admitting the health risks of smoking. If we are to live ethical lives in a world of markets, then we must ask what makes for ethics *in* markets. We are more likely to succeed if we think about markets as more than commercial affairs.

In light of this, let's revisit what Joseph Schumpeter described sixty years ago as a market for political leadership and control.[1] Centuries of place-shaped habits retard our embrace of what is obvious to each of us: elections are market and network mechanisms for choosing who controls governmental organizations and networks.

1. Joseph A. Schumpeter, *Capitalism, Socialism and Democracy*, Third Edition (New York: HarperPerennial, 1950), p. 269.

This observation is neither new nor startling. From *The Selling of The President 1968* to the widespread use of marketing consultants, from the rise of spin to the 2002 passage of the McCain-Feingold campaign finance reform law—our experience indicates time and again that the business of getting elected and re-elected is just that, a business. In the 2000 presidential election, the bulk of campaign funds were spent on a dozen or so states whose electoral-college votes were, according to each candidate's polling organizations, up for grabs. The money, then, went to the submarkets that mattered most. Politics is a business; politics is about markets; politics is a market. We all know it. It is obvious.

Politics is also a badly inefficient market that suffers from organizations with narrow visions obsessed with winning, weak customer service, shrinking market share, bad technology, terrible information, bloated cost structures, and poor product and service quality. It is no surprise that politics is a business we detest.

We are the most talented market makers and market innovators the world has ever seen. Our markets for political leadership and control can be as effective as our markets for automobiles, clothes, food services, computers, books, and marriage counseling—but only when we stop lamenting that it *is* a market and act to imbue the market for political control with *values* that stretch beyond value, feel good image management, false advertising, and winning.

We also understand what makes for effective, sustainable organizations. We know about vision, reengineering, teams, benchmarking, quality, projects, and more. We are learning rapidly about networks. We are discovering that effective networks have universal access, scalability, standards, security, and clear expectations about minimal kinds of mutual behavior. As with markets, we hamstring ourselves because we remain reluctant to *self-consciously* consider organizations and networks as *social formations*. We are familiar with questioning our lives and values in the contexts of town, state, and nation. Yet, we shy away from asking how we might live more ethically in markets, organizations, and networks.

As a student in the 1920s, the essayist Lionel Trilling was inspired by a teacher's exhortation regarding the moral obligation to be intelligent.[2] Trilling took this dictate to heart. Morality, of course,

---

2. Leon Wieseltier, ed., "Introduction," *The Moral Obligation to Be Intelligent: Selected Essays by Lionel Trilling* (New York: Farrar, Straus, & Giroux, 2000), p. ix.

encompasses more than intelligence alone. But, given the unprecedented nature of our new world of purposes, intelligence and its
moral uses are sorely needed. It is ignorance, for example, for government leaders, media organizations, and others to perpetuate
anachronistic debates about place-based illusions that ignore and
subvert what we know about the workings of markets, organizations,
and networks. Or it is cynicism. Either way, it is immoral.

. . . .

Our difficulties are self-inflicted. As in the Jewish Seder story of The
Wicked Child who stubbornly refuses to join other people in a thick
we, too many of us are in the habit of excluding ourselves from our
world *as it is today*. We prevent ourselves from carrying forward
many of humanity's best traditions into markets, organizations,
networks, families, and friends.

Reflect, then, for a moment about justice and the good life—concepts as old as humanity. All of us care about justice and the good
life; few of us conscientiously connect them to the organizations
where we work, markets where we shop and invest, and networks
through which we connect. In our organizations, for example, we
face challenges at the core of justice and the pursuit of good lives.
Downsizing, negative politics, unfair wages or benefits, bureaucratic
hassles, stress, narrow career paths, gender, racial and age bias, lack
of voice in decisions, double standards, and gross imbalances
between work and home: these are realities we confront every day.
These are the challenges in which we thicken our degrees of integration with fellow employees in a world of purposes.

*Too often we do not ask ourselves—we do not demand of our-
selves—what we are responsible for doing to make the organizations in which we participate more just. Nor do we think differently
about the we's who ought to act.* Instead, we submit to very real worries about job security, profits, and personal opportunity narrowly
defined, and about getting home or otherwise jumping into other
purposes and contexts of our lives. In our fears and habits, we narrow rather than enlarge the purposes we bring to our most basic
political entity: *our organizations*.

In a world of places, our ancestors grew familiar with and skilled
at deliberating and acting on good and evil, and justice, fairness, and
the pursuit of happiness. People self-consciously sought to improve
individual and shared lives through integrating beliefs and behaviors
across political, economic, social, religious, and family values. We

are out of practice in addressing such issues because we do not correlate them with markets, organizations, and networks. We do not look at what is so obviously different about the structure of our new world and ask, "So what do we do about it?"

We should adjust perspective. We need to rediscover our old habit of inquiry and apply it to our world, our new reality. We can begin by shifting *some* attention away from questions about justice and the state toward justice and the organization, justice and markets, and justice and networks. By tackling such questions, we are more likely to acknowledge government for how it operates today: a set of markets, organizations, and networks. Such new perspectives will help move beyond debates about government versus markets—arguments that fail to account for anything but the largest social formations in our lives. In doing so, we can reconnect the meanings of community and citizen to how, why, and for what purposes we live our lives. We need to enlarge our understanding of what markets are, what organizations are, and what networks are. By seeing and understanding them as our most basic *human* formations—and not just economic or technological phenomena—we can step into a future that integrates instead of divides value and values in a world of purposes.

3 The Split

The chasm separating value from values emerged in businesses more than 20 years ago. Starting in the late 1970s, companies experienced a rapid succession of traumatic shocks that—at first tentatively, then thoroughly— decimated longstanding assumptions about how best to finance, organize, and compete. Capital ceased being the scarce though familiar resource of yesteryear. The complexity, sophistication, and aggressiveness of financial markets mushroomed. A new market emerged: the market for corporate control. Out went the cozy ties among executives and their bankers who— unfairly, but actually —subsumed choices about value within a clubby world of shared values. In came the values-bereft Gordon Gekko, the ruthless investment banker in the movie *Wall Street*, who, like his real-life counterparts, promoted shareholder value and profited handsomely from it.

. . . .

The demands made on 1990s executives for financial performance would have given nightmares to their mid-century predecessors. So would the strategic and competitive requirements for success. Alongside persistent double-digit increases in available capital came the most explosive flowering of technology in history and a sea change in government policy. Powered by boundless expansions in the efficiency and application of information technology, companies with access to new ideas also had access to capital. Concurrently, governments undid 50 years of rules and regulations, thereby unleashing markets and eclipsing themselves.

Out went steady-as-she-goes monopoly and oligopoly capitalism. In came creative destruction—competition directed at upsetting, instead of reinforcing, the status quo. As one best seller put it, *If It Ain't Broke, Fix It!* Out went stability that required little strategy beyond protecting geographic position, co-opting government regulation, and signaling others in the club. In came a bewildering array of strategic options for defining and delivering value to customers. To ownership of the means of production and distribution was added control over the choices of consumption. Customers attained power to rival producers (although individual consumers did not recognize or use it as effectively as business customers). Value to the customer became the means to beget value to the shareholder.

In the early 1950s, when Charles E. Wilson left General Motors to become Dwight Eisenhower's Defense Secretary, he famously said, "I always thought that what was good for our country was good for General Motors and vice versa." At the time, neither Wilson nor many others had heard of ideas that would soon claim to be good for General Motors: total quality, customer service, innovation, speed, reengineering, horizontal organization, globalization, core competencies, teams, continuous improvement, benchmarking, outsourcing, downsizing, strategic alliances, systems integration, and eCommerce.

One of Wilson's successors at the helm of General Motors, Roger Smith, gained notoriety in the 1980s because, while he'd heard of such things, he considered them fads. When, for example, some folks from Human Resources decided to introduce quality into manufacturing, Smith pretty much ignored them as they hired someone to dress up in a mascot's costume and walk the plant floors as GM's "Quality Cat." They held a contest to name the mascot. One noteworthy entry: *Tuna Meowt*.[1]

Smith believed in cost-cutting. He bet on the past. He bet on what he could control. His faith in the tried and true was matched by the similarly backward-looking executives then running the Soviet Union. Smith watched as former GM customers voted with their wallets, competitors took market share, and, worst of all, GM employees lost pride, energy, and enthusiasm. One assembly line

---

1. Ben Hamper, *Rivethead: Tales from the Assembly Line* (New York: Warner Books, 1986), p. 112.

operator likened working at GM in the '80s to being paid for goofing off in high school.[2]

Organizations and their leaders can *always* perpetuate the status quo by clinging to the past longer than any of us think possible. GM is only now rising from the rubble of managing through its rear view mirror. It is doing so by tapping into the best part of its heritage: asking GM people to make great cars. During most of the '80s and '90s, however, GM was an exception proving a newfound rule: *Under the mounting pressures of competitive destruction, pre-1980s organizational orthodoxy could not hold.*

How organizations made decisions, allocated resources, and conducted work *had to change.* Out went painfully slow multiyear strategic planning and budgeting; out went steep, multilayered hierarchies constructed on narrow task-by-task divisions of individual responsibility. In came flat, horizontal, and fast organizations built around teams. Out went functional silos; in came cross-functional processes. Out went 9 to 5; in came 24 by 7. Out went the divine right of managers. In came employee empowerment, corporate culture, the best place to work and—pay attention—*values*.

According to the 1982 best seller *In Search of Excellence*, values were one of seven attributes of organizational design and behavior that explained the difference between success and failure. Values were the set of beliefs, attitudes, and behaviors among people that described "*the way we do things around here*." If values did not coordinate with strategy, trouble followed. GM's woeful performance illustrated this. The way things were done around GM could not possibly have promoted any promising strategy for recovering consumer, investor, or employee confidence.

In Search of Excellence was not alone in touting the contribution of employee values to customer happiness and shareholder value. *Reengineering the Corporation, The Discipline of Market Leaders* and *The Fifth Discipline* are other popular titles of the past twenty years echoing the same lesson. *In these books, values are a means to an end, the end being value.* The link is odd, linguistically if not managerially. Value is the supreme effect—values one cause among many. Value is not a type or kind or subset of values; the singular value is not part of the plural values. Rather, values are a tool to create value.

---

2. Ibid.

Executives more on their game than Roger Smith learned that (1) the capitalism of creative destruction demanded new strategies and (2) those strategies required new organizational approaches that, in turn, (3) could not succeed without a shift in behaviors and attitudes among employees. Much, then, depended on the we who shaped and made real "the way we do things around here." For example, faster and flatter organizations could not flourish if employees hesitated to act without moment-by-moment commands from bosses. Strategies for creating value depended upon employees *empowered* by the *values* of the organization.

· ·

One book neatly captures the linear logic by which values are a means to create value. Entitled *The Balanced Scorecard*, it argues that value is produced as follows: Shareholder value derives from customer value, which derives from the effectiveness of business processes, which derive from the skills and values of the people employed. The logic is sequential. The values and skills of employees produce results for processes. Processes produce results for customers. Customers produce results for shareholders.

The Balanced Scorecard advocates metrics and goals for all four links in the sequence: shareholders, customers, processes, and people. In that sense, it is inclusive of values and value. *But* The Balanced Scorecard *is neither balanced nor ethical.* It explicitly promotes shareholder value as *the* supreme objective. Values contribute to value, *but not the reverse.* Value is the single answer, the ultimate good.

Values? Yes, they matter—*as long as the benefits to shareholder value outweigh the costs to shareholder value.* In this scheme, values are split off from and subordinated to value. Value is produced by values, just as by technology, innovation, strategy, and so forth. Value stands apart, an objective. Value is the *end*, values one of many *means*.

The tragedy of *The Balanced Scorecard* is that of the wolf in sheep's gear—or the man in the pathetic cat costume. It is, however, far more sophisticated and, therefore, more pernicious than GM's "Quality Cat." It portrays itself as smilingly inclusive of values. Like the "Quality Cat," it cheers for values. Yet, its logic and teachings *entirely* subordinate values—and *"we, the employees"*—to being but one of many assets in service of shareholder value. Most people fail to generate or sustain enthusiasm about being strictly a means, one of a variety of assets. We have too many additional purposes for our lives; not insignificantly, we like to think of ourselves as ends.

. . . .

Books from *In Search of Excellence* to *The Balanced Scorecard* fueled a movement across the globe—the creation of "Statements of Values" in which organization's formally adopted the beliefs and behaviors employees were expected to practice. By the new century, most major organizations on the planet had a Statement of Values. The trend reached beyond the private sector—governmental and not-for-profit organizations joined in. The values defined in such statements were, for the most part, of a piece with one another: *respect, balance, integrity, teamwork, accountability, openness, customer focus, diversity, innovation, speed, and learning.* From Citibank to Shell, from KPMG to The Nature Conservancy, different organizations selected various words. All settled on the same core meanings.

Most Statements of Values focus on social values, the attitudes and behaviors that, according to the title of yet another best-selling book, we are supposed to have learned in kindergarten. Indeed, with regard to respect and integrity, the fact that *organizations* named them is, arguably, more notable than the specific values named. It indicated that we were coming to grips with what it means to live together—however partially—in societies, such as organizations, formed by purposes instead of places.

Other aspects in Statements of Values went beyond the social to the *political*. By formalizing expectations about "the way we do things around here," organizations established standards for political participation and consent under the leadership of the C-suite (CEO, COO, CFO, CTO, CIO et al.). Such values as teamwork, diversity, work/life balance, and accountability speak to political values more habitually associated with the rights and responsibilities of citizenship. Only we use different terms when speaking of citizenship—terms such as rights, responsibilities, voting, liberty, free speech, decision making, and consent. Few organizations, however, dwelled much on the essentially political nature of their Statements of Values because, by the late 20th century, politics was an entirely negative part of organizational life (indeed, life itself). Organizations spent hundreds of millions of dollars and tens of thousands of person-hours debating, discussing, choosing, and communicating values. Proportionately speaking, no money or effort was committed to integrating value and values. Consequently, Statements of Values often made little difference. In organizations whose values already contributed to value *and vice versa*, all that occurred was an articulation of what had gone unspoken—perhaps imperiling values by depriving them of mysticism. Meanwhile, the companies most in need of clear, constructive social and political values rarely progressed because they failed to integrate value as one among many values. Instead, they exalted value, especially shareholder value, as their idol.

This dispiriting summary holds no surprises. Imagine that you work in an enterprise (such as GM in the '80s) whose social and political values have cast your organization into a death spiral. How much faith and credit would you give to a massive exercise that, when all was said and done, forcefully and witheringly conveyed three headlines:

- "Here, at XYZ Corp, the shareholder comes first!"
- "People are our most important assets!"
- "This Statement of Values is to be posted on our walls!"

Language matters. "Assets." "Human Resources." "Human Capital." "People as Assets." "Shareholder Value." People are not adjectives, and people are not things. *At least not exclusively or by preference*. Can we usefully deploy the idea that human knowledge and skills are sources of capital and scarce factors of production and competition? *Of course!* But, when values flow strictly in one direction as a means to create value, and when people are seen strictly as assets, we violate ethical precepts that have guided the best part of our past for centuries. People are not tools. When organizations treat values as instrumental only and people as things—well, people do not need philosophy degrees to see through the sham. Employees can, and regularly do, detect false promises and insincerity, especially when the promises get no further than posters on company walls.

Instead of integrating economic and financial value as one of many values and *explicitly addressing political purposes*, organizations pursued a telling division of labor. Top management concentrated on shareholder value. They looked to marketing people to identify and deliver value to the customer and finance and operations people to make sure everyone delivered value to the shareholder. With few exceptions, the job of articulating values was delegated (some would say relegated) to Human Resources managers who often were uncomfortable and inexperienced in matters of

value. The linguistic split between value and values was institutional-
ized as a job split.

A swarm of sentimental and idealistic critics have taken the field
to condemn this. But, too often, the critics seek only to reverse the
sequence. They seek to have values be the single answer instead of
value. To them, economic and financial value should be the means,
and values—particularly family, social, and spiritual values—the
ends. Instead of the one-way, linear logic splitting off and subordinating values to value, they promote the opposite.

They ill serve themselves and us. Employees who intuitively
grasp the indignity of being assets also understand that companies
are not run exclusively for the benefit of those who do the work. Our
challenge is to reintegrate value and values, not to choose sides in a
destructive either/or battle between opposite sequences leading to a
single answer. We cannot restore value to its place as one among
many values by reversing the unethical logic of *The Balanced Scorecard*. And, perpetuating a dogma making values a means to the end
of value is unsustainable. Value must operate as one of many values—*all of which are **both** means **and** ends to and from one
another*. All human values—social, political, religious, technological,
legal, family, and economic—exist in a force field with one another.
No single one is superior to others.

Most employees embrace shareholder value as long as shareholders provide them with jobs, skills, opportunities, salaries, benefits,
and membership in a thick we. We should stop forcing people to an
either/or choice. Either you are a tool to create shareholder value.
Or, in line with love it or leave it political theory, you should quit to
find another job or start your own business. We ought to abandon
either/or in favor of both/and. We need to learn how to be *both* a
means *and* an end, and we need to insist that our markets, organizations, and networks reflect an ethics of both value and values. (See
the Ethical Scorecard, Illustrative Suggestion #1, in Chapter 17.)

. . . .

We live, as Peter Drucker says, in a society of organizations.[3] To
which I add, we also live in a society of markets and networks and
families and friends. Not surprisingly, the split between value and

---

3. Peter F. Drucker, *Post-Capitalist Society* (New York: HarperBusiness,
    1994), p. 49.

values in organizations echoes through markets and networks. There, too, value and values are estranged. In the markets with which we are most familiar—markets for products and services—our primary purpose as consumers is getting value for money. Few of us concern ourselves consciously with the values of the organizations that make, distribute, sell, and support what we buy. We are not in the habit, say, of considering the environmental values of oil companies when we purchase gasoline or the family values of financial service companies when we use credit cards. We worry about their values from time to time, but not usually at the point of purchase. Somehow the two sets of concerns remain separated.

The same division happens in media and political markets, organizations, and networks. Value is the dominion of business and economic news, and political news devoted to business and economics. Inflation, taxation, deregulation, reregulation, recession, growth, budgets, and deficits—all are the recurring themes of value sounded through the news. Whether packaged in sound bites or played out at feature length, the messages speak to value without reference to values. Meanwhile, following the commercial break or upon flipping to a different article, station, or Web site, we encounter news about values without reference to value.

These come in two flavors: (1) alarming trends, and (2) human-interest stories. The first are stories that scare us, that tell us values are deteriorating. Whatever the specifics, such stories point to underlying, systemic trends. News items such as the taking of American hostages in Iran, the Oklahoma City bombing, Montana militias, and attacks on the World Trade Center are about the recurring threat of terrorism. Headlines about dead lakes, smog, toxic waste, the greenhouse effect, acid rain, and oil spills chronicle the destruction of nature. Statistics and stories about divorce rates, sex scandals, latchkey children, Internet pornography, and priestly pedophilia recount the deterioration of the family.

The second variety illustrates good values packaged as human-interest stories. These provide anecdotal evidence that, well, things are not so bad. Positive human-interest stories suggest exceptional behavior, charming counterpoints to the drumbeat of deteriorating values. Evidently, human-interest stories are interesting because they remind us that something remains quaintly human about us.

Both categories of accounts—whether about bad or good values—rarely incorporate value. Meanwhile, stories about value, such as inflation, recession, stock market gains and so forth, do not connect to values. As consumers of news, of course, many of us connect value to values in our thoughts or conversations about such things. We might discuss, for example, the implications for family values raised by accounts of, say, executive perks and lifestyles. Or, we might remark to friends that there is an apparent pattern tying weak economic prospects for young men and women in the Middle East to recruitment opportunities for terrorists. But we are left to put the pieces together ourselves.

My criticism is not about thinking for ourselves. Of course, we must do that. Rather, it is a question of getting the information and analysis we need to think for ourselves in a world where *informed purposes* promise more than uninformed ones. In our world of markets, organizations, networks, families, and friends, we rely on the media to keep us abreast of a mind-bogglingly greater number of developments than concerned our ancestors who lived in worlds of places. Yet, by systematically isolating value from values, our media organizations, markets, and networks deprive us—their consumers—of the services and products we need to think and act as ethical participants in this new world.

Maybe sound-bite journalism is at odds with linking value to values and vice versa. Perhaps media organizations are stuck in old habits with unintended consequences, such as distinguishing among "news," "sports," "business," and "life." (Indeed, it is worth noting that sports sections do a better job of integrating value and values than others—probably because the business aspects of professional sports have so inescapably occupied the field of play.) Perhaps the editorial policies of media organizations are now handmaidens of business strategies relying on polarization, controversy, and celebrity to generate the ad revenues required to build shareholder value.

Whatever the explanations, the media's habit of divorcing value from values unfolds more than a problem of poor service quality unresponsive to consumer needs. There is a deep, underlying, and predictable behavior pattern here, one that habituates media organizations *and the rest of us* to the split between value and values. Repetition alone explains this. When so much of what we read, view, and hear are stories that focus on either value or values but not both, the separation becomes an expectation, a part of the reality of how we think about our day-to-day lives. It becomes "the way things are done around here."

The divorce is ugly. Look, for example, at the contest between value and values in recent presidential contests. History, at least the epigrammatic variety encoding memory these days, notes that Bill Clinton defeated George Bush in 1992 because the latter could not understand, relate to, or reverse deteriorating value. The image burned in our minds is of President Bush standing at a checkout counter bewildered by newfangled technology and oblivious to rising prices. Bush was inaccurately and unfairly branded by the media as clueless about value. The famous sound bite of 1992—"It's the economy, stupid!"—catapulted Clinton and *value* to victory. Pundits fussed over Clinton's dalliances, but got nowhere. Value elected Clinton again in 1996, even though the warnings about his personal values had so darkened daily headlines that Clinton was advised by political handlers to package himself as a promoter of values more than value.

By 2000, Americans had enjoyed an unparalleled run of prosperity. Value reigned supreme; good livings, as measured by value, were extended to tens of millions of people, many of whom, a decade earlier, had little hope of holding a job, investing in the stock market, buying a new car, or affording a trip to the dentist. *None of us should take this accomplishment for granted.* Value is not evil; value is good. And, value had delivered. Millions of small boats rose in a tide that provided dignity, opportunity, and other sources of material and subjective well-being.

Still, values suffered when value was king of the hill. This time the media stories were of the alarming trend variety. Just look at the headlines: Travelgate, Whitewater, Contract for America, Gingrich Shuts Down Government, Branch Davidians Burn in Waco, Terror in Oklahoma City, OJ, Monica, Impeachment. People were overwrought—not about value, but values.

I recall a conference of representatives from Red Cross chapters throughout North America held in the summer of 2000. The session's purpose was to imagine potential expansions on the well-known Red Cross mission regarding disaster services, blood supplies, and volunteerism. The chapter representatives divided into small groups and brainstormed. What happened was unexpected. Each group—independently—arrived at the same troubling question: What could the Red Cross do to help restore shared values in a world that all too regularly generated *human*, as opposed to natural, disasters?

The Red Cross folks overwhelmingly agreed value was not the main problem. Values were. In this, I think, they reflected the nation. In the subsequent 2000 election, Al Gore failed to straddle the widening gulf separating value from values. He simultaneously sought to redistribute Clinton-generated value while putting major-league distance between himself and Clinton's personal values. It didn't work. Values helped elect George Bush the younger to office. This time the bumper sticker exhorted us to "Restore Dignity to the Office."

It was close. Value won more votes than values, and many believe that Gore would have been President but for outmoded technology, local political hacks, and a controversial Supreme Court decision. Still, even if he held the office, his success or failure, like Bush's, would emerge from the chasm separating value from values—a divide that confers priority to the singular value over the plural values. Bush campaigned on a platform of values in a time of great value. In light of the dominance value has over values in our lives, he will only hold the office if he maintains and advances value, first and foremost. Or, if he finds a way to distract voters from problems of deteriorating value—for example, by capitalizing on a sense of insecurity to wage war.

. . . .

The rift is deep; it affects all who live in our new world of markets, organizations, networks, families, and friends. I am reminded of a twentysomething son of friends. As he made his way through college, he and his pals were increasingly absorbed with what seemed like a black and white choice: Should you pursue a remunerative career filled with the promise of wealth as a 24/7 workaholic in the global economy? Or, should you do something you might enjoy even though it seemed to imply dismal economic prospects? Should you pick value? Or values?

Like the East Germans, who grew dissatisfied with communism because they had access to Western television, radio, and music during the 1980s, our children are exposed every day in every imaginable way to the life of value. One account mentioned that teenagers see 3,000 advertisements per day. We don't need researchers, though, to tote up the value-laden messages and themes continuously—heck, intravenously—delivered through movies, TV, radio, music, magazines, and the Internet. But, unlike the East Germans, our children have no national or geographic wall separating them from value. There is only the either/or proposition pitting value against values.

The notion that, say, an investment banker might find meaning in his or her work and also—at work and away from work—act socially, religiously, environmentally, and politically responsible seems novel to those in their early twenties (indeed, to many of the rest of us too). The idea that teachers, government employees, auto mechanics, janitors, or midwives—or, increasingly, even doctors!—might thrive economically is equally disbelieved.

In response to this dilemma, a movement called the Graduation Pledge Alliance spread across campuses in the 1990s. It asks seniors to commit to social and environmental responsibility regardless of career pursuits. It is an example of self-exhortation without self-confidence—making stoic promises about values that we don't quite believe are possible to fulfill in a world where markets, networks, and organizations are so finely tuned to value.

There is a sweet naiveté in this pledge. Those of us over 30 know better. *But we do not convey our knowledge to our children.* Instead, we put them through years of education in which discussions of ethics are had in terms of citizen, community, and nation—in which we hardly mention, let alone develop, ethical action as employees in organizations, as consumers in markets, as network participants in networks, and as family members and friends living in a world of purposes. Intentionally or not, we ignore our world as it actually exists in favor of an idealized world of place gone by. Tens of millions of children and young adults, however, have *never* experienced a world of place other than in movies and television. The only world they know is a world of markets, networks, organizations, friends, and families. *That* is the world in which they need to find an ethical, hopeful path forward.

While college seniors confront their futures, many of their parents worry over the conflict between building greater financial security versus pursuing less remunerative options classed as making a difference. Adults, like their children, struggle with the conflict between value and values. Tellingly, in my acquaintance, however, are many adults who could diminish the pursuit of income and wealth in favor of a life of values, *if they choose to do so*.

When I inquire about this, I learn that most *enjoy* work and *their contribution to the organizations* in which they participate. They work in all manner of jobs: teachers, crafts, law enforcement, doctors, executives, supervisors, cooks, and more. And, while few express undiluted enthusiasm for every aspect of work, none experience work as the pain-filled, mind-numbing, and soul-killing drudgery described by 19th century philosophers and social critics. They do not work in the coal mines of industrializing England. Their participation in organizations yields *both meaning and money*—a reality we hear echoed any time we bump into a friend or acquaintance who has been downsized.

Yet, perhaps because so many inherited ideas incline toward categorizing life as *either* labor *or* leisure and as *either* doing well *or* doing good, many of us overlook and underappreciate how much we gain from the values we share with other people in the organizations where we work. Along with popular media, we romanticize a life of values unencumbered by the necessity of value. Like our children, too many of us believe we confront an irreducible either/or choice pitting value against values. What we somehow miss is what stares us in the face: *the opportunity, indeed the necessity, to reintegrate value and values by taking action in the organizations where we work.* Organizations are our towns—they are the social formations in and through which we *make a difference* today. We need to act in them knowing that *we* are the ones who determine "the way we do things around here" in organizations.

. . . .

Neither value-less values nor values-less value are worth much, and we know it. It is, I think, one of our dark secrets. It is the elephant in the room—the problem everyone knows exists but no one wants to mention. Value and values have parted company. More often than not, values are subordinated to the pursuit of value, especially in markets and organizations. Even efforts designed to promote values—such as crafting and publishing Statements of Values in organizations—are justified by the bottom line. When we are at work, we are told without embarrassment that we are assets in the production of value. We are asked to contribute to value through values such as teamwork, innovation, openness, diversity, and balancing work and life. The interpersonal aspects of such values are unremarkable. What *is* remarkable is that, unlike even a few decades ago, we encounter and practice such values far more in the organizations where we work than in the places where we live. Yet, these essentially *political* aspects of Statements of Values somehow elude us, perhaps because we associate politics with things negative and democracy with towns instead of organizations.

When we get home or go out, we see or read news stories that disconnect value from values even as they warn us about the scary consequences of deteriorating values. Like the Red Cross representatives I met in mid-2000, we wake up each day worrying about the next *human* disaster. We worry about a world that, as one Red Cross volunteer put it, "sits on our front porch." Yet, we recoil from the idea that politics is a constructive response to relentless trends the news media never lets us forget. And, because we fail to see or accept the reality of markets, networks, and organizations, we look past the venue where our politics can make the biggest difference: the organizations where we work or volunteer.

The habits acquired from living in markets, organizations, and networks imprint behaviors and beliefs at home and among friends. Our children think they face an irreducible choice: either value or values. We find it bewildering to balance financial needs with concerns about the environment, justice, spirituality, health, fairness, and one another. Yet, when we look to CEOs, government officeholders, media celebrities, and others who claim to lead us, we mostly encounter replays of the basic dilemma: the contest between value and values in markets, organizations, and networks.

It is not just that a genie has leapt from a bottle and we do not know how to put it back. We confront a profoundly different problem. *The bottle itself has changed.* We must find a new crucible for the errant genie—our new world of purposes and the markets, networks, organizations, friends, and families where we pursue purposes.

One approach I have seen succeed time and again echoes Gandhi's teaching *to be the change we wish to bring about.* In this, I think, we can take a cue from the quality movement that got such rude treatment in Roger Smith's General Motors. Among the hallmark lessons learned by people who successfully integrated quality into work are these: (1) *quality is not someone's job; it is everyone's job;* and (2) *quality must be tackled in the work we do **together.***

Reconnecting value and values is a concern for all of us—collectively and individually. It is something we must grapple with in our lives as we actually live them. We need to blend value and values in the *organizations* where we work or volunteer. We also must embrace this challenge in the *markets* and *networks* in which we participate and within our *families* and among our *friends.* We cannot succeed if we assume that reintegrating value and values is someone else's job. We will not progress by staring at others who dress up and entertain us as "Values Cats."

The second of the two quality lessons is equally vital. No organization *ever* implemented quality by focusing on individualism. Inevitably, major gains in quality arose only when people acted *together.*

For example, quality improved when activities such as customer service, product innovation, and logistics were reshaped by people who made quality *their shared purpose*. Individual responsibility was critical, but never enough.

Our new world of purposes has inherited a deep, abiding commitment to individualism. Individualism is *one* best part of our past. We cannot reintegrate value and values by abandoning our commitment to individualism. Yet, as the quality movement instructs, *individualism is not enough*. We must act *together*. In the best part of our past, acting together derived from many sources, including *political* values. To act together, we also relied heavily on shared beliefs, behaviors, and attitudes about "the way we do things around here." In this sense, the "Statement of Values" movement in organizations provides a chance to shape values of all sorts *in the organizations where we actually live together with people other than friends and family*.

Our new world has six social formations: markets, networks, nations, organizations, families, and friends. Of the six, organizations and families hold special promise for our future. It is in organizations and families that we spend the larger share of our time and attention. It is in organizations and families that we most persistently interact with other people who share in the achievement of our most critical purposes and with whom we inescapably share fates. Organizations and families give vitality to our strongest and most predictable shared values. They are our thickest we's. They are where we can act together most directly. If we can figure out how to heal the split between value and values in organizations and families by being the change we wish to bring about, we will take a huge leap toward imbuing our lives with what is best in our natures.

4 Explaining Values

In *The Fabric of Reality*, physicist David Deutsch equates knowledge with *better explanations*. Accurate predictions, he writes, are a byproduct of explanation and very important. But Deutsch insists that explanation is more crucial to understanding than prediction. He notes that the 17th century Catholic Church hierarchy okayed the publication of Galileo's heliocentric theory because they welcomed its predictive benefits. What frosted them—and led to the famous heresy trial, conviction, and recantation —was Galileo's contention that universal mathematical laws based on empirical observation had more *explanatory* power than Holy Scripture. *That*, not prediction, is what upset the Church hierarchy.

We need to seek better explanations if we are to rejoin value and values in our new world of purposes. Our new world is unprecedented. We no longer live in a world where place gives vitality to values. Instead, we live in markets, organizations, and networks, and among families and friends. These are our social formations. We know they influence our values, but we need to better understand why and how.

Far too often, though, our discussions of values do not provide better explanations. We fail to seek an understanding of what values exist, how they arise, and what any of us might do beyond exhortation and lament to influence them. We learn little about what explains values or makes them predictable.

Our ignorance begins with a disinclination to link value and values. We cannot discover better explanations without acknowledging that economic and financial value are exalted above other categories of values. Our ignorance continues with a habit of exhorting one another about what should be instead of first learning what is. We equate values with beliefs instead of admitting that values are the product (however messy) of belief, behavior, attitude, and speech. Our "should be" declarations rush to judgements about good versus bad without first explaining "what is" and "why."

Better explanations reserve comment on good versus bad until they figure out what is and why. Many men and women of the Baby Boom generation, for example, grew up believing "ladies go before gentlemen." Men opened doors or otherwise made way for women. Observations of actual behavior and attitude today suggest that, while this value persists, it is less shared than, say, 50 years ago. Regardless of whether any of us think this change good or bad, or important or unimportant, our observations suggest the degree to which this particular social value is shared.

Values as they actually are reflect the way we do things, the way we act, the way we speak, the way we think, and the way we behave. Consider drinking and driving. Perhaps your values about drinking and driving arose from years of drumbeat statistics, news stories, admonitions, and the experiences of friends and relatives. Perhaps they stemmed from a single incident. Perhaps you had never thought much about drinking and driving and *you* until, one night, you left a party a bit tipsy, missed a curve, and drove off the road. You were okay, just a bit shaken. But for you the eluded tree was a burning bush, a lucid personal message. You grew outspoken. From that moment you believed that driving under the influence is dangerous, irresponsible, and wrong. You joined Mothers Against Drunk Driving and now, whenever possible, you share your story and its lessons with others. Your teenage children consider you unreasonable about it.

Whatever your belief and however it emerged, it is improbable to live in our world beyond a certain age and not have a point of view and accompanying behavior regarding drinking and driving. We have decidedly strong and predictable values about drinking and driving because it is among our hallmark shared experiences. Alcohol and cars are embedded in our lives. We each must have some policy and we each must behave in some way that indicates whether we adhere to it. My guess is that 90 percent of us over the age of, say, 30 oppose drunk driving, believe we know our own personal limits, and nearly always stick to them. (That the estimation of personal capacities for drink might miss the proper legal or physiological mark raises an important issue of skill and knowledge. But it does not contradict that, with remarkably high consistency, our intentions, attitudes, and behaviors—our "are" values—are strong and predictable.)

In North America, 10 percent of the over-30 population plus an undoubtedly larger percentage of drivers below 30 is an unsettlingly large number of drivers careless about their blood alcohol level. There are 1.5 million DUI arrests each year in the United States; one-third of those nab repeat offenders. More than 17,000 people die annually from accidents involving drunk drivers. Just because many adults share a strong value about drinking and driving does not eliminate the menace. Still, think about the strength of this shared value, particularly in light of omnipresent anxieties over deteriorating values: Tens of millions of people share a recognizably similar belief structure and pattern of aligned behavior!

Calling our consensus over drinking and driving good would not spark much debate. Better explanations, though, emerge when we seek first to understand and only then to pass judgement. For example, pro-choice and pro-life adherents champion many competing values. The conformance of belief and behavior within each group is probably close to the drunk driving standard for strong, predictable values. Yet, unlike the drunk driving illustration, if I were to label either group's values as good or bad, I would instantly divert attention from what *explains* their strength. Explainable and predictable values might be good or bad or anything in between. Certainly, many pro-life adherents believe that pro-choice people have a set of predictable, yet bad, values.

. . . .

Our inclinations to exhort instead of explain erupt in the wake of gross failures. We see Bill Clinton distinguish sex from what he did with Monica Lewinsky, and we declare that executives (and interns!) *should be* better behaved. We hear George W. Bush distinguish insider stock deals and gimmicky accounting from what he did at Harken and what Dick Cheney did at Halliburton. In response, we assert that leaders *should be* less hypocritical. We learn that the first response of some Catholic dioceses to the sex abuse scandal in 2002 was financial damage control. We exclaim that abusive priests *should be* kept away from kids and bishops *should be* more interested in helping people than protecting church treasuries.

Each instance repeats a pattern. We exhort. We mix comments about individuals (Clinton, Lewinsky, Bush, Bernard Cardinal Law of Boston) with those about collectivities (executives, interns, political leaders, bishops, priests). We rush to "should be" and "good" versus "bad." We do not pause to ask what is and why.

Exhortations matter. People who articulate clear, compelling "should be" values have always done a service—especially when their own beliefs, behaviors, and attitudes reflect those values. Exhortation can work well in the absence of explanation *as long as it calls upon values already shared*. When parents, for example, exhort children to tell the truth inside a family that practices truthfulness, explanation is not required (however much it might help).

But exhortation stumbles in the absence of already strong shared values. In that case, explanation is sorely needed. Such is our situation today. Tens of millions of us have transitioned abruptly from a world of places to a world of purposes. We carry precepts that made sense in a world of places. Yet, when we convert the precepts into exhortations, our words bounce off ears deafened by the swirling realities of our new world of purposes. Our world has shifted. We cannot safely assume that the people we exhort share values with us.

We are at risk when we admonish in the absence of better explanations. Consider, for example, two anti-drug campaigns of the past few decades. The 1980s "Just Say No" effort sloganeered against illegal drug markets. First Lady Nancy Reagan and other leaders sought to win share of mind among children and teenagers. Theirs was a laudable effort—one that promoted a distinct alternative for kids targeted by drug markets, networks, and organizations.

As a strategy for shaping anti-drug values, however, "Just Say No" failed the test of a *better explanation* for how children's values emerge in our new world. "Just Say No" advertised in consumer markets. It directed messages at children and friends. Other than sloganeering, however, it mostly ignored the workings of markets, networks, organizations, families, and friends.

In our new world, advertising can effectively raise widespread awareness. "Just Say No" emphasized individual responsibility, a message consistent with one of our strongest values. But neither awareness nor individual responsibility are enough to shape and sustain *shared* values among people who, as we learned from the quality movement, must act *together* (see Chapter 3). For that to happen, messages and resources also must be directed at *groups*—

especially groups who are thick we's because of shared fates and shared purposes.

The "Just Say No" campaign stimulated *potential* conversations about drugs among adults and children. But it did not take enough steps to convert potential conversations into actual conversations or actual conversations into actual behavior. Many parents, for example, were likely to have "Just Said Yes" earlier in their lives. So were teachers, ministers, local governmental officials, and business managers. Discussions stimulated by "Just Say No" were likely to be awkward ones if, indeed, they happened at all.

It is a mistake in our new world of purposes to *assume* that individual values translate into group values. No one should take for granted that parent-child talks about drugs even occur in a world of working, shopping, playing, movies, TV, and chat. Adults are exhausted when they get home from work. Teenage children routinely flee to their rooms, which, not coincidentally, are wired to markets, organizations, and networks. In our reality, a child's room is as much part of the wider world as it is the home; a teenager's room is even more so.

Promoting awareness about what "should be" among individuals *without stimulating and supporting **group** follow-through is poor strategy*. It is like announcing an exciting new piece of communications software, then failing to educate consumers about how to use that software *together*. We know, for example, that the usefulness of any network rises in proportion to the number of people using it. Communications software is more valuable if you can reach thousands or millions of people rather than a few. In this sense, "Just Say No" might have fostered an extensive anti-drug network among young people and adults.

Building such a network would have required group action as well as individual action. It depended on conversations at home and conversations at school, church, and so forth. In a tightly knit world of places, family conversations were likely to reinforce discussions at school or church. In a world of places, it was reasonably likely that parents had ongoing relationships with their kids' teachers. Parents and teachers could rely on an echo effect. Not so in our new world. We might meet teachers once or twice a year. But we do not *know* them in the manner we know friends or colleagues at work. Our knowledge of our kids' teachers is thin rather than thick. It takes shape from roles (parent and consumer versus teacher and employee) rather than open-ended, persistent relationships.

We can make assumptions about the values of those who teach our kids. They, in turn, can make assumptions about our values. They and we can assume all of us are against drugs. But these premises are fragile in a world where drug use (including alcohol) is routine, supply is abundant, cultural messages are mixed, and the legalization of soft drugs is supported by millions. Nor do such assumptions easily translate into action in a world where action bears risks that go beyond the purview of drugs. Teachers, for example, who single out students for proscribed behavior regarding drugs risk unintended consequences. They cannot predict what might happen if their actions trigger reactions from angry parents, unsympathetic school administrators, a controversy-hungry media, or a confusing, slow, and unreliable legal market.

In this messy picture, we cannot confidently presume any pattern of shared beliefs and shared behaviors regarding drugs. Nor can we accurately predict how "Just Say No" messages get implemented, if at all, in the classroom or at home. In the absence of self-conscious, proactive *group* coordination, it is a mistake to assume that messages and actions at home reinforce those at school and vice versa. Nor can we assume that home and school discussions about drugs link in any predictable fashion with those at church, at the mall, or on the Net.

We live in a kaleidoscopic world of markets, networks, and organizations. Our markets extend beyond local boundaries. Rarely do the organizations and networks in any particular market coincide with neighborhoods or towns. Drugs are such a market. The "Just Say No" campaign advertised. But that is all. It neither reduced the supply of drugs nor attacked the profits of drug organizations and networks. It shut its eyes to the *value* reaped by those who promote instead of proscribe drugs. As a strategy, it exhorted individuals to "Just Say No." But it ignored the workings of markets, organizations, networks, families, and friends. "Just Say No" concentrated on "should be" values instead of seeking a better explanation for values as they actually get shaped and operate in our new world.

"Just Say No" led to another anti-drug campaign in the '90s— one that concentrated more explicitly on groups as well as individuals. It, too, exhorted parents to speak to kids about drugs. It, too, fell short of addressing the value aspects of drugs: the profits of producers and distributors. But as a consumer marketing effort, this second campaign took more effective advantage of how organizations, networks, families, and friends shape values in our new world of purposes.

It explicitly addressed individual and group belief and behavior. It openly acknowledged the difficulties parents might face in discussing drugs with kids and provided specific suggestions for how to approach the topic. This campaign recruited organizations to invite police officers and other adults into schools to discuss drugs and to set goals for children regarding anti-drug behavior. It taught kids how to work together to reinforce anti-drug values. Resources were provided to support such organizations and efforts. It encouraged parents to participate in the programs and to attend celebrations of success. Unlike "Just Say No," this second campaign did not assume that efforts at home would coordinate with efforts elsewhere or that shared ideas ("Just Say No") were sufficient to trigger shared purposes and action. Instead, it orchestrated coordination. It embraced *our* new reality, one in which shared values take strength from coordinated *group* action, especially in the thick we's of families, friends, and organizations.

Too often, we undercut efforts directed at values by limiting them to exhortations directed solely at individuals. As in the "Just Say No" campaign, we define "should be" values for improved individual lives much as we list out ingredients for better meals. Yet, we ignore the kitchens in which our lives get shaped—especially our lives *together* In our world, those kitchens are markets, organizations, networks, families, and friends. They are the contexts in which thick we's emerge who share values with one another because they actually, not just theoretically or remotely, share fates with one another. Better explanations for values—such as those in the second anti-drug campaign—happen when we take markets, organizations, and networks into account.

. . . .

What do actual beliefs, behaviors, attitudes, and speech indicate regarding political values? Clearly, we prefer democratic means to dictatorial ones for resolving differences and choosing directions. Yet, one of our favorite expressions suggests it is detestable to *politicize* any issue or question. It seems we live in a world that reveres democracy but hates politics.

The vast majority of us *believe* in two touchstones of democracy: voting in free elections and the liberty to do or say any thing we darn well please (see Chapter 12). Yet, our actual behaviors, attitudes, and speech match up poorly with our beliefs. We do not vote regularly or in large numbers. Rarely do more than 20 percent of eligible voters cast ballots in elections, especially state and local ones. Tens of millions of us have known for *decades* that we are estranged from, instead of engaged in, governmental markets, networks, and organizations.

In our organizations and families, neither voting nor free elections are commonplace. Nor do we regularly do or say anything we darn well please in organizations—although we do so more often in markets, networks, and families. By our twin standards of belief, then, we do not seem to behave democratically. There is much that is random and confusing in this picture.

Hey, we're human. We have failings. In any explanation of human values, the glass will be half-full, half-empty. We can always do better. But I think human frailty has less to do with explaining political values than a habit of mislabeling contexts. *I think we look at the wrong glass.* When we look at the glass of a nation of citizens, we observe beliefs, behaviors, attitudes, and speech that are weak and random. In contrast, when we look at a glass defined by markets, organizations, and networks, we see a more predictable pattern of actual belief and behavior.

We observe strong and predictable belief, behavior, attitude, and speech among people who:

- work in government service organizations;
- are members of unions, or party organizations and networks;
- participate in single issue advocacy organizations and networks;
- are employed by political action committees, lobbyists, or government affairs functions of companies and industry associations; and
- comprise well-identified demographic market segments (for example, college-educated women over 40).

In the first four, we find we's with strongly shared values about voice, participation, voting, and consent. In the fifth, there are market segments: collectivities of individuals who are not thick we's in the sense of participating in pursuit of shared purposes *they must implement together.* Collectivities of I's are thin we's pursuing *similar* purposes and interests in markets in a manner understood by organizations seeking their support. All five we's arise in organizations, markets, and networks, rather than nations or towns. Importantly, when we observe belief and behavior among people who do not fit these categories, we see a pattern of *similarly strong and pre-*

dictable values. It is just that the pattern indicates voting in elections is useless or doesn't make a difference.

In our new world of purposes, we find more widespread participation, voice, opinion, and choice in *nonpolitical* markets than in political ones. Nonpolitical markets do not rely on voting in elections. Millions of us actively participate through voice, resources, and effort in hundreds of markets from automobiles to zero-coupon bonds. In the 1980s, for example, tens of millions of people voiced opinions and made choices about Word versus WordPerfect. Similarly, the quality and variety of coffee available to coffee drinkers expanded over the 1990s in response to consumers who voiced opinions and made choices. In neither case did anybody vote in an election. Still, nonpolitical markets depend on widely shared patterns of actual belief, behavior, attitude, and speech that tell us much about our current democratic experience in markets—*about our market democracies*.

Increasingly, we participate with voice and choice in the organizations where we work, learn, or volunteer. There is a growing set of shared values regarding fairness, voice, due process, and consent in organizations (see Chapter 13). We expect to offer opinions and be heard when we contribute to solving problems at work. When we observe actual belief and behavior, we find a greater likelihood of shared values regarding democratic forms of participation in, say, project teams in organizations than in local, state, or national elections.

Actual behaviors and beliefs strongly suggest that our practice of local democracy has shifted from the towns and neighborhoods where we reside to the organizations where we contribute time and effort. Because we're human, this glass of the organization as political entity is surely half-full and half-empty. There are, for example, issues and policies such as brand, strategy, and due process often off-limits to democratic political values that are otherwise embraced routinely in problem solving to improve quality or customer service. We can do better. But we are more likely to strengthen the political values we practice every day of our lives in organizations than in towns.

Something novel is going on—something we cannot explain by studying a half-full, half-empty glass defined by voting, citizenship, town, and nation. We find better explanations for political values regarding voice, participation, and consent when we observe actual beliefs, behaviors, attitudes, and speech in *markets and organizations than in towns, states, or nations*.

. . . .

"Just Say No" would have thrived in a world of places. Families, friends, neighbors, community leaders, churches, and schools would have incorporated the anti-drug message into a fabric of *already strong shared beliefs and behaviors*. In a world of places, communities with strong shared values would have *actively* looked after one another's children.

Why? What explains the strength and predictability of shared values in the towns and neighborhoods of a world of places compared to the towns and neighborhoods in our new world of purposes? Or, put differently, what explains the greater strength of shared values inside, say, organizations where we work than in towns and neighborhoods where we reside?

Evolutionary psychologists and biologists argue that shared values reflect genetic inheritance. We know, for example, that something in our DNA makes yawning and smiling contagious. Smiling can lighten our mood. It increases our sense of fellow feeling and benevolence, social values we share with other people.

Evolutionary psychologists point, for example, to genetically inherited skills of pattern recognition to explain profiling—the practice of singling out individuals with certain characteristics. Over the course of the 1990s, a growing sentiment weighed against racial profiling by police. Then, following the September 11, 2001, terrorist attacks, people who sincerely believed racial profiling was wrong admitted doing it themselves at airports and on airplanes. Genetics helps explain this.

We know from genetics that we are social beings who cooperate as well as compete. Genetics, however, do not sufficiently explain when, why, and with whom we cooperate or compete. What, beyond genetics, causes us to share values with other people? Why do individuals break with or conform to the values of a group? Who are those groups? How do they come to be? When and why can we expect shared values to be strong and predictable versus weak and random?

There are several sources of shared values that have operated throughout history. Whether people live in a world of places or a world of purposes, shared values arise from:

- *shared relationships founded in shared fates,* especially relationships with other people we come to know well because critical aspects of our destinies are intertwined in inescapably obvious ways;
- *shared roles and status*, such as parent, employee, and customer;
- *shared ideas*, such as "Just Say No";
- *shared resources*, such as wealth or water; and
- *shared purposes*, such as making profits.

Consider the wave. In sports arenas around the world, there has been a shared expectation for several years now that, if an individual or group stands up and waves their hands in the air, others seated next to them will do likewise, causing a wave to propagate around the arena. Most people who participate in the wave have never met one another. Genetic mimicry helps explain this phenomenon. But so do other shared experiences. The wave draws on shared understandings about the role and status of fan and the shared ideas and purposes of sports entertainment. It taps into shared relationships. Friends and families who attend games respond in unison to the wave.

Each source of shared values operates differently in our world of purposes than in a world of places. In a world of places, the sources of shared experience were more likely to overlap and reinforce one another. Not always. Not certainly. But probabilities favored a congruence that promoted predictable shared values instead of an inconsistency that worked against them.

In a world shaped by place, people who lived in the same place shared relationships spanning multiple, reinforcing contexts such as home, work, church, and local government. Roles and status cut across circumstances. A teacher was likely to be a friend, a fellow church member, and a neighbor. In a world of places, shared resources, especially scarce ones, were mutually apparent. Water quality or road access, for example, likely garnered similar priority. Purposes more easily became *shared* purposes among those who lived near one another, whether those purposes were defense, economic development, or self-government. Ideas, too, were more likely to be shared among people who lived, worked, worshipped, and governed together.

By shared purposes and ideas, I mean commonly perceived and understood ones. Ideas and purposes can be shared without airtight agreement. The idea of witchcraft in 17th and 18th century Massachusetts villages inspired deep disagreements. So did purposes for how best to respond. But the proximity and intensity with which people lived together, like the rich fabric of shared fates, relationships, roles, status, resources, and ideas, made it more likely that witchcraft would be a strongly shared idea and the purposes shaped would be commonly understood.

The power of place over people made it probable that sources of shared experiences—relationships, roles, status, ideas, purposes, resources—would overlap and reinforce one another. This congruence helps explain why shared values overshadowed individual values in a world of places. History teaches that worlds of places were inherently collective, conservative, and cautious. We read about individuals like Galileo who suffered in cultures whose shared values seemed relentlessly bent on destroying individualism. A corollary suggests that new ideas came more slowly and in fewer numbers to a world of places.

In our new world, the sources for shared experiences operate in radically different contexts. They are anything but congruent. In a world of places, for example, shared relationships occurred among the same set of people who interacted with another in a variety of ways. In our world, shared relationships mostly happen at home, on the job, and among friends, but, critically, our relationships at work or school only randomly involve the same people as those at home or among friends. A friend once mentioned that his 10-year-old child asked him, "Daddy, when are you going to bring your friends from work home?" Millions of us don't bring our friends from work home. "Take your children to work day" aside, we don't bring our families— or other friends—to work.

Some of our shared roles are barely a century old, if that. We are consumers, investors, and networkers in addition to employees, family members, and friends. While the role of employee dates back a long way, its meaning to us would shock those who labored in centuries past. In our new world, we do not regularly see or interact with the same people in different roles. We are surprised to see a teacher at the mall or run into our car dealer at a game. Our role-based interactions tend to be unicontextual. They confine themselves to single contexts and single role sets (student and teacher at school, or customer and customer service representative over the phone).

Meanwhile, our world of markets, organizations, and networks has spawned entirely new shared ideas, such as brands and celebrities (see Chapter 9). Our markets and networks churn out ideas in unimaginably larger numbers and at faster speeds than ever before in history. If our ancestors found it hard to gain access to new ideas, we cannot escape them. Ideas flood over us, yet there is less likelihood that any given idea will run soul deep within us. In our world, a lack of information explains ignorance as often as a lack of ideas, perhaps more so.

We are more likely to recognize resources as mutually scarce in families or organizations than in markets (a phenomenon that bedevils environmental efforts). Many of us, for example, in the post-bubble economy of the past few years have a richer, more visceral and shared understanding of tighter budgets in the organizations where we work than the state and local governments who serve us. We read about budgetary crises in governments and, if we are unlucky enough to need those services, we feel them as consumers and beneficiaries. If we are not consumers and beneficiaries of governments, though, our experience of state and local budget cuts is limited to *shared ideas*. In contrast, as employees, we cannot escape the experience of budgetary cuts in the organizations where we work.

In our new world, purpose brings people together in thick we's more than place. Organizations and families—not towns or neighborhoods—provide the contexts in which we experience overlaps and reinforcement among shared fates, shared purposes, shared relationships, shared roles, shared resources, and shared ideas. Not surprisingly, then, organizations and families are the crucibles in which we discover our richest blends of strong shared values.

. . . .

Markets, organizations, and networks have transformed the sources of shared experiences. The contexts, purposes, and numbers of our shared relationships differ. The number, kind, and potential influence of our shared ideas differ. The nature and contexts of our shared roles and purposes differ. There is a jumbled discontinuity instead of the congruence that promoted strong shared values in a world of places.

This has happened in a startlingly short time frame. All of this makes it risky to exhort about what *should be* before seeking better explanations about *what is*. Yet, we hear so much about the deterioration of values in our regime of value that it is little wonder many of us wring our hands and raise our voices. Too often, when we speak up to clarify or instruct, we do no more than decry our condition without *explaining* that condition. We define the good values we *should be* practicing. We say the response to drugs *should be* "Just Say No." We opine that the ills of the underclass *should be* cured through individual responsibility, volunteerism, faith-based effort, and a thousand points of light. We tell one another that democracy's weaknesses *should be* cured by getting out the vote.

Our opinions and judgement matter. But it is insane to keep shouting at one another without understanding when and why strongly shared values are *possible* in this confusing new world. When we raise our voices, we tend to look past the actual contexts in which we live our lives: markets, organizations, networks, families, and friends. We miss what stares us in the face. We call for individual action, but miss the power of organizations and networks. We seduce ourselves with a cult of individualism that overlooks the necessity of thick we's who care—*organizations*—in making anything new or better happen (see Chapter 15). We celebrate points of light only to miss the greater glory of a *grid* of light that connects skills, resources, and opportunities through *networks* (see What Works, Illustrative Suggestion #22, in Chapter 17). In our stress or fury over what has gone wrong with values, we miss the potential to evolve our shared roles as consumers, employees, and investors and to revitalize shared values through how we govern ourselves in organizations, markets, and networks. We miss the chance to explain ourselves to ourselves in how we live our lives today.

5 Shared Paths

In his *Republic*, Plato recounts the story of Gyges, a shepherd from Lydia who unearths a magic ring that, when twisted, makes him invisible. Posthaste, Gyges deploys his new ring to seduce the queen, kill the king, seize power, and otherwise substantially improve his socioeconomic condition. *The Lord of The Rings* also tells the tale of a magic ring that turns the bearer invisible, but cues off good versus evil instead of ethical questions about justice.

. . . .

Gyges would not have committed murder, adultery, and theft had his fellow Lydians kept him in sight. He did it because he could get away with it. The speakers in *The Republic* disagree over whether he acted justly. Those who defend Gyges argue that might is right, and justice nothing more than the sum of individual pursuits of power, wealth, status, fame, and sex. Those who disapprove, including Socrates, argue that justice requires a balancing of many interests and values, both individual and shared.

Gyges would find plenty of opportunity to express his brand of individuality in our new world of purposes. In our world, value and values have parted company from one another. Value reigns supreme. Our largest social formations—markets—promote unfettered individualism and the self-interested pursuit of value. When we act in markets as consumers or investors, it is easy to be invisible to other people in our lives (see Chapters 6 and 7). Gyges lived in a world of places where shared values trumped individual values. Our markets are different. We revere individual values above shared values in markets. Individual choice is paramount. Much of our conception of self-government and the rule of law is dedicated to preserving individual choice from the strictures of shared values.

Putting aside judgements about good versus bad, we see actual beliefs, behaviors, attitudes, and speech that promote individualism in markets. We protect commercial speech in the face of group opposition (for example, pornography). We prohibit group infringements on individual choices for religious and spiritual well-being (for example, school prayer). We permit individual options that might be harmful to groups (for example, drinking, smoking, gambling, and polluting). We lessen or eliminate constraints on individuals that might arise from group commitments regarding marriage (for example, no-fault divorce) or children (for example, abortion rights). In our world, value regularly wins, particularly individual pursuits of value. It is easier for us to get a divorce than fire an employee because, in each case, individual economic freedom trumps shared values.

Our devotion to individual rights makes us reluctant to suggest that individuals fairly can be burdened by the values of groups—at least in markets. Note however that I reserve my comments to *markets*. If we look only at markets, we observe few shared values beyond our common dedication to individual freedom, individual choice, and individual pursuit of value. We live, however, in organizations and among families and friends in addition to living in markets. Our actual beliefs, behaviors, attitudes, and speech depict a dramatically different blend of individual and shared values in non-market contexts. *In organizations and among families and friends, shared values regularly override individual values.* Gyges would have needed his magic ring to pursue his private agenda in organizations and families. He would have had to be invisible to escape the strong shared values that emerge among people whose multifaceted and purposeful shared relationships make them constant witnesses to one another's lives.

. . . .

Strong and predictable shared values arise from persistent interactions among people known to one another. I use the phrase "shared path" to describe contexts where a consistent set of people known to one another persistently interact. Families and friends are shared paths in our world of purposes, just as they were in a world of places. Beyond families and friends, however, our shared paths mostly arise in organizations—a pattern quite different from a world of places.

We are much more likely to interact persistently with a consistent set of people in organizations where we work, learn, or volunteer than in neighborhoods, towns, or other places where we reside. A friend of mine, for example, runs a construction crew. Depending on the project, a half dozen or so men interact with one another over a series of months. The core group has remained fairly constant for several years. They have a strong common sense of shared purpose and shared values. Individualism matters. They know and respect each other's personalities and preferences. But across a number of issues—timeliness, quality, pitching in, pricing, goofing off—their actual beliefs, behaviors, attitudes, and speech reveal strongly shared values to which individuals are held accountable.

A few years ago, a brother of one of them joined the crew. A couple of months later, several men mentioned to my friend that the brother was proselytizing on behalf of his born-again beliefs. My friend called a meeting. The men discussed and debated the problem. They decided to ask the brother to make a choice: stop recruiting or stop working with them.

These are not anti-religious men. One is a deacon of a local church. But their shared values outweighed the brother's individual values. Their actual beliefs and behaviors proscribed a particular form of individualism as inconsistent with the common good. In taking action, they revealed how they chose to govern themselves through democratic means of voice and consent.

Two of the men happen to be neighbors. But place is irrelevant to the crew. Their persistent interactions occur because they work together, not because they live near one another. Their pattern typifies lives in markets, organizations, networks, families, and friends, where we experience shared paths in organizations and among families and friends.

Shared paths rarely arise in markets. We tend to operate as individual consumers or voters in markets. If we have persistent interactions with any consistent players, it is with *companies, brands, products, and services*, not people. Shared values in markets happen more because of shared roles (Chapters 6 and 7) and shared ideas (Chapters 8 and 9) than shared paths. Yet, neither shared roles nor shared ideas are as potent as shared paths in establishing strong, predictable shared values.

The asymmetry favoring individualism in markets is reversed in organizations and among families and friends. We make a mistake when we assume that the individualism rampant in markets operates as freely in organizations and among families and friends. Indeed, if we fail to specify context among markets, organizations, and networks, we can easily misconstrue trends about value and values.

Consider, for example, the rise in intergenerational selfishness. We regularly read or hear that retirement age people reject school bonds or live in gated housing developments that exclude families with school-age children. Time and distance have shattered multigenerational family gatherings. Commentators wonder about the long-term effects on kids who spend little time with their grandparents.

But this trend ought not surprise us. Simply (if painfully), it is far less likely that people from different generations share paths in our world of purposes than was the case in a world of places. Place does not forge intergenerational shared paths like it used to. Our shared paths happen in organizations, but few organizations have employees who span all age ranges, from the very old to the very young. Nor do organizations overlap with families. When older and younger people work together in organizations, the intergenerational experiences do not coincide with family. Once they retire, people work less in organizations alongside other generations. Meanwhile, when families scatter, the likelihood of intergenerational shared paths diminishes further.

Retired people do have shared paths. Quite often, with each other. People in gated housing developments persistently interact with one another. When retirement-age people band together to promote positions on, say, school taxes, their shared paths are pointedly generation-specific, not intergenerational. We see strongly shared values, but ones unfriendly to intergenerational values instead of the reverse. Like many challenges, then, intergenerational issues now play out in markets and networks. We worry over deteriorating intergenerational shared values; we worry, for example, that schools suffer as a consequence. Incorporating shared values into markets, however, is mighty hard—it demands organization and the time and money to participate.

Shared paths produce stronger, more predictable, and enforceable values for many reasons. *First, is the effect of repeated interactions, past and future.* People who have interacted in the past and expect to do so in the future form mutual expectations and obligations. They learn how individual beliefs and behavior are likely to get expressed in the context of the group's interests and purposes.

Several years ago, for example, I joined the Board of Directors of a start-up company founded by three people with modest business skills and big dreams. Ours is a shared path. The three executives, another Board member, and I have persistently interacted for a long time. Our interactions give specific content to the expectations and obligations we have of one another. The three executives expect to receive advice and counsel from me regarding a wide range of business issues. They expect me to show up for Board meetings and to be available by phone and email. I, in turn, expect them to listen and learn about finance, sales, and operations. But these are not legal obligations; there is no signed contract here. Our mutual expectations and obligations arise from shared values and shared purpose—from the experience of our shared path.

Through persistent interactions, we have discovered much about each other's honesty, dependability, openness, and respect. We know more about each other's character and motivations than when we began our shared path experience. They know I am interested in assisting them to learn and succeed as individuals and as a company. I know one of them is captivated by the chance to provide nonprofit organizations with better, lower-cost technology while another is also hoping to get very rich.

Second, ongoing interactions among a consistent set of people are more likely to have consequences beyond mere entertainment or one-off transactions. Obviously, the Board of Directors, like my friend's construction crew, deals with serious consequences. Each shared path involves inescapable aspects of shared fates. Yet, even loose, contemporary shared paths formed through regular dinners and movies with friends sustain and shape shared values. Such interactions give rise to declarations ranging across the political and economic, the social and religious, the environmental and technological. Talk matters. But so does action. Dinner-and-movies yields to occasions with more consequence than mere chat. Friends call on one another when the kids are sick, the car is broken, the electricity is out, or some candidate or cause needs support. When that happens, behavior gives ballast to belief.

Third, shared path interactivity ranges across many categories of values. There is more than economics involved in my friend's construction crew and the start-up company's Board of Directors. Value matters. But so do social and political values.

The shared paths at the church where one of the builders is a deacon encompass more than religious values. While the primary focus may be religious, a variety of individual and group social, political, economic, legal, family, and environmental beliefs and behaviors operate. The nature and extent of participation, the voice given and expected in decisions, the regularity and size of financial support, the responses to the good and ill fortune of others—these values blend together with the religious.

Shared values wax in strength when multiple categories of values blend together—especially when we integrate value and values. Shared paths almost always involve such blending; they thicken relationships by increasing the degrees of integration described in Chapter 2. People in shared paths at work, for example, inevitably discuss and act on social, economic, political, family, technological, and other values. Value and values commingle in their interactions. Even when formal purposes are economic or religious, the actual blend of values is much richer.

We need to look at this richer blend to understand the ethical challenges we face. Consider, for example, the decline in pro bono work at law firms. Many values are at stake when lawyers make choices about their time, including economic, social, political, and family values. Don't think for a minute that the drop in pro bono efforts, and the values it encompasses, is not discussed in law firms. This decline is talked about, critically, among lawyers who know one another and whose character and values are on the line in the conversations and action or inaction following such discussions.

In comparison to this kind of thick, personal interactivity in shared paths in organizations, our interactions in markets are thin. When you go to a restaurant and a host escorts you to a table, a waiter takes your order, a busboy cleans up, and a cashier accepts your payment, narrow beliefs and behaviors are involved. Any values you take away are unlikely to have a subject's name attached *other than the name of the restaurant* (a point with interesting repercussions for organizations and markets, including how and why we might seize on *brand* as a vehicle for integrating value and values).

When combined, the repetition of interactions among people in shared paths, the consequences of those interactions, and the likelihood that interactions encompass a variety of values all contribute to the strength, depth, predictability, and enforceability of shared values in shared paths. People in shared paths do a pretty good job describing each other's values—at least as they pertain to the purposes and activities of the shared path. Each of us, if asked, has articulate, precedent-based expectations regarding the behavior of others and how well behavior comports with beliefs. Each of us is more likely to act in accordance with shared expectations because of obligation and habit. Finally, each of us is more likely to regret, or at least be conscious of, failure or surprise.

. . . .

Shared paths are not Edens. There are dysfunctional shared paths whose strong, predictable values are bad and have severe negative consequences. Spousal and child abuse, for example, are strong, predictable behaviors in some shared paths. We are focusing first on explanations for predictable versus random values, instead of good versus bad ones. Even in healthy shared paths, people give vent to pride, envy, anger, temptation, hypocrisy, anxiety, and greed. We screw up. Still, it is characteristic of shared paths that, mathematically speaking, deviations are exceptions, and when they occur, we expect and accept chastisement.

The enforceability of shared path values stems from mutually reinforcing expectations and obligations and the possibility of shame and punishment. People in shared paths tend to discipline themselves; they do not require specialized or dedicated enforcement resources. Parents perform enforcement functions in families, as do captains on teams, leaders at work, deacons at church, and various individuals at various times among friends. Even criminals who conspire together have a code of values that is mutually enforced—something regularly depicted in movies and books.

Rarely, however, do shared paths demand dedicated, full-time cops—that is, one or more people whose sole function is enforcement. The appearance of such policing often signals an increase in number beyond the feasible limits of shared paths. Shared paths cannot operate among large numbers of people. Logistically and psychologically, a consistent set of people who number, say, 10,000 have neither the time nor wherewithal to persistently interact. Subsets of the 10,000 can, but not the whole group.

Throughout history, we observe cities and towns subdividing into smaller groups, such as neighborhoods, guilds, churches, and so forth. It is no accident that Aristotle's advice on the numeric limit of an effective city-state and Madison's about an effective Congress both suggested limits at several hundred. *This is also the barrier below which contemporary organizations most effectively do work.* Look closely at large corporations and you will find they organize and conduct work within this optimal range. Today, if you are an employee, independent contractor, or joint venture participant with Shell Oil, British Airways, the FBI, or the Salvation Army, you do not belong to a single shared path with thousands of people. But you do share one or more paths, each comprised of a consistent set of people with whom you persistently interact.

Recently, I read that public high schools near my home put full-time police officers on site. Among them is one school whose daily population (students, faculty, administrators, and others) is less than 400 and another exceeding 3,000. I believe I am reading two different stories. In the larger school, functional specialization is a reasonable organizational strategy to increase educational effectiveness. This larger school (like all schools) confronts the contemporary cocktail of sex, drugs, and rock n' roll. Yet, its educational performance remains impressive—reinforcing my sense that the full-time cop might be worth trying.

Reports about the smaller school, by contrast, bemoan deteriorating educational effectiveness, teacher burnout, an intransigent union, and vandalism and drug use among students. To me, adding a full-time cop is an act of surrender, a reddish sort of white flag indicating danger and capitulation to values that are weakening *because the shared paths within the school have degenerated*.

Number has always limited shared paths. What distinguishes ours from earlier ages is how purpose and time have substituted for place, blood, and belief in constituting shared paths. For most of human history, shared paths were located within the imperatives of geography, ethnicity, and divinity. Place and blood mattered most. Shared paths were total, all-absorbing associations, and individuals were fully in them.

Consider, for example, the 102 Pilgrims who embarked on the *Mayflower* in 1620. Today, we celebrate their story as a courageous blow for *individual* freedom of religious conscience. For them, however, shared *group* values must have been exceedingly strong. Theirs was a shared path that encompassed the most basic purposes of life: survival, procreation, salvation. Indeed, after they landed on Cape Cod, some of their number asserted independence from the group's authority and prompted the rest to draft and sign the *Mayflower Compact*, committing themselves to shared legal, political, civil, and administrative values.

The shared paths in our new world rarely have unlimited, all-encompassing purposes. *Our shared paths form around narrower, more specific aims and objectives.* At work, our shared paths are colored by economic and social purposes. At church, temple, or mosque, the primary purposes are faith and family. Among friends, the purpose might be companionship, enjoyment, and entertainment.

These narrowed purposes, however, still engender values cutting across many different categories: social, economic, religious, political, and more. It remains the case that *we most often articulate, understand, and define our shared paths according to a dominant value category*. Thus, again, at work we tend to describe our shared paths as economic; at home, as family; at synagogue, church, mosque, or temple, as spiritual.

The division of labor so critical to our world of purposes has spawned a division of purposes in our lives. In turn, the partial, pointed purposes in our shared paths reinforce the split between value and values. For example, we habitually *assume* that shared paths at work are about value and shared paths at home or among friends are about values. *Yet, our actual behavior belies these assumptions.* We join value to values in *all* of our shared paths. But, because of assumed and named purposes, we tend to subordinate values to value at work and the reverse at home.

. . . .

Our shared paths differ from those of earlier ages because time and attention have novel effects in our new world of purposes. When place and blood fenced people into shared paths, time was less relevant. People were integrated by the force of place. They were not—as we are—disintegrated and fragmented by time, attention, and purpose.

Presence was a given in a world of places. Not so in our world of purposes where people must *self-consciously choose* to be attentively present to participate in shared paths. A father who abandons his wife and kids is not present in the shared path of family (although he may be accounted for as a shared idea as in "Your father!" or

"Deadbeat dad"). A workaholic parent who interacts with his family for minutes each month may fit the same pattern. Or he may not. The shared idea of quality time admits the possibility for shared path sufficiency in such cases, even though the values harvested from quality time probably do not equate with those that arose from time-without-adjectives in a world of places. Even Norman Rockwell could not have depicted quality time without irony or doubt.

The collapse of geography under technology, markets, networks, and organizations frees us to participate in a greater number of shared paths with a broader diversity of people than occurred in a world of places. But sufficient presence and persistency limit the number of shared path experiences we might have. For us to claim a shared path experience, we must meaningfully be present persistently. Our world of markets, organizations, networks, family, and friends has sliced and diced our time, attention, and purpose; most of us are more likely to participate in, say, 10 to 20 shared paths rather than a hundred or more.

In addition to time and attention as a factor of presence is time as a yardstick for duration. Throughout history, people participated in shared paths that were what we might call open-ended and that they might have described as permanent unto death. People lived with one another in places. While some escaped these boundaries, most lived out their days with others from the same place. Like presence, duration was a given.

Our circumstances and contexts are constructed differently. Consider joining a raft ride down the Colorado River in the Grand Canyon. You will assemble with a dozen or so people for a weeklong adventure together. Within the limits of the trip, there will be shared path experiences. There will be talk; there will be demands on physical contribution; there will be unexpected challenges and obstacles. We know such raft rides are not the equivalent of the group journey on the *Mayflower*. Most of us, however, are not seeking an all-or-nothing group experience. We don't wish to live a life imprisoned by place. But we do want shared paths. Some of us have found true love, new beginnings, lasting friendships, attractive business opportunities, and spirituality in the company of other pilgrims on the Colorado River. Others have simply enjoyed themselves among people who became more than strangers for a brief interval of time.

Shared paths are the most fertile ground for strong shared values. When any of us persistently interact with a consistent set of people, sheer repetition plus orderly expectations and obligations strengthen values. There are important purposes and consequences in shared paths. Even special-purpose shared paths weave together political, social, economic, religious, technological, environmental, and other values. Enforcement is integrated into the shared behaviors and beliefs in shared paths. No dedicated police are required.

Shared paths are small thick we's. They shape and sustain strong, predictable values in our world, just as they did in a world of places. When we observe behavior that appears random or meaningless, we likely are looking at people who do not participate in shared paths or, as in the story of the smaller school near my home, people participating in shared paths that have deteriorated. In our world, small is not just beautiful. It is necessary.

But the explanation for the strong shared values in shared paths—small number—is also a great limitation. No matter how sincerely any us believe the values in *our* shared paths are good values, we cannot extend them by inviting large numbers of people to join us. We can and do promote values through markets, organizations, and networks. But we cannot grow shared paths beyond numeric limits.

We can, however, act in our own shared paths. Each of us can identify shared paths in which we currently participate, whether at home, among friends, or in organizations. We can reflect on how our shared paths blend value and values, and what we might do to enrich our purposes and experiences. We can, for example, discuss how our shared paths at work might better mix noneconomic and economic purposes. We can identify means by which shared paths at home, in church, or in other organizations might enlarge purposes to better integrate value and values.

We also can work through markets, organizations, and networks *to create shared path experiences for others*. Too often, as in the "Just Say No" illustration in Chapter 4, we restrict efforts regarding values to marketing *ideas to individuals*. If, for example, any of us wish to help unwed teen mothers, it makes sense to identify and spread key ideas about individual responsibility and family values through markets and networks. But, in our new world of purposes, we cannot assume ideas are enough. Nor can we assume our public philosophy of individualism is sufficient. Yes, of course, teens must take individual responsibility for their actions. *But teenage girls, just like the rest of us, are more likely to adhere to values that arise in shared paths.* Accordingly, we do a much better job of helping young women strengthen values when we assist them in finding shared path relationships. In our world, that means families, friends, and *organizations*.

This, in fact, is what happens today. Unwed teen mothers define a *market*. People who provide services in that market do so through *organizations*—through thick we's who make it their shared purpose to care. Many such organizations are governmental or not-for-profit. They have myriad purposes, strategies, and effects. Those that foster and spread shared path opportunities for teen mothers are doing critical work in helping teens build *together* the strong shared values needed for happiness in our new world of purposes.

Small thick we's outweigh large we's in any explanation of what generates and sustains the most predictable values in our world of markets, organizations, networks, families, and friends. It is in organizations and among families and friends—not in markets or networks—that we have shared-path experiences. Markets and networks disseminate ideas faster and to more people than any social formation before in history. But the journey of ideas from individual to *shared* values travels best in shared paths.

6 Consumers and Employees

The estrangement of value and values causes widespread uneasiness in our new world of purposes. Our anxieties trace more to people we don't know than people we do. Severely dysfunctional relationships aside, we are reassured by the blend of individual and shared values among friends, family, and work colleagues. We worry about strangers—about the unsettling probability that unknown people will act in ways that adversely affect us. *All of which makes it noteworthy that we rely on millions of strangers every day of our lives.*

Each day tens of millions of people who do not know one another's name come together in markets, organizations, and networks. Over the course of a year, hundreds of billions of interchanges among strangers happen in stores, restaurants, theaters, and elsewhere. Nothing like human interactivity on this scale could operate in the absence of exceedingly strong and predictable shared values. The actual beliefs, behaviors, attitudes, and speech, however, are not those of shared paths, the contexts in which a small but consistent set of people persistently interact (Chapter 5). Instead, these values arise from *shared roles*, particularly those of customer and employee. We may live in a world that makes us apprehensive about strangers. But not when we go shopping.

In late 2002, while visiting a city several hours from home, I decided to buy a new pair of shoes. I went into a store. After a few minutes of looking around, a salesman asked if I wanted help. I mentioned some styles and sizes. He retrieved them. I seated myself and removed my shoes. He laced up the new shoes and put them on my feet. He asked me to walk around. I tried out a few pairs, selected one, and gave him my credit card. He obtained the needed authorizations and handed me a receipt. We bid each other farewell.

None of this is exceptional. Each of you has had the experience many times. Our ancestors, though, would have been astonished at the values *shared* by the salesperson and me—two complete strangers. We did not know each other's names, families, neighborhoods, political leanings, or religions. We knew nothing about one another except that I was a customer and he was a salesperson.

Tens of millions of us share strong, predictable values attached to roles as customers and employees. The shoe salesman and I held fast to common beliefs and behaviors that were social (civility), political (freedom of choice), technological (the credit card authorization system would work), and economic (non-negotiable prices). Neither of us anticipated disruptive behavior from the other. We believed that I was free to enter his store, but not to loiter, and that he could handle my foot but not insult me in doing so.

The shared values we identify with the roles of customer and employee vary by context. Most of us anticipate haggling over prices at flea markets, but not in shoe stores. We are more vigilant about quality and honesty when purchasing "Rolex" watches from street corner vendors than jewelers. We understand the benevolence of those who sell us software may exceed the benevolence of those who service it. Still, when we look across the thousands of situations in which we are customers and employees, the pattern of actual beliefs, behaviors, attitudes, and speech is exceedingly strong. Our new world of markets, organizations, and networks is impossible without them.

Sociologists and anthropologists use role and status to explain how shared expectations, rights, and obligations arise in societies and cultures. Although sometimes blurred, status tilts more to position and role to function. Titles, such as Vice President or Manager, for example, indicate status within organizations while functional descriptions, such as marketing, sales, or operations, define role. *Shared values arising from role and status minimize overt conflict and disruption in favor of smooth sailing.* When everyone knows and keeps to their role and status, societies operate more efficiently and peacefully (although not always more fairly or justly).

The foundation for shared values in shared roles is not personal—it corresponds to *function and position.* In contrast, shared values in shared paths arise from *personal relationships.* In shared paths, repetition, consequences, and multiple value categories combine to build strong, predictable values among people who persistently interact. Repetition, consequences, and multiple value categories also matter to shared roles—but differently and more narrowly.

When I walked into the shoe store, I knew the salesperson's function was to assist me. He knew my function was to look at, try on, and possibly purchase shoes. Repetition, consequences, and multiple value categories operated, but not because we knew one another. It was not personal. Rather, each of us had experienced the roles of customer and salesperson thousands of times. We understood that the consequences of fulfilling our roles included, among others, his job performance, security, and income and my comfort, self-image, and healthy feet and posture. We recognized that a variety of value categories mixed in our transaction, including the various social, economic, political, and technological values noted above.

Because shared roles arise from function, the shared values they sustain are limited in scope. In shared paths, by contrast, we expect values to affect a broad range of circumstances. My expectations of the shoe salesperson were confined to buying and selling shoes. I anticipated he would behave in particular ways, but not because I actually knew anything about him personally. If some emergency had occurred, neither of us could have depended on the foundation of a *personal* relationship to guide our actions, either as individuals or together.

Shared roles and status have always generated strong shared values—albeit highly specified ones. This phenomenon is not new. People in worlds of places rely on shared roles and status to ensure peace and smooth functioning. But markets, organizations, and networks have profoundly transformed *our* shared roles and status, and the nature and consequence of the values we share as a result.

Our hallmark shared roles are customer, employee, investor, networker, family member, and friend. Some, like customer and networker, are relatively recent. Others, like family member and friend, have been around forever. Yet, even family member and friend—and the shared values they sustain—have changed dramatically because we live in markets, organizations, and networks instead of places. Our ancestors, for example, would require translations for such roles and status as significant other, latchkey child, and deadbeat dad.

Place no longer breathes much life into shared roles. Place-dependant roles and status, such as citizen and neighbor, do not sustain strong shared values. Neither has vitality because neither fits a world of markets, organizations, and networks. Each is a square peg in our new reality of round holes. Citizen and neighbor conformed well to places. They conveyed shared values regarding rights, responsibilities, and participation practiced among people who shared fates because they lived together in the same place. But we do not live in places. Citizen and neighbor still promise shared values. But it is because they are *shared ideas*, not shared roles.

. . . .

In the mid-1990s, a friend traveled to Colorado to give a public lecture on growth. A development boom to the west of Denver was fueling the local economy—as well as causing mounting frustrations over a threatened way of life. A bond proposal to widen roads prompted the invitation to my friend, and a few hundred men and women showed up the evening of his talk.

He started by asking for a show of hands from people who were antigrowth. No hands were raised. The audience was pleased with economic prosperity and, while aware that growth posed challenges, were prepared to vote for the bond. He then inquired about the population size of the area affected by the proposal. The estimates ranged around 75,000. He asked people to raise hands if they believed the area could support 1.5 million people. No hands. "How about 750,000?" No hands. Hands began to rise around 300,000 and, when my friend got to 200,000, nearly everyone had an arm in the air.

He invited them to explain their concerns about a population bigger than 200,000. They identified several environmental, social, and family values linked to water quality, air quality, traffic, schools, drugs, and crime. A lively discussion indicated a high degree of consensus. One woman summed it up: "We don't want big city problems."

At this point, my friend said he was confused. The audience had begun the meeting clearly progrowth. Now they were speaking just as eloquently against growth. "What," he wondered, "caused the shift?"

In the ensuing dialogue, *people pointed to role to explain conflicting perspectives*. When they were "bread winners," "investors," or "builders," they advocated continued growth. When they were "moms," "family men," or "sportsmen," *the same people* expressed antigrowth fears. As one real estate broker said, "I want to sell as many condos as possible between 9 and 5, and then, when I get home, I don't want anything to do with the people who buy those condos or the problems they bring with them."

In our new world of purposes, our shared roles correspond to markets, organizations, networks, families, and friends. Our most critical roles are employee, customer, investor, networker, family member, and friend. But—as my friend's audience discovered—*the values we share because of these roles mostly operate in the contexts in which we play them*. When we are brokers, salespeople, investors, and customers in markets, our shared values concentrate around value. When we are family members raising kids or friends relaxing at the park, the center of gravity belongs to values, not value.

Our shared values, as the real estate broker indicated, shift with role and context. Meanwhile, role and context change with purpose and time of day. The variations cloud understanding. It is difficult to make sense of ourselves without stepping back and using role and context as a guide. Ours is a novel challenge: If we do not integrate our many purposes and contexts together, we cannot shape a whole picture that makes sense. Yet, we cannot rely on place to paint the picture or forge our values together.

We are not different from our ancestors in having multiple roles and status. People who lived in a world of places did as well. But the *set of roles* they played at any moment were conditioned by places they lived. A person might have had many roles, such as family member, worker, friend, citizen, believer, and so forth. Yet, people were more likely to see themselves and others *in all or nearly all their roles simultaneously throughout a day*. The whole person, in terms of roles and status, was more consistently apparent.

Sociologists use *role set* to describe the many roles and statuses operating in a particular context. In the shoe store visit, for example,

I observed the fellow who helped me in a role set that included sales-person, employee, and work colleague. I also saw him as a networker in the card authorization system and a customer of shoe manufac-turers and distributors. In other contexts, he might well have been a father, husband, uncle, friend, or investor. But those roles and sta-tuses were not in his role set when he and I interacted in the store.

In a world of places, there were fewer disconnected contexts, and people had more complete and constant role sets. Consider a neighborhood pharmacy in the late 19th century. Yes, those who interacted in the pharmacy did so as customer and pharmacist. But, unlike the shoe salesman and me, their role sets also included family member, friend, neighbor, and citizen. In addition, they were likely to see one another in overlapping contexts beyond the pharmacy, in which the same or largely similar role sets operated to sustain shared values.

Living together in a place kept most roles in plain view much of the time. Because the fuller set of roles and status crisscrossed social, civic, family, political, and economic values, the odds favored a stronger blend of value and values. The pharmacist, of course, had to make a living. His purposes included generating profits. His con-cern for profits, however, was likely to blend with other values because—even at the pharmacy—his role set included neighbor, family member, friend, and citizen. *Unlike the 1990s Colorado real estate broker, the late 19th century pharmacist was not likely to live a life of value between 9 and 5 and a life of values when he got home.*

In our new world of purposes, we live in more contexts with shifting role sets that have less continuity. The people in the 19th century pharmacy lived in a neighborhood thick with shared values because of the force of place. We live in hundreds of markets, dozens of organizations, and scores of networks. As we transition from one context to another, we experience discontinuity and fragmentation. Our role sets shift depending on context. Like Gyges (see Chapter 5), we can make ourselves invisible to others who *see* us only in some of our many contexts and roles.

In markets, our role sets are thinner and shaped by specialized purposes. In the eyes of the shoe salesman, for example, I barely had any role *set* at all. I was a customer. In my eyes, he had several roles. Yet, each took shape from the primary purpose of our transaction: I was seeking value for money and he sought to provide it. Various other values operated. But, like our shared roles, they orbited around commercial value. In networks, too, the beliefs, behaviors, attitudes, and speech associated with shared roles tend to converge on narrow purposes. As drivers, for example, our purpose is getting from point A to point B. When the salesman used the card authorization network, his aims included approval and fraud prevention. When we dial a phone, our object is to connect with someone else.

It is unusual for role sets in *markets or networks* to include many of the roles we play in other contexts of our lives. In markets, we are often customers only. The people who serve us do not see us as friend, family member, volunteer, or investor. In *organizations and families*, by contrast, role sets are more comprehensive. In the organizations where we work, our matrix of roles and status include employee, colleague, friend, boss, subordinate, and family member (and various additional descriptors of function, task, and status). At home or among friends, we can be breadwinner, parent, sibling, spouse, friend, hobbyist, and more.

The thicker, more inclusive role sets in organizations and families sustain stronger and richer shared values than the thin role sets of markets and networks. In addition, as noted in Chapter 5, we are more likely to have shared path experiences in organizations and among families and friends than in markets or networks. Shared paths and shared roles reinforce one another. The shoe salesperson, for example, undoubtedly shared a broader blend of value and values with his work colleagues than he did with me. I was a stranger; his work colleagues were not.

Like any employee who interacts with customers, the shoe salesperson operated in parallel contexts simultaneously. In the *market* context in which he and I interacted, our values derived from the shared roles of customer and employee. Value was the primary purpose; our role sets were thinner. In the *organization* context, his role set included many of the roles and statuses of his life. His colleagues knew him—and he knew them—as family member, friend, consumer, investor, and so forth. The values they shared in their organization grew out of shared path experiences as well as shared role sets. Those values were thicker, not thinner. Earlier, for example, I mentioned that the strong but narrow values shared by the salesperson and me would not have aided us much in an emergency. In contrast, the rich brew of values shared among those who share their lives in the shoe store would have guided them in responding to emergencies—and probably had on several occasions.

The nature and blend of value and values in shared roles depend mightily on context. In markets and networks, we have special purposes and thinner role sets. We share exceedingly strong and predictable values with tens of millions of people who are otherwise strangers to us. But the scope of these values is limited and their character oriented toward value. On the other hand, the values we share in organizations and among family and friends arise from a richer, fuller set of shared roles as well as shared paths. In those contexts, our shared values draw vitality from a wide range of purposes that blend value and values together.

. . . .

Ethical dilemmas often trace to the shifts we experience across different roles, contexts, and purposes. As participants in markets, the people in the Colorado audience shared strong values that favored development. They were prepared to vote for the bond. In the context of home, they also shared strong values that opposed unbridled growth. In each context, their shared values were highly predictable; people who were otherwise strangers could depend on them.

These people were not hypocrites who said one thing, then did another. They said they favored the economic prosperity created by development in markets and they acted accordingly. They said they worried about home-based values threatened by growth and they did. It is just that, as they transitioned back and forth from home to market to home, their lives suffered from our age's characteristic and profound displacement. Value and values are estranged. Value reigns in the market, and values at home.

Conflicts in values also happen when people shift back and forth from organization to market to organization. The shoe salesman operated simultaneously in both a market and organization context. In the market, he and I shared predictable beliefs and behaviors oriented toward value. In his organization, he and others shared a richer blend of values of all sorts. My sense was that he did an effective job of integrating organization values with the narrower ones of market.

But the back and forth from organization to market to organization—like the back and forth of home to market to home—can cause trouble. We discovered in late 2001, for example, that several executives at Enron damaged themselves and others in an apparent clash between organizational and market values. These men promoted a blend of social, political, economic, and other values inside Enron. The Enron Statement of Values, for example, referenced integrity and concern for the customer. In dealing with California customers, however, some Enron executives manipulated prices and jeopardized the energy supplies of millions. Meanwhile, other executives lacked integrity in their dealings in capital markets. In their mania to generate value in markets, Enron executives lost touch with the ethics *supposedly* practiced in their organization.

Why *supposedly*? The people of Enron published a set of values for themselves. The beliefs and behaviors of various executives violated the stated values. That is clear. What's less clear—and always more interesting—is whether their actions varied from the *actual* "way things were done around Enron." Were the executives' values different from or the same as the *actual* shared values practiced in the organization?

The consequences of their actions damaged millions of people. In this sense, we must consider them economic and market terrorists. *The executives were strangers whose deeds reached into and shook up our lives.* What we have yet to figure out, though, is whether our sufferings stemmed from the values of individuals too mesmerized by value to practice the values of their organization—or if their actions echoed the strong, prevailing shared values of the Enron *organization.*

Were the Enron executives, like the men and women in the Colorado audience, struggling to reconcile two conflicting contexts of strong shared values—in this case, one of the organization and one of the market? Or were they behaving in markets exactly in the manner one would predict based on the actual values of their organization? Were we victimized by rogue individuals? Or, were our lives traumatized by the strong shared values of *employees of an organization*? What did Enron—and the brand of the thick we who worked there—actually stand for?

. . . .

In our new world of purposes, we depend enormously on values shaped by employees and volunteers in organizations. *By employee or volunteer, I mean anyone who participates in an organization through sustained time and effort.* Executives are employees with high status in organizations. Volunteers or members can be like employees based on contributions of time and work, as opposed to donations of money. Students are a type of employee, again assuming sufficient time and effort.

The word employee took a drubbing in organizations in the '90s. Human Resource executives sought to eliminate various 19th and 20th century connotations from the status of employee. They labeled people associates or colleagues in a sincere effort to dignify workers as partners and fellow stakeholders instead of adversaries locked in a we/they battle against management and capitalists.

Their aspiration echoes a theme of this book: We gain when employees see themselves as a thick we who share lives and fates in organizations. Still, I will stick with employee and volunteer. Not because I disagree with the intentions behind a word like associate. Rather, I wish to stress the contribution of time and effort as qualities that separate participation from nonparticipation in organizations. We routinely associate time and effort with the word employee. By including volunteers, participating members, and students as kinds of employees, I know I am stretching the word—perhaps too much. But associate poses hurdles too, and something like "organization participant" is jargon.

We share the role and status of employee when we participate through time and effort in organizations. Organization, too, is a broad word. Organizations, both formal and informal, come in many sizes, shapes, and kinds. A freelance professional, for example, might independently contract on a project-by-project basis. Each project is a form of organization. The shoe store I visited is an organization. The IRS and FBI are governmental organizations. General Electric, Proctor & Gamble, and Sony are multinational behemoths with hundreds of suborganizations. The aircraft engine division of General Electric is linked to but different from NBC, which is also part of GE. Meanwhile, CNBC differs from NBC and, a few years back when it operated, CNBC.com was a separate organization from CNBC TV.

Organizations provide us the chance to behave ourselves according to values we share in a society of other people. Our role sets in organizations include many of the roles in our lives. Unlike customers in markets or networkers in networks, our role sets in organizations include family member, friend, investor, networker, and customer as well as employee. Still, we key off the shared role of employee in organizations. Employee is the anchoring role—just as family member most often informs the many roles we play at home.

Unlike role sets in a world of places, however, our role sets at work and home do not include the role of *citizen*, let alone key off that role. Citizen lives on as a shared idea. But it has faded as a shared role. We tend to treat this as a dirty secret. We beat ourselves up for being poor citizens. Our criticisms are well-known. Too few people vote, serve as jurors, attend town meetings, or run for office. Too many who do vote are uninformed. Ignorance about the machinery of government and the names of officeholders is widespread. People treat citizenship as an entitlement—all rights, no responsibilities. We are a democracy that hates politics.

But our severe self-censure misses the mark. Beating ourselves up because we no longer fulfill the shared role of citizen is like taking drivers to task for not using hand signals. Advanced highway networks and automobile technology have made hand signals anachronistic. Analogously, the combination of markets, networks, and organizations has made citizen—as a *shared role in a world of places*—an artifact of an earlier age.

I expect it is the rare week in which one percent of you spend more than one minute in the role of citizen. This is not a condemnation. It merely recognizes the reality *we live in*. It should not surprise us, then, that our roles as customer, employee, investor, networker, family member, and friend are more vital to our shared values than citizen. To be sure, citizen remains a legal status and a powerful shared idea. But it is no longer a vital shared role that conveys expectations, rights, and obligations.

If you think about the *idea* of citizen as the *sum* of family, friend, consumer, employee, investor, and networker, then you logically arrive at the same point: Being better citizens means being better family members, friends, employees, customers, networkers, and investors. Yet, in our new world, we have a more pragmatic grasp of how to be better family members, friends, employees, customers, and networkers than better citizens because these are the roles we actually share with one another in the real contexts in which we live our lives.

As a shared idea, citizen conveys a mix of beliefs and behaviors about the terms of membership and belonging. Citizen connotes participation, voice, consent, rights, and responsibilities. Citizenship gives participants voice in decisions that influence their lives and holds them accountable for the implementation and consequences of those decisions. Our problem is not that tens of millions of us have somehow forgotten the blend of rights and responsibilities at the heart of citizenship. We practice the *meanings* in the shared idea of citizenship every day of our lives. We just don't practice them in towns, cities, states, or nations. *We practice them most when we participate as employees in organizations.*

. . . .

In our new world of purposes, we participate as employees and volunteers in organizations, as consumers and investors in markets, and as networkers in networks. As illustrated by the shoe salesperson, employees also participate in markets and networks as agents of their organizations. We also participate as family members and friends in many different contexts.

These roles shape exceedingly strong, dependable shared values without which our world would not be possible. But the nature of our shared values and their relative sway over individual values differs dramatically in markets and networks when compared to organizations and families. In organizations and families, our role sets include many roles we play in life. In addition, most of our shared path experiences happen in organizations and among families and friends. Together, shared roles and shared paths sustain a rich blend of strong shared values in organizations, families, and friends. Notwithstanding our strong public commitment to individualism, shared values regularly outweigh individualism in organizations, families, and friends.

In contrast, our roles as consumers in markets and as networkers in networks are narrowly gauged and directed at highly specific individual purposes. We use networks like the Web to connect and communicate—for example, email helps us sustain shared paths at work or at home. But the purposes of our shared path experiences trace to organizations, family, or friends instead of network infrastructure per se. Powerfully strong, dependable shared values emerge in markets and networks. Billions of interactions among strangers rely on them. But, unlike in organizations, families, and friends, our expectations favor individual values more than shared values and value over values in markets and networks.

As consumers, we are not oblivious to noneconomic values in markets. We share expectations of civility, respect, and freedom of movement and choice—just as I did when I purchased shoes. We also have strong shared values regarding quality and service—although the particulars differ by the brands, companies, products, and services under consideration. Nevertheless, our dominant orientation as consumers in markets is getting value for money. Like the audience in the Colorado illustration, we may blend value and values at home. But, once we go into the market, value trumps values, in my view, too much so.

We need to evolve our understanding of *being consumers* to more effectively blend value and values. Millions of us, I think, know that our purchases have consequences beyond value. We *live* in markets as consumers. We *govern* markets by the choices we make—a message drummed into us every day by thousands of ads. Markets are an inherent aspect of our *democratic* experience in this new world.

Consider, for example, the choice to buy or lease an SUV versus a hybrid automobile that uses electricity and gasoline. Millions of us realize this decision reflects a blend of values. In making a choice, we might emphasize the environmental (energy conservation) or personal (cars as image), the needs of family (seating and storage) or budget (price). We might inject technological (zero to 60) or legal values (opposition to legislative exemptions given SUV makers in calculating corporate average gas mileage). Some of us might stress religious or geopolitical considerations. A friend, for example, believes SUVs record *a vote* of support for a Saudi royal regime that ignores the socioeconomic conditions spawning terrorism.

The values-laden choice in automobile purchases is not new. Following World War II, many believed that family, religious, and political values weighed against getting a German car. In the 1970s and 1980s, millions understood that the choice between an American versus Japanese car expressed support or opposition to Japan's closed domestic markets—or support or opposition to poor U.S. manufacturing quality.

Consumer choice is an essential part of our *democratic* participation in markets. Choices about what form of life is worth living and how we govern ourselves are made each time we use our credit cards or checkbooks. (Indeed, it extends to our selection of *which* credit card or checkbook to pay with— a fact that explains the rise of affinity cards.) If we seek to shape *markets* into ethical human societies, we need to recognize that more is at stake in being consumers than getting value for money. We must also learn how to get *values* for money.

* * *

Who has time to sift so many considerations in each and every purchase? No one. We can do a better job of blending value and values as consumers. Each of us can pay more careful attention *sometimes*. Each of us could, for example, consider values and value in one purchase per year. Really. But any sustained practice of blending value and values depends on more than good intentions.

Consumers need information to compensate for lack of time. With information, millions of consumers have blended values and value in their purchasing choices. Not uniformly, mind you; our markets are *democracies*. Many North Americans bought Japanese cars in the 1980s as a statement about quality, while others rejected them because of patriotism or a sense of fairness. Either way, they cast *informed* votes. The blending of value and values in auto purchases during the 1980s could not have occurred in the absence of information. Information infused values into consumer choices otherwise skewed to value. Information about values was a difference maker—a phenomenon we have experienced time and again.

In the months following September 11, 2001, for example, sales of U.S. flags skyrocketed. Millions of consumers bought flags to express values about democracy, peace, free markets, tolerance, and more. Prices had not changed. Financial and commercial considerations had not changed. What had shifted was the *meaning and values* attached to the flag—meaning fueled by information. During those months, consumers were inundated with information about values. Flags were everywhere—on cars, in advertisements, on lapels, and on front lawns. The information linking values to flags was not a direct sales pitch. We were not swamped with TV ads exhorting us to "Buy this flag and show you are a patriot!" It may have felt that way, but there was no massive ad campaign with that pitch. Instead, the information that drenched us was more organic. The values attached to the flag were the subject of innumerable messages in markets, organizations, and networks, and among families and friends.

Similar, if less dramatic, examples abound. Information linking cigarettes to cancer, recycling to beverages, alcohol to driving, and antilock brakes to safety have influenced consumer choices. So has information linking tourism choices to Confederate flag imagery in South Carolina and Georgia. Every holiday season, information helps consumers avoid unsafe toys.

I believe tens of millions of us are ready to respond to information about values in our shared role as consumers. I believe we wish to do so. But we live in *thousands* of different markets. We purchase thousands of products, services, and brands. As consumers, we act mostly as individuals. As *consumers*, we have neither the resources nor the time to research and disseminate all the information that we need to blend value and values in purchase choices.

Organizations, however, *do* have the resources, time, and influence to inject information about values into markets. This is obvious. We are not novices at being consumers. We understand advertising, marketing, and public relations. We are thoroughly familiar with the efforts organizations make to provide us information. We are also accustomed to the motivation of organizations: They want our business. They want to sell us their products and services. They want to deliver value to us in exchange for our money, time, and loyalty.

So, we come full circle. As consumers in markets, our shared roles sustain powerful shared beliefs and behaviors that orient toward value more than values. We confidently interact with strangers in markets every day of our lives. But we have learned that our new world of purposes is vastly complex and interconnected. We worry about the values of strangers, like those Enron executives whose actions disrupt our lives. We wish for a world that better integrates value and values.

We are ready, I think, to evolve our shared role as consumers to blend concern for value with concern for values. In our shared roles as employee, family member, and friend, we already integrate value and values more strongly than we do as consumers, investors, or networkers. As employee, family member, and friend, we also practice participation, voice, consent, and mutual rights and responsibilities in the manner of our shared idea of citizenship. It is in our organizations especially that we practice the art of governance (see Chapters 12 and 13).

That is good news. Organizations have the resources to provide information to consumers about values and value. Organizations also have the motivation. *In our new world of purposes, organizations that compete on the basis of blending values and value will gain sustainable competitive advantage because we, their consumers, stand ready to respond.*

The main question, then, is who will guide organizations to adopt and implement such strategies? Who is responsible for the choices organizations make about value and values, and how those choices get communicated in markets and networks?

The answer is obvious. *We are—in our shared role as employees and volunteers.* As employees, we shape the competitive strategies of our organizations. These don't happen *to* us. *Employees* shaped the cultures of Enron, WorldCom, Tyco, and other companies whose executives broke laws. Employees shared in the creation and practice of values. As employees, we bear responsibility for the deeds of our organizations. *As consumers, we rely on employees to govern organizations.* We cannot accept employees who claim to be "just doing my job" any more than we can accept that equally passive defense by people living in nations that sponsor holocausts and wars.

The fate of markets, networks, nations, organizations, families, and friends rests in our hands as consumers, employees, investors, networkers, family members, and friends. Not in our shared role as citizens. That is an anachronism. We live in a different world. We share different roles. Yes, value has historically driven markets. We can explain this to ourselves. But, as we ponder the futures of our children, let us also explain how and why we might blend value and values through everyday actions as consumers and employees. Like my friend's Colorado audience discovered, roles help us understand the split between value and values. Now, however, we must do something about it.

7 Investors

The Root of evil, Avarice,
That damn'd ill-natur'd baneful Vice,
Was Slave to Prodigality,
That Noble Sin; whilst Luxury
Employ'd a Million of the Poor,
And odious Pride a Million more.
Envy it self, and Vanity
Were Ministers of Industry

— **Bernard Mandeville, Grumbling Hive, 1705**

The relationship between value and values was upside down when Bernard Mandeville penned his tribute to vice. Investors existed, but the role was not widely shared. Investors (and their sharper cousins, speculators) came from narrow reaches of society. In contrast, tens of millions of us have become investors over the span of a few decades, including more than half the households In the U.S. Investor is a *suddenly* shared role, and our crash course has centered on the pre-eminence of shareholder value.

Mandeville's world was rooted in place; values nailed down value much as the Lilliputians did Gulliver. Over the entire planet, social, religious, military, family, and other values dictated how people put bread on the table. Children were born into fixed roles and status. Moneylenders, profit takers, and speculators were reviled. Neither land nor labor was routinely alienable. Capital was not just scarce, *it was barely understood* and certainly not an -ism. Markets were mostly places or events, fairs attended on the outskirts of towns.

Value toiled like Cinderella. Mandeville, a Dutch emigrant to England, was too early to be cast as fairy godmother. Or, perhaps too impious—some accused him of Satanism. The part went instead to Adam Smith, the world's first great economist. He was the first because economics had remained submerged in a world that subordinated value to values. Today, we comprehend economics as a force of nature. Economists, financiers, executives, and their political partners rule us through value. But in the 18th century, economics lay hid in darkness. A world of markets, organizations, and networks remained well offstage.

Smith, much as Newton had done a century earlier with physics, unleashed economics by identifying its most elemental force: self-interest. He acknowledged excesses; he regretted vice. But he shunned the in-your-face trash talking of Mandeville. Smith sought to enlighten, not scandalize. *The Wealth of Nations* defended self-interest as a virtue. He made investment, trade, capital, and profits respectable. His other great work, *The Theory of Moral Sentiments*, reasoned equally well on behalf of benevolence—humankind's natural sympathies for one another. But Smith's writings about fellow feeling did not unlock the universe. His tract on self-interest did.

Following Adam Smith, people learned (albeit slowly) that markets were not fairs or bazaars. Markets were *forces* that converted self-interest into abundance, just as photosynthesis transformed sunlight into sugar. *The Wealth of Nations* appeared in 1776, along with Jefferson's *The Declaration of Independence*. Together they sired liberal market democracies. To Jefferson, political liberty was the oxygen of self-interest, which, in turn, built happiness, an 18th century word focused on property and wealth. Beyond life itself, the unalienable rights were liberty and the pursuit of happiness. These were the twin engines: political liberty and self-interested market economics.

Together they loosened dynamics that routed the social, religious, political, legal, and family values that had enslaved value for millennia. Individual liberty and market opportunity have now enshrined value; it sits atop the mountain. Value governs our world of markets, organizations, networks, family, and friends. Value even subjects the political values of liberty to the discipline of markets. The tables have turned.

Our challenge inverts that of Mandeville, Smith, and Jefferson. We need to unleash the force of values without once again subjugating value. We need to restore a sense of we to the unrestrained I. When Smith wrote *Wealth*, it would have been unimaginable to him for value to rise to such a mighty height as to isolate itself *across the whole of society* from benevolence, propriety, and the other values in *Moral Sentiments*. Did Smith anticipate individuals doing harm through self-interest? Yes. But he and Jefferson lived in an age when town, community, church, and culture were grounded by "we" values shaped and sustained in places. Neither foresaw a value so triumphant as to make strangers of people who lived next door.

We are in the grip of an unsustainable ideology of value and individualism whose officialdom is as resourceful as any lord mayor, priest, general, or shaman who ruled when values held sway over value. *Shareholder value is a centerpiece of this orthodoxy.* Its followers, as Pogo instructs, are ourselves, especially in our shared role as investors. Mandeville's ribaldry seems quaint, not shocking, to tens of millions of us who chuckle at contemporary versions such as "Look out for No. 1," "Greed is good," and "Show me the money!"

These exhortations entertain; we smile at them. But something troubling goes unspoken. Value fundamentalism is an ideology; it insists on a single answer. Common sense shouts that value is propped up by unsustainable dogma. Greed is not good. Its less excessive cousin—self-interest—is good insofar as it makes markets efficient. But greed is sinful. Our challenge is figuring out where self-interest leaves off and greed begins in a world of markets, organizations, networks, families, and friends—a world where character and values are less transparent than Smith's and Jefferson's world of places—and when and how our experience of "we" differs.

Historically, the rise of value in markets makes sense. We can explain it to ourselves. Smith's main lesson was about the power of self-interested pursuits to make markets efficient and effective. As he famously wrote, "It is not from the benevolence of the butcher, the brewer, or the baker, that we expect our dinner, but from their regard to their own interest." Markets, he argued, were providential systems for value creation even if, on the surface, he noted, "The great affair, we always find, is to get money."

He knew money could be an obsession. Still, Smith's butchers, brewers, and bakers *lived in places with one another.* They operated within markets mostly constrained by place and place-based values. They lived in towns and did business with suppliers and customers from the town and surrounding countryside. They knew one another from frequent interactions in the shared paths (Chapter 5) and shared roles (Chapter 6) dictated by place.

Character—good, bad, or mixed, but highly predictable—was the fruit of such interactions. So were predictable values. People interacted with familiar people in church, school, government, entertainment, clubs, and more. Commerce was only one way they learned about the values they shared. Shared paths, shared ideas, and shared roles reinforced one another to produce strong, predictable beliefs and behaviors that, again, were not necessarily good or bad. Indeed, value had been hemmed in and made poorer by the strength of other values. Smith wrote *The Wealth of Nations* to liberate value from the place-based values that had kept it down.

Today, however, markets are not bounded by place or the values of place. We live *in* markets, not in places that contain markets. The bakers in whom any of us might invest as shareholders typically are not human beings whose names and character we learn through daily interactions. Our commerce is with *organizations* and *brands* such as Entenmann's, Arnold, and Sara Lee.

Consider Sara Lee. As of 2002, the company operated in nearly five dozen countries and employed more than 140,000 people. Sara Lee is not only a baking concern. Its brands and offerings also include apparel, meats, and body care products. The vast majority of Sara Lee's employees are not bakers. They have many roles: marketing, communications, human resources, engineering, facility services, finance, legal, business development, purchasing, information technology, supply chain, research and development, and sales.

*We do not know them—or their character or values—*in any manner remotely similar to that fostered by the interactivity of place. Nor do they know us. We experience their products and brands, not them. If they understand us, it is through market research instead of the persistent, interpersonal interactivity of school, church, work, entertainment, and government.

The vast majority of us who interact with Sara Lee do so in our shared roles as customers or investors. *Only the people who work for Sara Lee learn about one another's character and values through shared paths, shared roles, and shared ideas—through repeated interactions as employees.* It is only when we consider Sara Lee *as an organization and people in the role of employees* that we can imagine character and values revealing themselves in a manner that echoes the place-based reality of Adam Smith's world. *In our new world of purposes, millions of us rely on the 140,000 employees of Sara Lee to develop and sustain shared values that promote the mutual well-being of all of us.* We eat the food they make on trust; if we invest, we pin part of our financial future on trust. If Sara Lee employees drop the ball, we suffer.

Unlike Adam Smith's neighbors, we cannot rely on *people we know* to determine if we should invest in the companies where those people work. Instead, we must rely on the character, values, and prospects of companies and brands, and on what we understand about their products, services, and competition. In our current

orthodoxy, however, we tend to inquire less about the *values* of organizations in which we might invest than about *shareholder value*.

As investors, most of us acquiesce in the dogma making shareholder value *the* objective in capital markets. Sara Lee, for example,
proclaims in its 2002 annual report, "Our primary purpose is to create long-term shareholder value." Yes, Sara Lee's executives promote
values such as integrity, trust, and corporate citizenship. They seek
to hire and retain employees motivated by opportunity and skills.
They market products that are environmentally friendly. But Sara
Lee embraces the dogma of our age. The company and, by extension,
the 140,000 people upon whom the rest of us depend openly and
proudly subordinate all values to the single overriding objective of
building shareholder value. That is our reigning orthodoxy—*even
though it is rife with illogic and unsupportable claims*.

. . . .

The glorification of shareholder value took hold in capital markets in
the 1980s, just a decade before tens of millions of us became
investors. I recall a conversation from those years with a senior
director at McKinsey & Company, a management consulting firm
where we worked together. At the time, he and I were advising a
British company about opportunities in the United States. The sole
criterion for our recommendations would be shareholder value,
which, I learned, was to be evaluated by analyzing the discounted
cash flow effects of any potential U.S. expansion. Discounted cash
flow meant the sum of future cash the British company would gain as
adjusted ("discounted") by the risks they would have to take. If the
risk-adjusted cash generated by opportunity A outweighed the risk-
adjusted cash generated by opportunity B, then A was preferred
because of its superior impact on shareholder value.

Shareholder value and risk adjusted cash flow are cornerstones
of our capital markets orthodoxy. At the time, I was struck by the off-
hand remark of my McKinsey colleague that, *"businesses—all businesses—are mere cash flow generators."* According to the dogma of
shareholder value, organizations such as Sara Lee have no higher
purpose than generating cash.

Jobs? Innovation? Quality products and services? Technology?
Customer service? Design? Employee morale? Paying taxes and
obeying laws? Preserving the earth for future generations? Making a
difference? Sure, they matter. *But only if, and to the extent that,*

they increase or decrease risk-adjusted cash flow and shareholder value. Value trumps everything else. Value is the single answer.

Capital markets—like all markets—benefit from risk taking and self-interest. You invest your money and you take your chances. Boiled down, discounted cash flow turns on predictions investors should make before placing bets. First, you must predict future cash—that is, the cash that will come in by making and selling products and services minus the cash that will go out. Second, you must evaluate the *risks* that might affect the accuracy of your cash flow predictions.

A business that, say, sells auto insurance might predict many millions in cash to flow in over the coming years. But such forecasts always include assumptions that could be wrong—to either the disadvantage or the advantage of the business. For example, an auto insurance company might plan on exiting California or New Jersey because of costly claims. Yet it faces a risk that state legislative action could upset the plans. To manage that risk, the company spends money to influence legislators. In other words, there is a *political* risk to the company's cash flow predictions.

There are as many risks to projected cash flow as colors in the rainbow. In addition to political risks, shareholder value is affected by financial risks, competitive risks, technology risks, information risks, innovation risks, labor risks, legal risks, pension risks, medical risks, currency risks, and safety and security risks. As we learned from the 2002 fiascoes at Tyco, Enron, WorldCom, and others, there are also integrity risks.

This litany is incomplete. For example, many distinct risks parade under the umbrella of political risk. Predicted cash flows might rise or fall with regulation, deregulation, or reregulation. Shareholder value can be affected by taxation or by government going into competition or the reverse, privatization. There are geopolitical risks, such as ongoing tensions in the Middle East or between the two Koreas. Whether a nation like Argentina devalues its currency or suffers hyperinflation is as much a political risk as a currency risk. There are risks within risks and risks that compound other risks. *There are as many varieties of risks as people trying to understand and make sound predictions about shareholder value and discounted cash flow.*

The good news for efficient capital markets is that *patterns* distinguish the risks confronting one industry from another. The risks faced by insurance companies resemble one another. The risks confronting one biotech company are similar to those of another biotech company. But the *pattern* of risks faced by biotech companies differs from the *pattern* for insurance companies. Today, biotech organizations confront greater risks than insurance companies.

Promoters of shareholder value emphasize the patterns. One popular technique puts patterns of risk onto a single scale—something called industry betas. Betas tell investors whether any particular industry is, relatively speaking, more or less volatile than the market as a whole. By equating overall market volatility with the number 1.0, analysts point to numbers greater or less than 1.0 to measure industry-specific volatility.

In late 2002, I looked up the industry betas for biotech and insurance. The biotech beta of 1.12 meant that the biotech industry was likely to have 12 percent more volatility than capital markets as a whole. The insurance beta of 0.82 indicated that insurance had 18 percent less volatility. When compared (i.e., 1.12 versus 0.82), biotech is more than 35 percent more volatile than insurance.

If you invest in biotechs, you can expect a higher return for the higher risk. If you can't take the heat and want a surer but smaller return, you can invest in insurance companies. Betas are not limited to industries as a whole. Investment advisors will share company-specific betas to help guide your choice of one insurance firm versus another insurance firm or one biotech company versus another biotech company.

It is elegant and helpful when used wisely. But that is a huge caveat. Look again at what any beta is telling you. *Beta is a **single measure** of the combined effect of all risks facing a particular industry or company compared to the combined effect of all risks facing the market as a whole*. By itself, beta does not distinguish among hundreds of different risks. Nor does it shed light on particular risks.

There *is* a constructive logic to risk-adjusted cash flow analysis. It *does* help investors navigate capital markets. It *does* make capital markets more efficient. We ought not toss out its advantages by engaging in either/or conflict. But its practitioners too often finesse themselves (and us!) by ignoring the messy, yet determinative, realities underpinning the construct of risks so critical to their predictions. Shareholder value advocates too easily come to believe that "all business are mere cash flow generators." They snare themselves with the elegance of their insights and take their eyes off the ball of what *explains* the risks they so earnestly enumerate.

That explanation—what drives risk and determines if risks enlarge or diminish projected cash flows—concerns values of all sorts (including, of course, value).

Look again at the risks described. The behaviors, beliefs, and attitudes—the *values*—of human beings explain potential adjustments to predicted cash flow. For example, whether California and New Jersey legislators accept the exit plans of an auto insurance company depends on the political, social, family, and economic values of the legislators themselves as well as governors, state insurance regulators, lobbyists, and voters (and nonvoters, too).

In this case, the values that determine political risk for an auto insurance company reflect those of people and organizations *external* to the company. Discounted cash flows and shareholder value are also sensitive to *internal* values; that is, the strength and predictability of beliefs, behaviors, attitudes, and speech of people inside organizations— to "how we do things around here."

Consider the risks in the telecommunications industry. In a decision a few years back, Verizon Wireless selected Lucent instead of Nortel to provide $5 billion worth of high-speed, high-capacity wireless infrastructure. Were the cash flow predictions for Verizon, Lucent, and Nortel affected by competitive and technological risk? Yes! Was this decision an economic and financial one influenced by self-interested concern for shareholder value? Yes! But this decision, *like all decisions made in organizations*, was intensely subject to political, social, cultural, and other values.

Such billion dollar business-to-business choices take months (sometimes years) and involve hundreds of people who shift across social and political coalitions. In addition to price and technical performance, decisions turn on the integrity, trust, faith, skills, reputations, and relationships of employees. Without doubt, people consult self-interest—that is, the value for themselves and their companies. But there is more to these decisions than value and self-interest alone.

Investment options sometimes reflect risks beyond the influence of human values. Property and casualty insurance companies, for example, must anticipate hurricanes and tornadoes. Yet, in our complex world of purposes, even the effects of hurricanes and tornadoes cannot be predicted without considering litigation, operational and emergency response times, construction practices, medical infrastructure, and efficiency—all of which shift under the force of human values.

The risks that explain the betas of discounted cash flow analyses are the stuff of human beings. *The capitalism of shareholder value is in reality the capitalism of values—all values, including, but not limited to, value itself.* "Money in common language," wrote Adam Smith, "signifies wealth.... (a) popular notion so familiar to us, that even they, who are convinced of its absurdity, are very apt to forget their own principles." In obscuring other values, shareholder value devotees have forgotten their principles. Risk-adjusted cash flow is equally well described as *values*-adjusted cash flow, because human values of all sorts describe and determine the risks themselves.

. . . .

In 1990, three partners of my McKinsey colleague published a book entitled *Valuation*. By then, the dogma of shareholder value had begotten the market for corporate control, the arena of capital markets made famous in the movie *Wall Street*. The market for corporate control sparked a wildfire of mergers, acquisitions, plant shutdowns, and downsizing that ultimately transformed jobs from lifelong arrangements into less certain affairs. The stakes shot up. Today, executives of companies that fail to deliver shareholder value do so at their own peril.

The authors of *Valuation* were blunt. Business managers, they insisted, have but one job—*manage value*.[1] Theirs is the kind of single answer that plays well in a tough guy, macho culture where "Greed is good" and winners rake in billions. It quickly became an obsession in boardrooms and executive offices around the globe. Sara Lee's devotion to shareholder value is the rule, not the exception.

But the dogma is a snare and a delusion. Yes, self-interested pursuits in markets produce wonders. Managers who ignore value *should* fail. But the dangerous fundamentalism enshrined in *Valuation* is illogical, irrational, and unsustainable. If executives obey its dictate and sum up their challenge with those two words—manage value—then who, we as *investors* ought to ask, will attend to the *values* conditioning risks? Who will guide the human messiness and excellence that determine the very risks identified in discounted cash flow analyses?

---

1. Tom Copeland et al, *Valuation: Measuring and Managing the Value of Companies* (New York: John Wiley & Sons, 1990), p. 23.

The orthodoxy of shareholder value is as simplistic as it is short-sighted. Yet, it has so captivated capital markets that the cynical now watch with delight as sincere men and women like the executives of Sara Lee defend shareholder value with constructs such as *The Balanced Scorecard*. As discussed in Chapter 3, *The Balanced Scorecard* is unbalanced and unethical. However well intended, it exacerbates the split between value and values. It thoroughly subordinates values to shareholder value. It makes people into assets and human values into financial instruments.

When confronted with such criticism, defenders of shareholder value question one's political values, one's toughness, and one's intelligence. Of course, they say, values matter. Without values, nothing would work. But, they assert, the responsibility for values in our liberal market democracies lies properly with individuals. Managers must attend to value; let each individual make his or her own choices. In a sophistical trick as old as human time, defenders of the dogma gloss over the dangers of isolating and enthroning value. Instead, they rush to the horrible hypothetical. Who, they ask, would prefer to live in Afghanistan or Iran or Bolivia? Take it or leave it: shareholder value and individualism, or poverty, tyranny, and the road to serfdom.

Then, they move on to street smarts and brains. Intimations that values ought to share the mountaintop with value elicit a dismissive attitude. I recall, for example, the prototypical comment of one shareholder value tough guy that if he "heard the word empowerment one more time, he'd vomit." Values are soft; value is hard. Get tough.

Or, they warn, get a grip. Of course, shareholder value proponents point out, values play a role. Just read *The Balanced Scorecard*. Organizations must attend to values, just as organizations must mind technology, strategy, information systems, processes, innovation, marketing, finance, operations, and other means to the end of shareholder value. Organizations ought to have Statements of Values (see Chapter 3). Value *is* the single, overriding objective. But of course, they say, values do need attention.

Don't you get it?

Then, in the next breath, these philistines simultaneously delegate the job of shaping values to others and return to their higher calling of managing shareholder value. When people attempt to shape values with proposals about work/life balance, child care, environmental costing, wiring schools for the Internet, moving swiftly to build hybrid cars, divesting holdings in pornography, or working hard to keep people employed in the face of economic reversals, the high priests of value invoke their incantation: Will it help or hurt shareholder value?

Theirs is an arrogant philosophy. It subordinates and obscures the foundation—identifying and understanding risks—that explains its own sustainability. These men and women are the ones who ought to get a grip. Value cannot and does not exist in a vacuum. Sustainable value creation is impossible in the absence of shared values that integrate with value itself. We cannot calculate risks without reference to values. We cannot manage organizations, understand customers, or respond to markets without reference to values.

The horrible hypothetical thrown in our faces about North Korea or Iran or other *places* is an either/or ploy unresponsive to our both/and reality. We do not ask to defeat value. We do not seek to go to the barricades in the manner of the antinationalist and anticapitalist revolutionaries of the mid-19th century. We give thanks for the benefits showered upon us by markets.

But our capital markets imperil those benefits. *They threaten to eat our seed corn.* Among the many strategies for building shareholder value tried over the past few decades, we have witnessed time and again a virulent strain. Its variants rise from greed unguided by any interest in, or sense of responsibility toward, others—from the pursuit of value without concern for values. This is what made Enron, WorldCom, Xerox, Dynergy, Adelphia, Arthur Andersen, Merrill Lynch, and other companies newsworthy.

Because we live in a world of markets, organizations, and networks, the value-obsessed mantra of capital markets swamps other markets—*including the governmental and nonprofit sectors*. For example, we cannot rightly explain why the American Red Cross misrepresented its fundraising purposes in the wake of the September 11th tragedy without looking to *its need for capital* and the subordinating of integrity to the dictate "manage value." Nor can we evaluate the energy or defense policies of the Bush Administration without reference to the pursuit of shareholder value by their industrial partners and supporters.

The Wealth of Nations is filled with quaint observations about the workings of capital. For example, Adam Smith writes that, "upon equal, or nearly equal profits, most men will choose to employ their capitals rather in the improvement and cultivation of land, than either in manufactures or in foreign trade." The reasons recounted for preferring farming over trade include "the beauty of the country," "the pleasures of the country life," "the tranquility of mind," and the country as "the original destination of man."

Smith integrated value with values. He highlighted the many benefits of self-interest operating in markets. But he wrote about capital invested in a world of places. We no longer live in that world. We live in a world of markets, organizations, networks, family, and friends; a world shaped by capital markets that have exiled and sub-ordinated values from the objectives of investment. In our world, capital is not allocated for reasons of beauty, pleasure, tranquility, or spirituality. We do not prefer investments in cultivation over trade in order to bring us closer to "the original destination of man." Our capital is directed at a single purpose: its own accumulation. In our world, "all businesses are mere cash flow generators." In capital mar-kets where shareholder value is orthodoxy, value has no purpose other than itself. It has no values.

. . . .

During the 1990s, people in more than half the households in the United States became *investors*. The logic of the numbers is inescapable. As investors, *we* determine where to put financial resources. *We* choose whether and how to evaluate organizations in which we might invest. *We participate in the democratic governance of the capital markets in which we live.*

There is, however, an additional lesson in the dramatic numbers: *Tens of millions of us are novices at being investors.*

We confront a profound dilemma. Contrary to arrangements in the age of Bernard Mandeville and Adam Smith, our capital markets exalt value over values and thereby exacerbate the risks and dangers in our new world of purposes. None have escaped the trauma of a world reeling from the irresponsible pursuit of value for its own sake. In our shared role of investor, we have motivation and power to heal the split between value and values in capital markets. But, for now, we lack *capability as investors.*

Millions of us lack the time, skill, and experience to confidently direct investments. We do not comprehend the machinations of shareholder value, discounted cash flows, and industry betas (let alone zillions of other ideas and techniques). Nor do we *know* the people who work in companies like Sara Lee in which we might invest. We can only hope to know the *values* of these companies and their brands. To do so, however, most of us turn to advice and information provided by others. In addition to being investors, then, we also are *consumers* of investment advice and information. We live in markets for financial advice and information. We depend on financial services and media organizations that currently promote the orthodoxy of shareholder value.

Sara Lee's proud homage to shareholder value is no accident. Its Board and executives comply with the orthodoxy demanded by the organizations and people most active in capital markets. If you ran a company whose stock was publicly traded, you too would find it difficult to *appear* to dilute your concern for shareholder value. It is more likely you would declare your singular devotion to shareholder value and run your organization accordingly.

The choice to promote a more ethical blend of value and values is not impossible. But sticking to it invites scorn from investment advisors, financial intermediaries, and business media—that is, the people and organizations in our capital markets who will quite publicly convict you of ignoring the dictate in *Valuation*: manage value. These are the same organizations upon whom we depend as consumers of investment advice and information. *Shareholder value fundamentalism, then, is the price of entry into capital markets set by those who control the gates of information.* It is too high a price.

Dogma shifts. It was popularly believed in Smith's 18th century England, for example, that markets were local affairs. Now, we must rid ourselves of shareholder value as a single answer. All of us—*and especially those who inform and advise us about investments*— need to wake up. Shareholder value as practiced today is illogical and irrational on its own terms. It is promoted and sustained by people and organizations who act as though their *only* interest is self-interest. *It is a mighty wedge dividing value and values*.

In our shared roles as investors and consumers of investment advice and information, I believe we will respond to leaders who seek to dethrone shareholder value and reform our capital markets. But we must have organizations and leaders to respond *to. We depend on the emergence of new leadership in the organizations who guide and participate in capital markets*.

The leaders of Sara Lee, for example, can act. They can declare an integrated view of value and values instead of a singular devotion to shareholder value. They can scrap the unethical *Balanced Scorecard* in favor of a purposeful pursuit of both value and values according to the Ethical Scorecard (see Illustrative Suggestion #1 in Chapter 17). So, too, can leaders in financial service organizations, such as Merrill Lynch or Deutsche Bank, media organizations, like CNBC, Fortune, the Los Angeles Times, and Bloomberg News, and pension and other investment funds, such as Calpers or Fidelity.

The people who most directly influence whether such leaders emerge are the people *employed* in organizations. In a world of democratic *places*, the local citizenry participated along with their leaders in the blending of value and values. In organizations, no one is better positioned to restore values to a healthy relationship with value than *employees* (who, as explained in Chapter 6, include executives). *Just as millions depend on people inside Sara Lee to insure quality cakes, so too must we look to the 140,000 employees of Sara Lee to identify and support leadership that moves beyond the dogma of shareholder value.* The rest of us depend on them to govern the values conveyed and delivered by their brand. Similarly, we rely on thousands of employees at CNBC, Fortune, Merrill Lynch, Calpers, Deutsche Bank, and other organizations large and small to save our world of markets, networks, organizations, friends, and families from the dangerous fundamentalism of shareholder value.

8 Ideas and Purposes, 1

In the late '90s, Budweiser aired commercials featuring friends whose fondness for one another was summed up in an oft repeated greeting: "Whazzzzup." The TV spots were well-conceived and well-executed. Millions of people instantly liked them. One variation played on the word wasabi, the horseradish condiment served with sushi. In it, a Whazzzzup guy is on a date at a sushi restaurant. When the waiter offers him wasabi, he bursts out with a huge smile, "Whazzzzabi!" First the waiter, and then others, join in. Good feelings all around. (Except for the young woman, whose expression tells us she prefers more propriety from her all-too-male companion).

During the years these spots ran, an acquaintance was on business in Tokyo. Sure enough, he told me, one evening at a sushi bar he hailed his waiter with a loud "Whazzzzabi!" Instantly, people were "Whazzzzabi-ing" each other. Everyone was in on it. Thanks to Budweiser, "Whazzzzup" and "Whazzzzabi" became shared ideas that influenced behavior, attitude, and speech in modest ways around the globe.

Is this anecdote a big deal? No. But the markets, networks, and organizations explaining it are. Together, they have *permanently* altered the forces that determine when we share ideas and how shared ideas influence shared values. In our new world of purposes, ideas supersaturate the air and multiply beyond measurement.

Some, like Whazzzzabi, are mere wordplay but nonetheless facilitate shared social values among millions of people who might not have tolerated one another in a world of places. Others, like shareholder value, foster entrenched beliefs, behaviors, attitudes, and speech that divide value from values (see Chapter 7). Still others, such as the shared ideas of product, brand, and market, have morphed and reconstituted. Unlike even twenty years ago, for example, products and services now overlay every aspect of life. Today, there is no human activity, including conceiving and sharing ideas, beyond the range of becoming products and services. None.

Ideas have always influenced values, especially when people who share some understanding of ideas use them in consequential circumstances. Consider holistic medicine. Not many people in market democracies had heard much about holistic medicine 40 years ago. Most who had (especially doctors) believed in Western medicine and considered holistic medicine a crackpot idea. Today, because of markets, networks, organizations, friends, and families, millions of people, including physicians and other health professionals, share a welcoming understanding of holistic medicine. When we walk into a doctor's office or chat with friends, the odds favor us sharing some common understanding of holistic medicine and how it might promote health. These odds also apply to random interactions with strangers, say, at a mall or, more likely, in the doctor's waiting room. Unlike three or four decades back, we now share ideas and values regarding holistic medicine with people we do not know. Like shared roles (Chapters 6 and 7), shared ideas facilitate shared values among strangers as well as acquaintances.

*But unlike shared roles and shared paths, which **inevitably** forge shared values, shared ideas only create possibilities.* When two or more people share some understanding of ideas, the odds increase that their beliefs, behaviors, attitudes, and speech will be mutually recognizable. But they are just odds. We might, for example, share some sense of ideas about deficit spending or Reality TV and yet have quite dissimilar values regarding them.

Unlike shared paths, there is no limit to the number of people whose values might get shaped by an idea. Shared paths (Chapter 5) typically include a handful of people. By contrast, Whazzzzabi and holistic medicine may be understood in similar ways by *hundreds of millions of people*. As a matter of possibility, this has always been so (as evidenced, for example, by the spread of religious ideas across place-bound cultures). *But it is now an everyday experience because we live in markets, networks, and organizations whose purposes depend upon the rapid spread of ideas.*

Nor is there any limit beyond interest and intelligence to the number of ideas we might share. Perhaps you participate in a dozen or so shared paths. But you have reasonably similar understandings of *thousands* of shared ideas that influence your values, whether trivially, profoundly, or anywhere in between. The infinite plasticity of language explains this potential. But, again, our world has made the possible real in unprecedented ways. In our new world, billions of people share an understanding of ideas essential to the purposes and mechanisms of markets, networks, and organizations that, themselves, spawn and spread ideas without regard to barriers of place or language. Whazzzzabi is a linguistic pun filtering African-American cool through Japanese cuisine. Even 50 years ago—let alone a 1,050 years ago—this would have been improbable. If it did spring to anyone's mind, its reach would have been trivial by comparison.

Along with uncapped mathematical possibilities comes a mile-wide, inch-deep corollary. An inch is an inch. Whazzzzabi engendered fellow feeling among millions in not unimportant ways. The diners in the Tokyo restaurant that evening had a chuckle. Still, the strength and predictability of values arising from the shared idea of Whazzzzabi pale in comparison with the shared values in shared paths. Moreover, there are ideas and ideas. Holistic medicine, do-it-yourself, and democracy foster broader ranges of values with more serious consequences than Whazzzzabi.

The consistency of people participating in shared paths, as well as the persistency of their interactions, inevitably generates and stabilizes shared values. (For good or ill: As mentioned in Chapter 5, dysfunctional shared paths traumatize people who, nonetheless, have highly predictable beliefs, behaviors, attitudes, and speech.) We come to *know* the people with whom we interact regularly and repeatedly in shared paths. Ideas, by contrast, dance and flit around like fireflies. *They are mere possibilities.* As an animating idea, Mike Myers' "Not!" operated much as Whazzzzupp. Today, it amuses fewer people than before and requires explanations to 10-year-olds. "Edsel" is a another example; as are "The Beatles," "Martin Luther," "détente," "Copperheads," "phrenology," "federalism," "Barney," "The Enlightenment," "Forty Acres and a Mule"—and the ideas in every book ever written, movie ever made, TV show ever aired, song ever sung, and product, service, brand, and celebrity ever marketed. One Internet message each September alerts professors, teachers, and administrators to a long list of ideas that, however dearly shared among them, are beyond the comprehension of matriculating freshmen.

The dynamics conditioning how shared ideas influence shared values include exposure, comprehension, belief, and action. *First, ideas cannot influence values in the absence of awareness.* Notwithstanding the immense disseminating power of markets, networks, and organizations, thousands of ideas never interact directly with *you*. You may or may not have been exposed to "synthetic securities," "nobarizing," "closing the commons," "DINCs," "Trapper Keepers," "risk-based accounting," "six sigma," "seigneurage," "been-to," or "Metcalfe's Law." If not, there is *no* possibility for belief, behavior, attitude, or speech in these ideas for you.

Second is comprehension. You may have heard about "parent-child" and "inheritance" but had *no understanding* about their meaning among database programmers. We must distinguish a lack of *any* understanding from misunderstanding. The idea of "liberal," for example, includes a range of meanings many people consider antithetical to the idea of "personal responsibility." This is a misunderstanding. Nevertheless, it is *a shared misunderstanding* that influences shared values in predictable ways. It invites politicians, commentators, talk radio hosts, and religious leaders to gain *value* for themselves and their organizations by spreading and reinforcing the misunderstanding. Some may find the strong, predictable behavior of such men and women contemptible. But they *are* predictable behaviors in our new world of markets, networks, organizations, friends, and families. It is the nature of ideas that our values cannot incorporate them without *some* comprehension, yet *any* understanding—even an inaccurate one—will do.

Third are belief and action. We can comprehend an idea without believing or acting on it. More people today than in the 19th century grasp yet reject the idea that criminal tendencies are traceable to cranial bumps. On the other hand, more of us than them understand, believe, and act on the idea that criminal acts are corroborated by fingerprints and DNA. *We also can understand and believe an idea without acting on it.* We know from surveys and elections, for example, that millions of people believe in the idea of democracy yet fail to register or vote. *In addition, we can act on ideas without believing them.* I'll wager that some politicians and talk radio celebrities do not personally believe liberals disdain personal responsibility, yet still act on the idea because it sells in the markets in which they participate. In this practice, by the way, they are not alone. Millions of people work in organizations that generate value through appeals to misunderstood ideas such as people as assets and shareholder value.

Ideas carry possibilities for shared values. Whether or not they animate reason and passion enough to convert exposure and comprehension into belief or action has always been up to us. None of that, I think, has changed. *But nearly everything else has.* Indeed, our world is so profoundly sensitive to ideas and information that a scientific theory known as *memetics* now argues that memes (ideas and information) replicate, mutate, and compete for survival just as genes do—and with comparable long-term effects for the human species. Memetics takes ideas and information into biology and evolution. It's intriguing. But we do not need to be memeticians to acknowledge that we live in an information age.

This and the next chapter explore how ideas and information influence values. This chapter reviews the implications for exposure, understanding, belief, and action caused by a shift from a world of places to a world of markets, networks, organizations, friends, and family. In particular, markets, networks, and organizations spawn a juggernaut of ideas aimed at creating value. The number, kind, and pace of ideas far outstrip our capacity to comprehend or control. In our new world, our purposes—and not the places we reside—best predict which among the infinity of available ideas we share with others.

Ours is a world chaotic with ideas. Ideas chase us; we chase ideas. We reject or embrace ideas because of problems we must solve—particularly problems of value required to live in markets, networks, and organizations. Unlike people in a world of places, we have extraordinary opportunities to pick and choose ideas without fear of reprisal from power or popular opinion. Yes, we encounter groups whose strongly shared ideas and values constrain our ease and freedom to express ourselves. We sometimes confront the call to dissent. But in our world, dissent matters mostly in organizations and among friends and families, rather than in places.

In Chapter 9, I explore how ideas about value and values relate to products, services, brands, and celebrities. Today, people with ideas to share beyond friends and family must *market* those ideas. They must accept that, in our world, ideas themselves *are* products, services, and brands. Discussion, debate, leadership, publication, and education in places we reside make sense. But, unlike in a world of places, such steps might be irrelevant and, in any event, are insufficient to spread ideas and transform them into shared values. *Because we live in markets, networks, and organizations, we must market and sell ideas if we hope to see them flourish.*

This entire book is about ideas, not just these two chapters. I am especially concerned with ideas that can heal the split separating value from values. I am advocating, for example, that we take the best meaning from shared ideas such as citizen, community, and democracy and incorporate them into our understanding of markets, organizations, employees, consumers, and investors. Like the rest of the book, these two chapters refer to specific ideas. But my main objective has less to do with any particular idea and more with how differently we now find ourselves oriented to ideas. In particular, our *purposes* in markets, networks, and organizations, and among friends and families explain much about the ideas we share and how they affect our values. Our challenge today has more to do with using ideas to integrate value and values than generating ideas themselves. The ideas are there. The question is how and for what purposes we use them.

· ·

In 1644, two decades before wrapping up *Paradise Lost*, John Milton had a lot to complain about. His wife had left him, his eyesight was failing, and his countrymen were at each other's throats. That year, however, he chose to vent against a different evil: Parliament's Licensing Order requiring prepublication approval of thoughts and ideas. "Though all the winds of doctrine were let loose to play upon the earth," Milton argued in *Areopagitica*, "So Truth be in the field, we do injuriously by licensing and prohibiting to misdoubt her strength. Let her and Falsehood grapple, who ever knew Truth put to the worse in a free and open encounter?".

Scholars invoke Milton in the cause against censorship. Censorship has always been a predictable behavior of powerful people. But censorship is also a bedfellow of popular opinion, especially in a world of places where (1) ideas are more likely to be shared by people who live among one another, and (2) shared paths and shared roles harmonize with shared ideas to produce strong perceptions of "the way we do things around *here*." The adage "when in Rome, do as the Romans" was not an idle suggestion over most of the past few thousand years. In our new world, by contrast, it is trivial unless we substitute organization for place. "When at IBM do as the IBMers" remains wise counsel.

In Milton's time, the way things were done around England was up for grabs over ideas such as the "one true faith" and the "divine right of kings." His dissent is admired because, though staunchly anti-Catholic himself, he railed against censorship of religious truth by Protestants controlling Parliament. Two centuries later, John Stuart Mill penned another rousing defense of free discourse. Mill used *On Liberty* to defend dissent as necessary to a fuller range of truths: scientific and secular as well as religious. His target was less a censorious government than closed-minded popular opinion. "Let us suppose," he wrote, "that the government is entirely at one with the people, and never thinks of exerting any power of coercion unless in agreement with what it conceives to be their voice. But I deny the right of the people to exercise such coercion, either by themselves or by their government. The power itself is illegitimate."

In a world of places, power and popular opinion conspired to control interactions among ideas and people. Shared paths, shared roles, and shared status were highly congruent with shared ideas. Ideas added up to shared worldviews about truth. In contemporary management lingo, people in a world of places suffered from groupthink. Dissent was honored *because* groups had so disproportionate a say over the ideas that influenced values.

Individual opinion mattered. *But in a world of places, individual opinion and action rarely occurred beyond the context of groups in which individuals participated.* People responded to ideas *together* according to the orthodoxy of the places they lived. Orthodoxy summed up the ideas knitted into shared truths and shared values—ideas so strongly shared that individuals were cautious about contrary ideas lest they be seen as errant. Individuals had the refuge of conscience. Philosophers and theologians bestowed moral weight on individuals for honoring ideas in the privacy of their own minds, especially ideas in conflict with power or popular opinion. Many English men and women in the mid-seventeenth century, for example, found the idea of unseating King Charles repugnant. Those who wished to speak and act, however, *had* to weigh the consequences of dissent.

In a world of places, to *act* individually regarding ideas out of favor with power and popular opinion *was* to dissent. Other than private conscience, there was little alternative. For this reason, we celebrate dissenters. The risks of dissent were so high that dissent was regularly a *group* affair. Shortly after publishing *Areopagitica*, Milton joined with groups so enraged by Charles' claims of divine authority that they revolted. The pilgrims who sailed on the Mayflower several decades earlier struck a blow for the idea of *individual* religious liberty *as a group*. In the following century, Thomas Jefferson wrote on behalf of a group who had gathered in Philadelphia when he informed the English King and Parliament that "*We* hold these truths to be self-evident."

We often criticize groupthink as a form of orthodoxy, and we deride orthodoxy as little more than truth decked out with more syllables than facts. We discredit people who lived in a world of places for favoring tradition over empiricism in choosing truth. I began Chapter 4, for example, with the well-known story of Galileo's trial and recantation (a significant emotional event for Milton who, years before penning *Areopagitica*, met and learned from Galileo about the risks of open dissent with power over truth). A less familiar, more light-hearted, and probably apocryphal anecdote tells of a Middle Ages gathering of scholars debating the number of teeth in a horse's mouth. Following a thousand-year tradition, the learned men argued various alternative interpretations of Aristotle (who, uncharacteristically, left this particular fact vague). When one recommended that, instead of consulting Aristotle, they ought to go outside, peer into their horses' mouths, and count, the others exclaimed, "Blasphemy!" and banished him forever!

In recounting this, I do not mean to reprise the misunderstood idea of a Dark Age in which thought took a longer snooze than Rip Van Winkle. Humor, inquisitiveness, invention, creativity, risk— sources of new ideas operated in a world of places. New ideas obviously flowed; otherwise, we would not live in our new world of markets, organizations, networks, families, and friends. But fresh ideas came slowly. People who lived in places resisted new ideas *together*; they also revered existing ideas together as part of truth. Arguably, people in a world of places cherished ideas more than we do because so many more of their ideas were shared and acted upon in shared values. As a body, ideas were more serious, less quixotic, better integrated, and longer lasting; if new, they were distrusted. Place kept ideas under strict regulation. Power and popular opinion barred the doors to new ideas. Dissent was a risky, if courageous, option. Yet dissenters, like other individuals, tested ideas in *groups* that determined "the way we do things around here."

In our new world of purposes, we have extraordinary opportunities to influence ideas that influence values by acting as *individuals*.

Groups still affect our attitudes toward ideas, especially thick we's in organizations and among friends and family. But, each of us *has the option* to act on ideas every day without reference to *groups*. Like people before, we too can take refuge in conscience. Unlike them, private thought is *not* our sole alternative to dissent. We can act on ideas anonymously in markets and networks, and do so without fear.

In the absence of media attention or personal display, what we say or do in markets and networks is not exposed to the approbation or censure of people who live down the block or around the corner. In fact, our responses to ideas are less likely to be of interest to fellow town or city dwellers *than to the organizations who make it their purpose to pay attention*. What we say or do about ideas matters profoundly to organizational success in markets and networks. As a consequence, organizations far afield from where we reside are more likely to know about our attitudes regarding ideas of interest to them than people who live next door.

Markets, networks, and organizations are *sense and respond* social formations. Organizations spend billions of dollars and millions of person-hours on market research, surveys, polls, focus groups, and other sensing efforts to identify, shape, disseminate, and manage ideas. Organizations assiduously attend to how consumers, investors, and networkers *actually act* on the ideas incorporated in products, services, and brands. Success depends on it. Organizations ranging from shampoo makers to political campaigns to holistic medicine associations seek to identify and shape ideas they can extend and link to shared beliefs and behaviors.

Organizations are in the business of using shared ideas to foster strong shared values. That is how our markets work. Organizations are not attempting, however, to use shared ideas to mold groups whose shared values arise from shared fates and shared purposes. Organizations are not building thick we's. Rather, organizations use ideas to identify, understand, grow, and build market segments—*collectivities of individuals, of I's*—whose similar interests and motivations make their behavior as consumers and investors in markets and networks strongly predictable.

These efforts can be quite sophisticated, especially when conducted with information technology through networks. Consider collaborative filtering. Collaborative filtering is an analytical technique that relies on statistical inference to predict consumer preferences. Movie Web sites, for example, use collaborative filtering to make recommendations. For users who have selected and rated as little as a dozen or so films, the better collaborative filters sift through data on thousands of other users to provide surprisingly accurate predictions of personal reactions to movies. In a broad way, collaborative filtering is analogous to using poll data to forecast election outcomes on the back of a few thousand respondents. Both draw inferences about belief and behavior—values—from patterns in *defined* market segments. Organizations using such marketing techniques are not trying to foster groups with shared values arising from intragroup interactions and shared fates. Rather, they seek to induce predictable results from *collectivities of I's* who share demographic and behavioral characteristics and preferences.

We might consider this sinister. Like Hamlet dealing with Rosencrantz and Guildenstern, we might worry that the most sophisticated organizations find it so easy to get their tunes out of us. Yet, even as we fret, we must remind ourselves that organizations operate in markets and networks *to serve us*. They compete for *our* business. And, critically, as *employees, we* work in and for them. Indeed, as employees in thick we's, we *are* them. Our shared values as consumers or investors may reflect the thin we's of collectivities of I's. But how and to what purposes organizations use ideas to promote value and values in products, services, and brands *is* a thick we affair. It reflects our shared purposes—and on our character—as employees.

. . . .

In a world of places, competitors mostly battled over feature, function, and distribution. Products and services were undifferentiated *commodities*. Henry Ford's dictum rang through the land: "I don't care what color car they want so long as it is black." Cars, stoves, electricity, cereal, shampoo—yes, there were some differences in products and services. Advertising magnified such distinctions through ideas and language that fostered what Thorstein Veblen derided as a broad leisure class motivated by pecuniary emulation, conspicuous consumption, and invidious distinctions. There was a lot of smoke and even more mirrors. On balance, though, products and services had a commodity-like sameness directed at meeting the undifferentiated needs of as many people as possible.

Not today. Consider shampoo. There may be, in effect, an infinite variety of shampoos because, by the time any of us had sampled and compared each variation, so many new variations would exist that our sampling might never end. Shampoo is not a commodity.

Like most products and services, shampoo is an aggregation of features, functions, information, and *ideas*. Physical and *psychological* factors of hair type, gender, sexual orientation, age, color, scent, ingredients, environmental impact, cross-cultural relations, distribution channels, access, marital status, and personalized services compound with one another. Nor is shampoo only a product. Organizations ranging from stand-alone barbershops and beauty parlors to Supercuts and Hair Club for Men provide services. In our world, if you wish to start a shampoo company or, more likely, advance a shampoo concept in an existing organization, feature, function, and distribution are necessary but not sufficient. You had better have at least one promising *idea*.

Are ideas still magnified and distorted by advertising? Yes. Messages in TV, radio, magazine, newspaper, and Web pages are constrained by space and time. Advertisers must select only some of many possible ideas to communicate. Exaggeration is inevitable because of the dictates of choice. For example, Weight Watchers might emphasize safe and healthy weight control in its ad messages. Cell phone companies might emphasize instant messaging or video games. Food product companies might highlight home-style cooking. Political parties might push jobs as a hot button to sell economic programs. In each case, however, our experience of the products and services extends well beyond the chosen ideas. By selecting a few messages, those few are exaggerated. Exaggeration is built into the logic of advertising.

But exaggeration need not be misleading or false. There is no logic of limited space or time requiring organizations to disseminate and instill *misunderstanding*. For example, many automobile manufacturers intentionally market the idea of safety in promoting SUVs, even though studies show SUVs are relatively less safe than midsize sedans. Safety is an idea that speaks to social, civil, technical, family, and religious values. If asked why automobile manufacturers disseminate inaccurate claims of safety, most of us answer, "Because they are trying to sell cars."

Put differently, automobile manufacturers—*the thick we's of automobile-producing organizations*—focus primarily on value. That forms part of *their* shared values, their character. Automobile manufacturing thick we's use ideas about values such as safety misleadingly to promote value. This is obvious. But they are not alone. *The use of ideas about values to generate value in markets is among the strongest, most predictable beliefs, behaviors, attitudes, and speech in our new world of purposes.*

Organizations use ideas to make promises about experience. If experience contradicts the promises, the associated products, services, and ideas suffer. So do brands. Tens of thousands of consumers, for example, have experience-based reasons to believe in the safe and healthy claims of Weight Watchers. Millions refer to experience regarding promises of their favorite shampoos. Those injured in accidents involving SUVs have reason to discount the safety claims of automobile manufacturers.

Companies that cross the line separating exaggeration from deception risk failure because *experience* in a world of markets, networks, and organizations depends so heavily on products and services. Ideas come alive in products and services. Differentiated claims based on ideas promise differentiated experiences. If experience falls short, we have other choices because markets, networks, and organizations are sense and respond social formations.

We have power as *individuals acting alone* in markets and networks to adopt, reject, or otherwise affect ideas based on experience. *But our power to influence ideas through individual action in markets and networks is better explained by the idea of voting than the idea of dissent.*

Unlike people in a world of places, we have the option to act anonymously in endorsing or opposing ideas in markets and networks. In contrast, the dissent practiced by Milton and defended by Mill *was dissent* because it involved individuals who acted *in groups of people they knew*. When, as happened a few days before I wrote this, a telemarketing representative phones me and hears my anger over the idea of invading privacy, I am not dissenting. I am giving customer feedback. I am *casting a vote* in favor of the idea of privacy and against the idea of uninvited telemarketing. And I am doing it *alone* in the context of markets and networks without concern for reprisal or argument (or even support!) from any group of people I know.

I could opt to dissent. I could speak directly with people I know who work in organizations that telemarket. I could raise ideas ranging from privacy to hypocrisy and engage them in a discussion over the value and values of telemarketing. I could ask them to let me speak to people they know at the companies where they work. In addition, I could join organizations in the growing movement against telemarketing. I could abandon my anonymity and lead or join boycotts of telemarketing service organizations and their client companies. All this is possible. But in our new world of purposes, I do not need to dissent to shape the ideas that shape values. Nor do I need to dwell in the privacy of my conscience. I can shop.

. . . .

Our freedom and power as *individuals* in markets and networks to influence ideas that shape values is among humanity's most extraordinary achievements. It sits in the center of our popular philosophy of individualism and is actively opposed mostly by fundamentalists, who, not coincidentally, remain obsessed with the idea of truth. But to acknowledge and celebrate our power to act alone as individuals is not to say we ought *always* to exercise it alone. If we are to reintegrate value and values in our world, we increasingly need to open up individual consumer, investment, and networking choices to dissent and free discourse in the *groups* in which we participate.

In a world of places, people reacted to ideas together in groups. That was simply part of their reality, a default condition of life together. Among the many downsides were curtailments of individual freedom and widespread ignorance due to a *lack* of ideas. On the other hand, for good or ill, ideas were more likely shared ideas that, together with shared paths and shared roles and status, engendered strongly shared values.

In our world, by contrast, we increasingly must *self-consciously* decide to subject individual actions in markets and networks to groups in which we participate. This is not a legalistic point about rights. Whether groups consist of friends, family, or fellow employees, we need not grant rights of censure or control to consult with others. Rather, in our fragmented and kaleidoscopic world, where shared paths, shared roles, and shared ideas are most congruent in organizations, friends, and families, the issue we face is how to take the wisest advantage of opportunities to integrate value and values. How do we take advantage of our shared paths and thick we's in order *to learn and develop ideas by acting together* as opposed to alone? Friends, families, and organizations are the contexts to which humanity's proud tradition of dissent and open discourse trace. Because we share our strongest and broadest range of values in shared paths, our *failure* to invite open discourse about consumer and investment choices can itself be an unintended contradiction—a betrayal of value at war with values in our lives.

Consider ideas about health, beauty, self-image, diet, weight, and individual responsibility. These inspire many celebrated values. We need think only of the last wedding, graduation, dance recital, or school play to smile on excellent possibilities for belief, behavior, attitude, and speech in youth, beauty, health, and individual responsibility. Yet, we know the same ideas serve up dangerous cocktails in markets, networks, organizations, friends, and families. We confront an epidemic of eating disorders because strongly shared ideas and shared values about self-image and self-control combine to sicken and kill young people. The menace affects boys as well as girls; steroid use is on the rise among teenage boys captivated by the idea of looking "buff."

The ideas themselves are neither good nor bad nor anything in between. They are just ideas. They merely hold out the possibilities of shared values. Nor are the particular ideas new. Youth, beauty, health, and individual responsibility have inspired good and bad values since the dawn of time. The Judgement of Paris to choose beauty over wisdom and power, for example, led to the kidnapping, rape, and other ills chronicled in *The Iliad* and other ancient tales of the Trojan War. But, for most of human history, ideas ran a gauntlet of group opinion in places people lived together. In our world, by contrast, these ideas course through markets, networks, and organizations ranging from dieting to entertainment, medicine to education, and advertising to sports. We interact with the ideas *in these contexts* nearly every day of our lives. Unlike our ancestors, we have the very real option to pick and choose our way alone. Indeed, individual, not group, experience is often our default condition. We must consciously (even conscientiously) *choose* to subject awareness, comprehension, belief, and action about ideas to the *groups* in which we participate.

In deciding to join Weight Watchers, for example, a fortysomething single mother *might* reinforce or contradict ideas and values she shares with others. Simply by starting a Weight Watchers diet, she may appear to her 15-year-old daughter (especially to her 15-year-old daughter!) to contradict beliefs the mother has articulated about eating disorders. The daughter's response may be a misunderstanding. If so, then, as Mill noted in *On Liberty*, open discourse is a powerful antidote.

Weight Watchers abhors eating disorders. It promises safe and healthy weight loss through a counting system supplemented by weekly meetings with other customers guided by a Weight Watchers' group leader. By discussing this with her daughter, the mother might convert misunderstanding to shared understanding. By inviting her daughter to participate in a dialogue, the mother betters the odds that her daughter will see her actions as consistent with expressed concerns about eating disorders. This is neither a sure thing nor hassle-free. Open discourse among parents and teenagers, we know, is fraught with surprise—and opportunity for dissent. Still, the shared path of family members remains the core extension of our lives together in places. The powerful and seductive anonymity of markets and networks might be an illusion at home. Or it might not: Working mothers can join Weight Watchers or utilize other dieting or exercise approaches without their children gaining in awareness or understanding as a consequence.

In discussing the choice, mother and daughter convert shared awareness and comprehension into mutually understood belief and action. They take the risk to integrate ideas into the values of their shared path, whether for good or ill. Perfect agreement is not the point; disagreement has never been inconsistent with mutual understanding and shared values. Open discussion reinforces shared political values between mother and daughter regarding free discourse and dissent—especially if there is disagreement.

Not only might the mother dispel misunderstanding due to a lack of information, but daughter and mother might also deepen awareness, comprehension, belief, and action about eating disorders in ways that have larger effects. The daughter might ask why Weight Watchers doesn't do more to market *ideas* to teenagers about safe, healthy weight control and broader conceptions of beauty and healthy self-image. The daughter might share ideas with her friends; the mother might introduce her daughter's concerns at the next Weight Watchers meeting.

In our new world, purposes foster shared paths more than places. Customers who succeed with Weight Watchers stick to it. Sticking with Weight Watchers means attending the weekly group, which is likely to become a shared path. The narrow purpose of that path may be weight loss. But, like all shared paths, persistent interaction among consistent members produces discussion and action across a range of values (see Chapter 5). Beliefs and behaviors regarding hard work, discipline, goal setting, integrity, and candor are part of the group's experience together. To this, the mother might add ideas about eating disorders among teenagers and what opportunities (and responsibilities) might exist for Weight Watchers to pick up on her daughter's suggestions.

Mother and daughter, then, might take ideas from their shared path into other shared paths. This, according to the science of memes, might get replicated. The Weight Watchers group leader might email other group leaders and suggest they raise similar concerns in their groups. Weight Watchers group leaders might informally disseminate ideas and shape shared values in many different groups. One or more might take advantage of formal processes at Weight Watchers to raise concerns and opportunities to a different level. Or a Weight Watchers manager monitoring discussions about eating disorders in chat rooms on the company Web site might see a new product or marketing opportunity.

Weight Watchers cares deeply about the ideas associated with its brand. Insights from the mother-daughter discussion *might* wend their way through weekly group discussions into the sense and respond efforts of the company. Weight Watchers might ask its board of advisors to consider eating disorders, and based on their recommendations, the company might form an alliance with the National Eating Disorders Association to co-market an awareness program in schools. Or, Weight Watchers might craft a set of specially customized services targeted at children of Weight Watchers members. They might hire an advertising firm to coin slogans like Whazzzzup to capture the imaginations of young people and convince them to "Just Say No" to eating disorders.

I could go on. So could you. Markets, networks, organizations, friends, and families forcefully shape awareness, comprehension, belief, and action regarding the ideas in our lives. *If we wish to convert shared ideas into shared values, we must act in these social formations.* If a mother and daughter wish to influence each other's values with ideas, they must introduce the ideas into their shared path. They must risk open discourse, dissent, and disagreement. If either or both wish to spread an idea further, they must do so in other shared paths and in markets, networks, and organizations. Markets, networks, and organizations are sense and respond formations. They are listening. They may or may not respond as we wish; that is a risk we take. But, in our new world of purposes, ideas that flourish inevitably do so because of how they get disseminated in markets, networks, organizations, friends, and families.

"Never doubt that a small group of individuals can change the world," Margaret Mead once said. "Indeed, it is the only thing that ever has." Like the world of places that has passed us by, ideas must be sounded by individuals and groups. Unlike in a world of places, however, we cannot assume that individual and group deliberation are coincident. We can influence our world as individuals acting alone in markets and networks. We are not limited to choos-

ing between risky dissent in groups versus private deliberation. Yet,
Mead's observation holds. In our world, too, small *groups* hold the
key to ideas that might spread to millions. But today, group action
is a matter of choice, not fate. We are not cast into groups in which
dissent or private conscience are the only options. We must *choose*
to act in groups if we are to discover ideas that make a difference to
values.

9 Ideas and Purposes, 2

In the 1980s, when I was researching *Fumbling the Future*, a book chronicling the invention of personal distributed computing at Xerox, I asked one of the key developers what motivated him. He said that, unlike scientists who carve out truth claims, he preferred inventing *good things to have*. In this, I think, he headlined a core shared idea of our new age. Tens of millions of us go to work every day to create, make, sell, and service good things to have. It is not that we dismiss the idea of truth. There are truth markets, truth networks, and truth organizations. There are plenty of scientists seeking empirical truths and politicians and spiritualists promoting revealed truths. Still, how we actually spend most of our time and attention suggests that seeking and disseminating truth is a niche compared with our pursuit of good things to have.

Markets, networks, and organizations are extraordinarily well tuned to invent, promote, sell, and service good things to have. Markets operate through competitive differentiation and segmentation, something nicely captured by the shared ideas of *mass customization* and *market of one* that gained currency in the 1990s. Each inspires organizations to make, sell, and service products and services that *fit the customized needs of a market of one—that is, every individual on the planet*. The vision promises a world designed and operated to meet *your* needs. Good things to have are good, in part, because they tailor to *individual* needs, wants, desires, and experiences.

This is not, by the way, a vision of indolence. Markets, networks, and organizations do not beaver away as if each person on the planet had no more exalted dream than a life of passivity. We have inherited either/or ideas about labor and leisure that imply life is fulfilled when the first is entirely eliminated in favor of the second—notions that trace to histories of slavery and other brutal realities of 19th and 20th century industrialization. But these shared ideas contradict our actual experience. Today, marketing, advertising, and strategy promote human motivation spanning a spectrum from *do-it-for-me* to *do-it-with-me* to *do-it-myself*. My niece and her husband, for example, recently went looking for a carving block for their kitchen. My niece wanted to purchase one (do-it-for-me); my nephew preferred to make one himself. In contrast, they share do-it-myself motivations with regard to athletics. They prefer the labor of preparing for and performing in marathons to the leisure of watching professionals on TV. For them, athletics are a form of labor *and* leisure.

Infinite possibilities arise when aspirations like a market of one take wing under this range of motivations. When the Xerox developers began tackling personal distributed computing in the early 1970s, there were some good things that had not yet been created: cell phones, digital watches, VCRs, camcorders, DVDs, pocket calculators, air bags, nonsmoking sections in restaurants, Web access, Prozac, microfleece, lip gloss, adult diapers, mortgage-backed securities, supply chain management, warehouse stores, ATMs, reality TV, MTV, music videos, antisnoring devices, nicotine patches, bioengineered food, the Segway personal transporter, Internet banking, email, hypertext, EZ Pass, titanium hips, and in vitro fertilization.

An *uncountable* number of products and services have emerged and, along with them, an uncountable number of ideas that *might* get shared. Yet, generating good things to have is not the whole picture. *Organizations that succeed in gaining market share by providing good things to have also work to protect their positions.* Organizations fight tenaciously to hold on. Even as they search for new drugs, for example, pharmaceutical companies spend huge resources on politicians (campaign contributions), doctors (paid junkets), and patients (advertising) to perpetuate intellectual property and market share for existing drugs. Organizations, then, are not solely or exclusively focused on good things to have. In addition, *they are focused on opposing the identification and dissemination of good things to have by **other** organizations*.

They battle over ideas. An astonishing and audacious idea launched the invention of personal distributed computing at the Xerox Palo Alto Research Center. Robert Taylor, a psychologist, challenged Xerox researchers to transform the primary purpose of computers from computing to communication. He asked them to reinvent the pencil, paper, and the telephone. Their work, along with parallel and subsequent efforts by so many others, changed the world. The idea of computers as a communications medium sired *networks*, social formations as formidable as markets, nations, and organizations. Less than a few decades separated Xerox PARC's efforts from a world besotted with ideas about a new economy and society built around the World Wide Web. Billions of dollars were made (and lost). Values of all sorts—social, political, religious, economic, family, and technological—were affected.

Networks have turbocharged the proliferation of products, services, and ideas. Ideas rapidly become shared among hundreds of thousands of people spread over the globe—even without the supporting infrastructure of television, radio, newspapers, and magazines. With a link to the Web, each of us is a publisher in a many-to-many network. Television, by contrast, is a one-to-many network; it broadcasts from one location to many. When you use the Web to send or receive the latest joke—or job opportunity, baby picture, product offer, or religious plea—you are bypassing one-to-many networks. None of this suggests that major media is leveled or decimated. Ideas promoted and supported by television, radio, newspapers, and magazines still enjoy better odds of wider dissemination than ideas trafficked through email. But, in our newly networked world, ideas travel at blinding speed from many people to many people without regard to place.

Among other consequences, networks pressure organizations to convert ideas into good things to have faster than ever before. The average time from new idea to first commercial sale has shrunk dramatically. A battery company executive once told me that, prior to the '90s, the last new battery had taken *four decades* from idea to commercialization. In the '90s, several new batteries hit the market in two to four years—a tenfold or better increase in speed. Other organizations reduced new product and service cycle times from decades to years, and years to months. The shared idea of *fast cycle time* did not exist in the 1960s or 1970s. It is now as widely used as shareholder value, reengineering, supply chain management, and customer service. Together with others, these shared ideas have produced strong, predictable shared values in organizations regarding problem solving, out of the box thinking, teaming, empowerment, buy in, and contingent, instead of lifelong, employment.

Ideas about what products, services, and markets are have reconstituted. In a world of purposes, products, services, and markets overlay *all aspects of life*. Every human activity can be enhanced or eliminated by good things to have. Products and services are essential to the material and immaterial bases of our lives. We *sometimes* experience the material basis of life apart from products or services. But rarely. Some of my friends, for example, bring do-it-myself motivations to growing tomatoes or, like my nephew, to making furniture. *Even so, every do-it-myself-er is still a do-it-for-me customer of one or more organizations, such as those providing seeds, trowels, fertilizer, wood, glue, and clamps, as well as how-to manuals and related advisory services*. In a world of markets, networks, and organizations, *none* of us are pure survivalists. Quite the contrary: Most of us most of the time *must* rely on organizations to do-it-for-me.

This transforms the meaning of products and services beyond our inherited understanding. For example, the air we breathe swirls with winds stirred by markets, networks, and organizations trading in pollution rights, or heating and cooling the great indoors. Water? It is bottled and branded, regulated and managed, and bought and sold in all three natural states. The same holds for earth and fire—and other substances nominated over the centuries by philosophers and scientists as primary materials of reality.

Every human possibility invites good things to have. What exists as a potential product or service today becomes real tomorrow *because someone somewhere has an idea and organizes to pursue it in markets and networks*. The acorn still embodies the potential of the oak. Most likely, though, that realization depends on how ideas about acorns and oaks translate into good things to have coming our way from organizations we know as forest services, zoning and land use agencies, seed companies, nurseries, gardening schools, tree sprayers, and residential and commercial developers.

When everything is or might be a product or service, the *idea* of markets encompasses life itself—from biology to government and communication to enlightenment. Human cloning, for example, is inevitable. It will happen, and it will happen fast. There *is* a market in cloning; there are organizations and networks devoted to speeding up, slowing down, or eliminating cloning. How the market for cloning evolves depends on such forces. But the market exists—and will always exist because people in organizations will find customers who consider cloning a good thing to have.

The good-things-to-have phenomenon extends beyond for-profit firms to not-for-profit and governmental organizations. They, too, innovate and improve. They, too, protect established positions. Governmental organizations, for example, struggle to establish and protect positions in markets and networks for cloning. So do various not-for-profit organizations. Across all sectors, then, we find the dual purposes of organizations: *meet customer needs and protect competitive position.* Some more actively pursue the first, some the second. But *all* organizations pursue a blend. The dual purposes pose a both/and challenge to organizations to create and protect positions built on converting ideas into good things to have for individuals variously motivated by do-it-for-me, do-it-with-me, and do-it-myself.

. . . .

Humanity has crossed a threshold. Under the compulsion to seek and protect good things to have in markets and networks, organizations generate *more ideas than we can identify, understand, or use.* Ideas were more manageable in a world of places; they simmered in a soup of power, popular opinion, and shared values about "the way we do things around here." It was seemingly feasible for some people to know everything. Today, ideas supersaturate the ether and multiply beyond measurement because power and popular opinion operate in *organizations,* not places. None of us can know every idea—not even every idea spawned *yesterday.*

Ironically perhaps, strong shared values about the shared idea of truth in place-confined cultures provided an unintended service to ignorance. The leaden pace at which ideas evolved is captured in a fun way by contrasting the acceleration of knowledge to the evolution in human brain capacity. Knowledge is said to have doubled from the life of Jesus to the life of Leonardo da Vinci—a span of 1,500 years. Knowledge doubled again between da Vinci and the American Revolution (250 years), doubled again between the Revolution and the advent of the automobile (125 years), doubled again between the automobile and the Cold War (50 years), and doubled again between the onset of the Cold War and the election of John Kennedy (10 years).

Today, estimates vary. Some people claim knowledge doubles every five years, others, every 18 months. Meanwhile, according to fossil evidence, brain capacity has increased *three and a half times* from the dawn of humanity to today. Compared to the *four-thousandfold* expansion in knowledge over the same horizon, which will become *eight-thousandfold* soon and *sixteen-thousandfold* a bit later on, our perspective on the twin ideas of understanding and ignorance must alter.

Ignorance always has arisen from an imbalance between capacities such as intelligence and effort on one hand, and, the nature, quantity, relevance, and timeliness of ideas and information on the other. Human brain capacity has expanded; we are more intelligent. Scientists assert that we use little of the capacity we have. Compared to other species, our brains are enormous. We outstrip other species in capacity to understand—which also means that we outstrip them in capacity to misunderstand.

Yet, knowledge now doubles every few years. Moreover, those who count such things ignore thousands of ideas and reams of information roaring through media, entertainment, advertising, and marketing. Slogans and sound bites may not be knowledge—but they *are* information and ideas. *Our world of markets, networks, and organizations churns out an infinity of ideas and information.* The imbalance between ignorance and understanding is less a matter of raw intelligence and more about the number, scope, and pace with which ideas and information emerge, propagate, and flow in markets, networks, and organizations.

Consider the potential for ignorance regarding pharmaceutical company efforts to find and sell good things to have. Pharmaceutical companies have responded to burgeoning consumer demand for life-enhancing drugs that combat everything from depression to erectile dysfunction. They have gained handsomely in terms of *value*: They are among the most profitable companies in the world. Yet, concerns about their *values* surface because of (1) kickback-like rewards to doctors who promote their drugs, (2) research and development trials conducted without oversight by independent agencies with sufficient resources to maintain objectivity, (3) campaign funding provided to politicians in exchange for extending legalized monopolies, (4) product development processes that favor marginal advances on existing drugs over research into fundamentally new ones, and (5) marketing and advertising campaigns that draw attention away from possible health risks while misleading people about the actual cost of new drugs.

Few of us lack the intelligence to understand these strategies and tactics. We understand kickbacks, false statistics, payoffs to politicians, and small print advertising. So, how do we explain widespread ignorance?

Characteristic of our world of purposes, I think, our ignorance traces to lack of time, energy, or will. Millions of busy people default to a do-it-for-me motivation in pharmaceutical purchases. As consumers, we rely on doctors for guidance and explanation—doctors who might enjoy emoluments tied by pharmaceutical companies to the advice given. Pharmaceutical companies might intentionally hide or distort *information* we need to understand the benefit and cost of new drugs as well as the risks in using them. This is not a new form of behavior. We know, for example, that tobacco companies fought tooth and nail for decades to keep information about links to cancer from the smoking public.

Pharmaceutical companies also *make information available in ways difficult to access*—for example, by including it in the small print. Perhaps we lack the will to find information in small print because advertising beguiles us with promises of feeling or performing better. We may lack will because of strongly shared beliefs and attitudes regarding the ideas of statistics and politics. Many people believe that statistics are *always* biased to favor the objectives of those "making them up."

We have unprecedented opportunities as consumers and investors to act on ideas *individually* in markets and networks (see Chapter 8). We can vote individual attitudes and beliefs with individual behavior. If we believe in the idea of objective pharmaceutical research, we have myriad opportunities to support it in how we act as consumers and investors. If, on the other hand, we deem objective research less critical than, say, enhanced sexual performance, we might comprehend the dangers of pharmaceutical industry practices and, nonetheless, make an *informed* choice to purchase their offerings. That is the glory of individual liberty in markets and networks. It sustains visions about a market of one; it explains why tens of millions of us go to work every day in organizations pursuing and protecting good things to have.

Markets, networks, and organizations put the onus of responsibility and opportunity on *us*. We can choose sexual enhancement at the cost of objective pharmaceutical research. We might say, "That's not so great an outcome." But *we* are the ones choosing. We must recall, however, that the *design* of markets and networks includes a preference for *informed* choices. If we wish to make rotten choices, that's how the system works—so long as they are *informed* rotten choices.

Unlike place-bound people whose ignorance traced to a paucity of ideas bottled up in "the way we do things around here," we confront ignorance linked to the superabundance of ideas and information. We ought not look contemptuously on people in a world of places as ignorant. *Ignorance is also a condition of our lives.* In our world, however, ignorance comes from too much information rather than too few ideas. The ideas are there, and the information to interpret and understand the ideas is there. Whether we find the ideas and information we need to make ethical choices, however, is a matter of the *purposes and values* we bring to our lives in markets, networks, and organizations, and among friends and family.

When we are motivated by do-it-myself or do-it-with-me rather than do-it-for-me, the odds favor understanding over ignorance. My father-in-law, for example, brings a do-it-with-me attitude to the pharmaceuticals he needs for various ailments. He does careful research and discusses what he finds out with his doctors. My niece and nephew abhor environmentally damaging glues. Still, the odds of my nephew making an informed choice about glues in assembling his own butcher block table are superior to those of my niece because her do-it-for-me approach *entrusts the choice of glues to butcher block table makers and the thick we's who work in those organizations*.

*Most of the time, we **must** rely on other organizations to do-it-for-me.* It is the default condition of our lives. We cannot possibly tap *all* the ideas and information needed to make informed choices about the products and services that overlay life itself. We are forced to rely on the *character* of people in thick we's of organizations that provide us good things to have. We are forced to trust that people working in the pharmaceutical industry will not endanger us in ways hidden from our comprehension.

The idea of character, of course, has always related to values. In our world, however, we rarely have personal experience of the *character* of human beings upon whom we rely to live (see Chapter 6). Instead, we *experience* their products and services. We judge the character of their organizations by how well that experience matches up with their ideas and promises. Only, we do not call it character. We call it *brand*.

Brand is a shared idea responsible for highly predictable beliefs and behaviors in our new world of purposes. Our world is impossible without brands. If the idea of brand did not exist, it would spontaneously generate. In Chapter 6, I described how shared roles as customers and employees explain values that enable millions of strangers to confidently interact in markets and networks. The shared idea of brand facilitates the same phenomenon.

Think for a moment about how much you depend on brands. You cannot know *how* thousands of products and services are created and distributed any more than you can know the people providing them. You might bring do-it-myself motivation to, say, repairing your car or building your computer. But most of the time, you rely on organizations to do-it-for-me. You rely on thick we's who understand how to make, distribute, and support products and services. You rely on their expertise *and their values*. Yet, you cannot personally know them or their values. Instead, you rely on the brand of their thick we.

The idea of brand has morphed over the past quarter-century. Brand is not limited to consumer markets. Brand makes a huge difference in business-to-business markets and networks, too. From the 1950s through 1980s, for example, it was well known in industry that you "could never go wrong purchasing IBM." This widely shared idea governed political values inside organizations. Managers who chose IBM were protected from political fallout if IBM products and services fell short of expectations. By the late '80s, other brands—Microsoft, Oracle, Dell, HP—had emerged as similarly mistake-proof. IBM faltered. But IBM has battled tenaciously over the past decade to replace the idea of IBM hardware with the idea of IBM solutions and services and, as a result, has re-established its favored status. IBM rebranded itself by shifting the nature of the good things to have it produces and delivers.

Brand is not merely about image and logos. The most advanced practitioners equate brand with *experience*. Image matters; image makes promises. But powerful brands convert promises into experiences in line with the expectations fostered through ideas and promises. Some years ago, for example, Nike branded itself with the idea "Just do it." The company worked hard to infuse employees and partnering organizations with the aspiration of identifying and making *real* a compelling, unforgettable, and formative athletic *experience* for people who wore Nike shoes.

The powerful idea of brand is not limited to multinational corporations. In the aftermath of September 11th, for example, the leaders of the FBI introduced a new idea to the meaning of the FBI's brand. *Prevention*, we learned, would be as important as prosecution. Like any organization hoping to convert brand promise into brand experience, the FBI must figure out how to actuate the idea of prevention into an *experience* delivered by thousands of FBI employees and their partner organizations.

The idea of brand carries forward a best part of our past: the idea of goodwill. From individual entrepreneurs to governmental, nonprofit, and for-profit organizations, a vital brand conveys the *trustworthy character* associated with goodwill. No asset is more important to sustainable performance. And, yet, brands *are* ideas. Brands are *intangibles* blending ideas into values of all sorts. Yes, brands promise value for money. But, to succeed as references for good things to have, brands also promise and deliver quality, service, integrity, attentiveness, dependability, and more—character itself.

. . . .

Because brands *are* ideas, they evolve in ways beyond the control of those who create and manage them. Like characters invented by authors, brands depend a lot on the experiences of audiences. Authors have testified for centuries about the ornery independence of characters. Sometimes inherent personalities of characters resist management; other times, readers or viewers take over. Consult Jim from *The Adventures of Huckleberry Finn* and you can almost hear him tell you, "Mark Twain hisself couldn't civilize Huck, no sir. Tweren't no show in his tryin' neither." (Indeed, Twain tried and failed.).

The same thing that hems in authors constrains organizations that create brands, political parties that create slogans, and celebrities who create themselves. Consider Beanie Babies, the branded population of stuffed creatures contrived a few decades ago. Beanie Babies inhabit the world and refuse to go away, perhaps to the dismay of their originator, who once called for a vote by collectors to see if they had had enough. The vote overwhelmingly registered an unsatisfied appetite for more Babies to buy, collect, trade, and display. If Babies are discontinued, we can be sure the *market and network* for pre-owned Babies will persist. Until customers cease trading, the ideas associated with Beanie Babies—"lovable," "cute," "complete set," "rare"—will endure in the shared experiences of those involved.

Individual and group responses to ideas—ranging from the important ("objective medical research," "eating disorders," "safety") to the ephemeral ("Beanie Babies," "complete set")—occur in markets, networks, organizations, families, and friends. Yes, we ponder ideas in the privacy of our minds. But we influence ideas in what we do and say in markets, networks, and organizations and among families and friends. The private imaginings about the idea of shareholder value among Enron executives mattered less than the actions they took to inflate Enron's stock price. Or, consider the Unabomber, Theodore Kaczynski. He spent years boiling privately over ideas about technology, nature, academia, and more. His reflections, however, remained as isolated as his Montana cabin until he started mailing out letter bombs.

We no longer live in places where *groups* shape ideas in a contest of power and popular opinion over truth. In our world, ideas explode upon us like Kaczynski's letter bombs. Think again about Twain's Jim and Huck. If you were a parent, student, teacher, or principal in American public schools in the 1980s, you might *suddenly* have had to take a stand on the curricular inclusion or exclusion of *Huckleberry Finn* and, in so doing, articulate and defend specific political and social values. Thousands of people have been animated in comparably agitated ways by the state flags of South Carolina, Georgia, and Mississippi. And why not? Can you imagine the *brands* of General Mills, 3M, the IRS, the AARP—*or any other ethical thick we*—nostalgically recalling race-based slavery?

Or think about Tiger Woods. In late 2002, Tiger Woods was abruptly forced to weigh value and values as he reflected on the 2003 Masters golf tournament. The Masters is hosted by the Augusta National Golf Club, which, at the time, did not permit women members. Woods is the most celebrated golfer of his generation. Because of his African-American and Asian-American heritage, he was targeted by organizations active in political markets to take a stand against discrimination and intolerance. Woods won the Masters in 2001 and 2002. No golfer had ever won the Masters three years in a row. As a sportsman, Woods must have hungered to break that record. As a person, he cares deeply about values. But Woods' choice was not simply personal. Not in our world. Woods is a *celebrity*—a highly specific kind of brand—whose value and values play out in the ideas associated with his name in markets, networks, and organizations.

We must distinguish Tiger Woods the individual from "Tiger Woods" the *shared idea and brand*. The quotes may irritate or amuse. But, inasmuch as celebrities are characters, they unfold according to expectations and obligations beyond their full control. Tiger Woods did not invite interest groups to cajole him about the Masters. Still, "Tiger Woods" the idea has generated tens of millions of dollars for Tiger Woods the man, as well as for organizations who promote *their* brands by association with values Woods embodies: excellence, competitive drive, sportsmanship, and *opportunity for all*. We can hope that Woods' decision regarding the Masters included conversations with people from affected companies who asked, "What does 'Tiger Woods' stand for?"

In a world of markets, networks, and organizations, celebrities *are* ideas. They are *brands*. This is as true of Tiger Woods as Tom Brokaw, and of Snoop Dogg and N'Sync as Martha Stewart and Dubya. The human being is only part of the equation. No one, of course, does "David Letterman" better than David Letterman, but the two are not identical. One is an individual; the other is a shared idea. That consumers get disgruntled when "David Letterman" fails to live up to "his" values was demonstrated by the negative reaction to an interview with Hillary Clinton in early 2000. Many viewers complained when David Letterman (the man) spoke *respectfully* to the First Lady of the United States instead of, as expected, "David Letterman" (the *brand*) disrespecting a New York Senatorial candidate. Viewers *experienced* David Letterman, an imposter, instead of "David Letterman," the brand promise.

Consumers did not stop watching "David Letterman." But consumers do sometimes *vote* in markets and networks against celebrities when the real human being steps too far beyond the promised experience. We must look to both O.J. Simpson's alleged double murder and consumer condemnation to explain the demise of the wise-cracking, carefree, ex-jock shared idea of "O.J. Simpson" in favor of the now widely shared idea of "O. J. Simpson, killer." O.J. Simpson may have gotten away with murder, but "O.J. Simpson" didn't. There were two trials—one of the man, one of the shared idea—and each reflected social, political, personal, racial, and economic values in a variety of markets, organizations, and networks.

Murder is a far cry from entering a golf tournament. In our world of purposes, though, the actions and choices made by celebrities and those who manage them—*like the actions and choices made by companies about their brands*—trigger opportunities for consumers to express their own values. As noted in the Weight Watchers illustration in Chapter 8, consumption is a political act if it *purposefully* relates to specific ideas and values.

Think, then, about Martha Stewart. Martha Stewart is the founder of Martha Stewart Living Omnimedia, Inc., an organization competing in the market for home decorating and entertaining. "Martha Stewart" is a celebrity and a brand. In 2002, we read that Martha Stewart the woman may have violated securities laws and may have misled investigators about it. Once this hit the news, consumers and investors were given an opportunity to reflexively determine the effect of Martha Stewart's acts on the value and values of "Martha Stewart." There was a dramatic drop in the stock price of Martha Stewart Living Omnimedia, Inc.—most likely because institutional investors feared that Stewart's legal difficulties, like Simpson's, would lead to serious erosion in business.

Consumers, networkers, and investors express attitudes and beliefs about values through responses to Stewart's situation. So do employees. K-Mart, for example, has distributed the "Martha Stewart" brand for years. Now, K-Mart employees from cashier to inventory buyer to chief executive must make and defend choices about the relationship between Stewart and K-Mart and about what ideas and values the K-Mart brand stands for, such as integrity, legal compliance, and self-interest. In this, K-Mart employees have individual and group purposes, including whether and how K-Mart's pursuit of profits is affected by the values linked to Martha Stewart the person and "Martha Stewart" the idea. These choices are hard ones; Martha Stewart branded merchandise has been credited with revitalizing the fortunes of K-Mart. Murder ruined the idea of "O.J. Simpson." How greed and obstruction of justice affect the idea of "Martha Stewart" is now playing out in markets, networks, and organizations, in which consumers, investors, and employees ponder *worth and worthwhileness*.

. . . .

Celebrities are individuals. It is easier to get our heads around how their values link to their brands than it is for us to evaluate *values* in the mix of brand promise and brand experience with regard to organizations. For one thing, information about celebrity values is more readily available because of the media's passion for celebrities and controversy. Gossip, if not always accurate, nonetheless serves us well in keeping celebrity values front and center.

Our actual behavior suggests we are less interested in the values of organizations than in the value they offer in their good things to have. Some good things are loved; some are merely necessary. Sometimes we seek to do-it-myself, but all of us must rely on organizations to do-it-for-me most of the time. We have little choice but to *assume* that good things to have are, indeed, good, and, if experience turns out otherwise, take our business elsewhere. We *presume* that the brands we favor *promise and deliver* on values such as integrity, safety, dependability, lawfulness, and more. Our assumptions explain our surprise when we learn that trusted brands have fallen prey to venality (Arthur Andersen), environmental negligence (Exxon), tax minimization (Stanley Tools), bureaucratic infighting (FBI), racism (Texaco), or crony favoritism (the SEC).

In our reflexive world, how we respond shapes the fortunes, fates, and values linked to brands and the ideas and promises brands represent. Sometimes, as with Texaco and racism, millions of us move on as consumers and investors without much change. We make *informed* choices: We understand that Texaco executives acted to perpetuate racism—and we purchase their products anyway.

Other times, our *informed* choices cause organizations to rethink their brands. Stanley Tools reconsidered an initial decision to avoid U.S. taxes because of strong reaction in markets and networks in the wake of September 11th. The questions were clear. *What did Stanley's brand, and the character of its employees, stand for with regard to the idea of patriotism?* Should a thick we who branded their organization by waving the flag get a free pass in minimizing financial support provided "to the nation for which it stands"?

Most of the time, however, our choices and responses *are not adequately informed*. As consumers and investors, for example, many of us are ignorant about the practices and values of pharmaceutical organizations because we lack information. We lack information because we lack time, energy, and will. This is a necessary corollary of markets, networks, and organizations that create and protect market positions through providing good things to have to people who *must* presume on organizations to do-it-for-me.

We have no choice. We must trust thick we's in organizations to apply *values*-based standards of good to good things to have. Our fate—the fate of the planet—rests in their hands. In light of this, the FBI's shift in brand promise from prosecution to both prevention and prosecution is instructive. In our new world of purposes, we depend on *employees* in organizations to *prevent* harm from brands gone venal or sour. Yes, we have extraordinary power as consumers, investors, and networkers to vote preferences. But, as consumers or investors, we have little power or opportunity to *prevent* abuses that arise in organizations. It is only as *employees* that we are positioned to do that.

"We, the employees" must prevent abuses and assure "we, the consumers" that good things to have are good. Thick we's of organizations have the motivation and the purpose. Employees are best positioned to carry out that purpose. They cannot afford to bring do-it-for-me motivations to their jobs. They cannot afford ignorance due to lack of information or ideas. They have the resources to get and understand information. Employees in pharmaceutical companies, for example, have enough resources to make *informed* choices about practices ranging from doctor kickbacks to research conducted in the absence of disinterested parties. They can make informed choices about balancing value and values in how they fund politicians. In our world, brands—the character of organizations—depend on the purposefulness of employees. We—consumers, investors, networkers, friends, and families—rely on employees to recognize and take responsibility for applying ideas and information to good things to have in a manner that blends value and values.

The good news and the bad news—and everything in between—is that they, the employees, are us, the consumers, investors, networkers, family members, and friends. And we are them.

10 Civil Society

In the winter of 2003, millions of people around the globe voiced support for or opposition to a U.S led war against Iraq. Among the objectors were a father and his adult son who donned T-shirts bearing peace slogans while shopping one day in an Albany, New York, shopping mall. A security guard from Macy's alerted a security guard employed by the corporation that operates the mall. The corporation has a policy against disruptive behavior. The corporation's security guard located the two men and asked them to take off the T-shirts. The son agreed. The father, whose T-shirt read "Give Peace a Chance," did not. At the request of the security guard, a police officer arrested the father for trespassing. A few days later, hundreds of shoppers gathered to protest. The corporation dropped the charges. Less than a week after that, the corporation fired the security guard who had acted with the approval of his boss (who was not terminated).

The heavy-handedness of the security guards and police broke the link between healthy market democracies and civil societies. The incident highlights a growing concern among sociologists, political scientists, historians, and others who fear that declines in civic engagement have accompanied worrisome deteriorations in family, social, and political values. In *Bowling Alone*, for example, Robert Putnam catalogues across-the-board collapses in political party participation, serving on committees in local clubs and voluntary organizations, attending public school and town meetings, reading and writing letters to newspapers, signing petitions, and running for and holding public office. He points to drops in family experiences, such as eating dinner together, and social interactions, like visiting friends. While Putnam reports rising attitudes of tolerance, most of the consequences of civic disengagement are troubling: neglected children, faltering education, spreading mistrust, ill health, income and wealth inequality, religious insularity, and disrespect for law. He even charts a steep jump in people who give the finger to others.

Anger, anxiety, and apathy corrode civility. As Putnam's title suggests, a sense of being alone in a harsh world crowds out sharing, caring, and togetherness. The security guards and police gave the thumb, not the finger, to the father and son that day in Albany. It was an angry, uncivil moment in which the liberties of the father and son were shamefully violated by men exercising police authority. The incident is not supposed to be "the way we do things around here" in liberal market democracies where free speech and dissent are among our most cherished liberties.

So, what happened?

. . . .

In *Democracy's Discontent*, Michael J. Sandel explains that such incidents arise from weak civic skills and poor judgement that, in turn, stem from *the lack of practice in governing together toward the common good*. Individual liberties are best tested in groups. The constant struggle matches I's, who want to go their own way, against we's, who share a sense of their common good and how to pursue it together. By participating in we's, people learn the skills and judgement needed to balance individual liberty with the common good. If that engagement vanishes, Sandel argues, erratic behavior serving neither liberty nor the common good fills the vacuum.

Legally protected individual liberties have flowered in market democracies over the past three centuries. But, according to Sandel, along with layer on layer of legal assurances have come doubts regarding the legitimacy with which groups can establish and pursue the common good. In particular, prevailing legal and philosophical frameworks discourage government organizations from adopting substantive, content-filled versions of the common good that might limit or proscribe individual liberty and choice.

Consider marriage and family. Government groups are not to impede choices about the role of marriage and family in each individual's unique vision of the good life. If individuals wish to live together without the legal or religious sanction of marriage, okay. If they wish to get married, okay. If they wish to divorce, okay. If they wish to have extramarital affairs, okay. If they wish to have children out of wedlock, or with others to whom they are not married, okay. If they wish to be married and yet live apart, okay. If they wish to have children but see little of them, okay. If they wish to sacrifice so their children have better lives, okay.

Government is not to take stands other than procedural fairness. In particular, government must avoid substantive positions on how people should live and toward what ends. This, Sandel writes, generates governments of means instead of ends and laws protecting individual rights instead of *group* freedoms. In the absence of demonstrable harm, substantive positions are suspect. Local ordinances against smoking in public places, for example, are justified because harm outweighs liberty—not because governing groups write "tobacco-free society" into the common good. It is a philosophy tuned to me's pursuing individual happiness instead of we's governing together toward some substantive common good.

Sandel believes the United States has become a procedural republic. He compares it to substantive republics, which, in theory and practice, form among people *whose shared fates compel them to pursue content-filled visions of their common good*. Plato's *Republic* was substantive, not procedural. It constructed the common good on substantive choices rejecting nuclear families and embracing a strict hierarchy of social roles, state control of education and the arts, and equality of men and women. "We, the people" of the United States, in contrast, are not to impose answers about the good life on the now-sovereign I.

As argued in 2003 by the plaintiff contesting the University of Michigan's admissions practices, for example, the University acting on behalf of the "we" of the State of Michigan could not *explicitly* include race as an element of the common good of a diverse student body because that infringes the liberties of I's who might otherwise gain admission. The 14th Amendment to the U.S. Constitution—a codicil *explicitly* added to make "we, the people" *substantively* diverse—is turned on its head in a procedural republic gone mad with individual liberties played out in markets.

Under this view, the widespread public philosophy of individualism becomes a fundamentalist cult. Individual rights, individual liberties, and individual choice trump *group* values in the conception of what is good. This live-and-let-live philosophy, Sandel notes, is embraced as much by an egalitarian left seeking freedom and dignity for all as a libertarian right advocating unconstrained individualism. It is fueled by the utilitarian pursuit of the greatest good for the greatest number, where good is defined by value and number counts only individuals (see Chapter 14).

The only thing common in the common good becomes procedure. Group values and group choices go missing in action, a shift that *drives out the civic engagement required to learn and practice skills and judgement crucial to balancing individual liberties and group purpose*. There are plenty of problems government groups might solve. We all know that. But who wants to participate in governing organizations when wide swaths of potential solutions are out of bounds and procedures for problem solving insist on avoiding real or imagined insults to individual liberty and dignity? Who wants to govern together in local, state, and federal jurisdictions when governance becomes all process, no substance?

Evidently, too few of us.

. . . .

On the other hand, who wants police power invested in men like the security guards and police officer in Albany? Legal protection of individual liberty was won at great cost. Tens of millions of people died in a history dark with the evil of groups pursuing content-filled versions of the good—a history of group oppression of individuals, as well as group violence against other groups. Centuries of violence, revolution, imperialism, colonialism, slavery, racism, fascism, and communism; two hot world wars and one cold one; and McCarthyism, naked capitalism, and jihad motivate political theorists and practitioners from left to right to strip government we's of the power to define and enforce substantive definitions of the common good.

As Isaiah Berlin explains in *Two Concepts of Liberty,* free societies rely on two interrelated principles. First, no power is regarded as absolute; only rights are. Second, there are boundaries of activities within which liberty is inviolable.[1] The boundaries define what Berlin calls negative liberty: areas of individual freedom off-limits

---

1. Isaiah Berlin, *Four Essays on Liberty* (New York: Oxford, 1969), pp. 119–172.

to government intrusion. The Bill of Rights enumerates negative domains of liberty, including free speech. The rule of law, meanwhile, ensures individual liberty by making rights and not power absolute. In the Albany T-shirt story, the guard and police officer betrayed freedom: They abused their power and invaded an area of negative liberty guaranteed by the Bill of Rights. They coerced the T-shirt wearing son to take his shirt off; they arrested and evicted the father from the mall.

Coercion and exclusion endanger I's who participate in groups. Putnam writes about this in *Bowling Alone*, as does Sandel in *Democracy's Discontent*. When groups coalesce around substantive answers to the common good, there is no escaping the possibility of coercion and exclusion. Nor is there any guarantee of avoiding yet one more pitfall: *bad* answers to what constitutes the common good (such as imperialism, racism, and fundamentalism).

Berlin explores this pitfall in what he calls positive liberty. While negative liberty sets up government-free zones of individual activity, positive liberty asks, *"Who shall govern and toward what ends?"* Human beings wish to be their own masters, doers who govern themselves. Liberal market democracies answer, "Who shall govern?" with representative government—*governors elected by and under the direction of the governed*. "We, the people" govern ourselves indirectly by ensuring swaths of negative liberty and participating in the selection, influence, and control of those picked to exercise governmental authority. By resting ultimate governmental authority in "we, the people," market democracies optimize positive and negative liberty against incursions from the powerful and the popular. That, at least, is the design and intent.

Positive and negative liberty sit in tension with one another. For example, as a doer fully in charge of my pursuit of the good life, I may seek tranquility and harmony with nature. You, on the other hand, might wish a life fulfilled by machinery, including snowmobiles, motorcycles, chainsaws, and wood chippers. The content in our respective individual conceptions of the good life are of little consequence unless we happen to reside next door to one another.

The prevailing government approach to our conflict lies in zoning and land use laws that, according to democracy's design, are made and enforced *by the two of us and others whose fates we inescapably share in place-based thick we's*. Negative liberty is not sufficient to resolve our contrary versions of how each of us wishes to employ positive liberty. Something has to give. In theory, the resolution gets struck by the thick we in which we participate that—*together*—governs by balancing individual interests with the common good.

Polarities invite both/and, as well as either/or, responses. Long-standing democratic theory and practice favors the both/and approach in which thick we's deliberate, decide, and implement solutions balancing positive and negative liberty as well as individual and shared versions of the good. But there have been many either/or approaches. Fascism, communism, theocracy, and other tyrannies justify eradicating freedoms protected through negative liberty with a sleight of hand *premising the common good on the positive liberty of groups*. Unlimited government power held by the few is defended as necessary to emancipate the many who are not yet masters of themselves. Self-mastery, according to this either/or approach, is impossible until people are free of vices and passions, and inculcated with the right virtues.

To illustrate, imagine that a group of back-to-nature enthusiasts take power and outlaw the use of tranquility-destroying machinery. We who have power declare—in the name of our *group's* positive liberty—that individuals with uncontrolled passions for machinery (*you!*) are not *free enough of those passions* to be masters of yourselves. We arrest you for disruptive behavior and remove you to a camp where we subject you to rigorous (say, even sadistic) re-education. Only if and when *we* decide that you appreciate tranquility do we permit you back into our society of *truly* free people.

This either/or approach is all positive-liberty-and-the-common-good-of-groups and no individualism-and-negative-liberty. It is a scenario that makes our skin crawl. So much so that Sandel believes we now err on *a different side of the either/or divide*. "We, the people" choose all-negative-liberty-and-individual-good. Substantive answers shaped by groups with an eye to their common good are suspect. In our mania to protect negative freedom, we sterilize the substantive half of positive liberty's two questions: *toward what ends?* Habitual distrust drives us into a procedural republic so obsessed with live-and-let-live individualism that people no longer participate in governing *together*. Positive and negative liberty spin out of each other's orbit. Security guards need but ask and police officers handcuff and cart away people for wearing T-shirts. "We, the people" cease being *thick we's* bound up by shared fates. Instead, we are various *collectivities of I's*—market segments—who occasionally vote, but otherwise look to governmental organizations to do-it-for-me instead of *governing ourselves*. Shared values deteriorate. Society turns ugly.

. . . .

Individuals must have liberty to pursue unique dreams of the good life. Individuals must have protections from coercion, exclusion, and other depredations of groups. Individual possibilities must be free of indignities born of group-on-group violence. The desire for dignity and respect, for example, caused tens of millions of people across the planet to put up with coercive, illiberal regimes led by mid-to-late 20th century despotic revolutionaries because those leaders were racially, religiously, or nationally like the people themselves. This is the phenomenon of "he may be a jerk, but he's *our* jerk." (Substitute for jerk the racial, religious, or national epithet of your choice.).

But the democratic project stalls when passion for individual freedom and dignity shifts into extreme proceduralism. As sovereign I's pursue the good life, "we, the people" cease participating in thick we's concerned with the common good. Proceduralism drives out *shared* problem solving. Individuals turn apathetic. Civic engagement declines. Freedom and dignity atrophy into lonely, vulnerable affairs. The rugged individualist becomes a Unabomber or hate-mongering talk radio host. Security guards and police officers incarcerate shoppers for wearing T-shirts. On the other hand, if we risk substantively defining the common good—say, a ban on divorces or mandating organizations to perfectly mirror demographics—individual freedom and dignity suffer.

Round and round we go. The cure for apathy—rebalancing substance and process in the common good—is a contagion threatening individual freedom and dignity. The fear of that disease, in turn, engenders bowling alone. *Our fates are interdependent, but not actively shared*. We avoid the war of all against all—of caring and hatred aligned with place-based we's thickened by religion, race, nation, class, or culture. Instead, we condemn ourselves to a rat race of I against I in which, in the worst case, no individual cares much about any other individual beyond friends and family. Tolerance rises. But, again in the worst case, it is not a caring form of tolerance. It is live-and-let-live for slackers.

To break the cycle, Sandel implores people to get involved in government and take the risk of defining substantive content in the common good. Only that, he believes, can revitalize the skills and judgement—the shared social and political values—essential to self-governance and civil society. To underscore his plea, Sandel invokes de Tocqueville's *Democracy in America*.

"The native of New England," observed de Tocqueville, "is attached to his township because it is independent and free: his co-operation in its affairs ensures his attachment to its interests; the well-being it affords him secures his affection; and its welfare is the aim of his ambition and of his future exertions. He takes part in every occurrence in the place; he practices the art of government in the small sphere within his reach; he accustoms himself to those forms without which liberty can only advance by revolutions; he imbibes their spirit; he acquires a taste for order, comprehends the balance of powers, and collects clear practical notions on the nature of his duties and the extent of his rights."[2]

De Tocqueville described strong shared social and political values shaped by reinforcing ideas, roles, and relationships in a New England township. He applauded some shared values (optimism and freedom), while others made him nervous (conformity and slavery). But whether good, bad, or in between, the values were predictable. The New England native was likely to practice them, whether in his township or *when traveling to other towns*.

The italicized point is key. Strong, habitually shared values increase the odds of predictable behavior regardless of context. Again, I am speaking only of the odds associated with habit. Values learned in shared paths that harmonize with values fostered by shared roles and shared ideas produce predictable belief, behavior, attitude, and speech in interactions among people who are otherwise strangers, like the security guard and the T-shirt wearing father and son. If we wish to explain the security guard's behavior, for example, we need to probe the strength and predictability of free speech as a shared value in the many contexts of his life. Based on his abuse of the father and son, my hypothesis is this: *weak and random*.

Mid-level social formations such as de Tocqueville's New England town blend shared paths, shared roles, and shared ideas among people who are not necessarily friends or family. Values and habits strongly shared in towns bridge individual and small group experiences to larger formations, such as states, nations, or markets. Democracy's 18th century design centered on *place-based* mid-level formations. The New England township was the characteristic thick

---

2. Alexis de Tocqueville, *Democracy in America*, Volume 1 (New York: Knopf, 1945), p. 68.

we *then*. People who were not necessarily friends or family *governed together* in that social formation because they shared fates, because they *had* to. In townships, people learned the skills and judgement—the shared social and political values—needed to balance self-interest and *their* common good in the manner they deemed consistent with both negative and positive liberty.

The common good of a New England township was not overly procedural. De Tocqueville's New England native and his fellow townspeople had *no choice* but to *substantively* respond to challenges affecting their shared fates. The welfare of the township—the common good—was "the aim of his ambition and of his future exertions." Live-and-let-live individualism may have been highly regarded in their conception of the common good, but it did not drive out shared responsibilities to *substantively* respond to social, religious, economic, technological, and other challenges. People who lived together in the township—who shared fates—had many problems to solve *together*. They were a thick we, not a collectivity of I's. They had to govern themselves *or hand the job over to someone else*.

To Sandel, a widespread lack of participation in governing together produces this worrisome result. Too many people, he thinks, have handed the job of government over to someone else. In response, he, Putnam, and other civil society advocates exhort us to "Get Involved!" Their recommendations run in a straight line from de Tocqueville's 19th century New England township:

- Democracies are governments.
- Governments form around legal jurisdictions.
- Legal jurisdictions map to places.
- Therefore, we must reconnect our lives to the jurisdictions in place and take shared responsibility for self-governance and civil society.

The path ahead lies directly in front of the path behind.

Notwithstanding their homage to 19th century arrangements, Putnam and Sandel admit profound differences in how we live today. "From Aristotle...to Jefferson," Sandel writes, "the civic conception of freedom found its home in small and bounded places, largely self-sufficient, inhabited by people whose conditions of life afforded the leisure, learning, and community to deliberate well about public concerns. But we do not live that way today....(Our) vast society is not self-sufficient but is situated in a global economy whose frenzied flow of money and goods, information and images, pays little heed to nations, much less neighborhoods. How, under conditions such as these, could the civic strand of freedom possibly take hold?"[3]

It is an excellent question.

His answer, however, like that of Putnam, is *place-based*. Sandel promotes involvement in local government. Putnam favors participation in voluntary associations. Amitai Etzioni, another voice contributing to this debate, emphasizes community. "Communities," Etzioni writes in *The Spirit of Community*, "are best viewed as if they were Chinese nesting boxes, in which less encompassing communities (families, neighborhoods) are nestled within more encompassing ones (local villages and towns), which in turn are situated within still more encompassing communities, the national and cross national ones." [4]

Non-place-based possibilities get raised, but as exceptions. For example, after celebrating the Chinese nesting boxes of neighborhood, town, and nation, Etzioni suggests there is also "room for nongeographic communities... such as professional or work based communities." Putnam, too, glances at the workplace. "We need," he says, "to challenge the notion that civic life has no part in the workplace." But when Putnam puts flesh on this, he snaps back to form. "Why not," he asks, "have employer-provided space and time for civic discussion groups and service clubs?"[5]

. . . .

These critics document troubling behaviors inconsistent with liberty, democracy, and civil society. *Yet, they miss the root causes of those behaviors.* Tens of millions of us no longer share fates because of place. Our failure to govern together in place-based governmental jurisdictions symbolizes this sea change. We ought to worry about it. But we cannot carry forward the best parts of our democratic and civil society past through naïve calls to revitalize *places* that no longer connect us to one another in the common good of a thick we.

---

3.   Michael J. Sandel, *Democracy's Discontent* (Cambridge: Belknap, 1996), p. 317.

4.   Amitai Etzioni, *The Spirit of Community* (New York: Crown, 1993), p. 32.

5.   Robert D. Putnam, *Bowling Alone* (New York: Touchstone, 2000) p. 407.

Thick we's form *only* among people who inescapably and palpably share fates. Only then is there a *common good. Only then **must** people who participate take shared responsibility for balancing individual liberty and group purpose.* It is in thick we's that people learn and practice the skills and judgement necessary to the health of market democracies and civil society. Many people, of course, still participate in the thick we's of places, including tens of thousands in some New England towns. For them, shared fates and the common good remain place-based. Not surprisingly, *such people govern together well*—as Putnam himself notes in chart after chart in his book. *They* do not bowl alone.

For them, Etzioni's image of nested Chinese boxes lives on. But his metaphor is preposterous for the millions of us who *live* in a chaotic, kaleidoscopic world of markets, networks, organizations, friends, and family. Our world of purposes reconfigures age-old sources of shared values: shared paths, shared roles and status, shared ideas, shared purposes, and shared fates. Our shared paths exist at home, among friends, and in the organizations where we work or volunteer. Our shared roles are customer, investor, networker, and employee in addition to family member and friend. Citizen is a potent shared idea. But, for people who live in a world of purposes, citizen is not an actively shared role—as civil society critics convincingly demonstrate.

For millions of us, organizations—not places—are the mid-level social formations in which we share fates and pursue a common good with other people not necessarily friends or family. Sandel's contention that we lack practice governing together is mistaken. We practice the skills and judgement of balancing self-interest and the common good *every day we go to work*. We have no choice but to do this—*in organizations*. In those contexts, our shared fates depend on these skills just as surely as did the shared fates of de Tocqueville's New England native and his fellow townspeople.

The political and social values we practice in organizations bridge our experiences at home or among friends to our experiences in the larger social formations of markets, networks, and nations. If free speech and dissent, for example, are welcomed and respected in organizations in which we participate, we are more, not less, likely to respect them in other contexts. We know that hierarchy and command and control are among predictable shared social and political values in organizations. *But, increasingly, so are democratic values.* In a world driven by technological, geopolitical, socio-demographic, capital, environmental, and other potent forces, the common good of organizations requires problem solving and collaboration that thrive on free speech, dissent, consent, participation, liberty, rights, and responsibility. Today, organizational performance rarely happens through mindlessly giving and taking orders in a "my way or the highway" hierarchy (see Chapter 13).

Private and not-for-profit organizations are *not* procedural republics. *Proceduralism*—known as bureaucracy or red tape in organizations—is a sure sign of failure now or failure to come (see Chapter 13). It is a symptom that ought to worry us about governmental organizations. People in organizations cannot escape debating and choosing substantive responses to the challenges confronting them every day. We describe such challenges with words like vision, mission, and strategy, and continuous improvement, customer service, innovation, reengineering, and learning. Self-interest and the common good depend on how well we—*the thick we of organizations*—substantively respond to them (see Chapter 12).

In a world of purposes, the links binding civil society to democracy and liberty depend more on the shared values in organizations than in places. Civil society advocates look at this reality without *seeing* it. Consequently, they do better at identifying disturbing signs than at explaining root causes. I do not believe, for example, the security guard would have arrested the T-shirt wearing father *if both men worked together in the mall-owning corporation.* If the security guard's boss had donned the T-shirt on a day off, I doubt the guard would have asked the police to handcuff *him*. Nor would the boss have okayed his own arrest. That makes for good farce—something we laugh at on TV or in a movie. But it does not contribute to the common good of organizations.

The arrest revealed troubling personal values. *But the failure belonged as much to the thick we in which the guard participated as the guard himself.* It betrayed social and political values in tune with "my way or the highway" command and control instead of democratic problem solving and initiative. It revealed an organization—a mid-level social formation—out of touch with customers and a thick we confused about *their* common good.

The common good of the mall-owning corporation—like the common good of the stores in the mall—suffered. That was clear from the message delivered by the protestors who objected to the corporation's violation of strongly shared *customer* expectations. Arrest for wearing T-shirts is not what shoppers anticipate when they head out to a mall. The protestors wore T-shirts with a slogan supporting the father on the front and "Please don't arrest me" on the back. Executives and employees of the mall-operating corporation and tenant stores must have shuddered. Hundreds of shoppers threatened to take business elsewhere. It was a classic case of how *values* get attention when linked to *value* in a world of markets, networks, and organizations. Customers were insisting that more than price and quality mattered. The mall-owning corporation heard them.

The protest exemplified civic engagement in a world of markets, networks, organizations, friends, and families. The protestors sacrificed anonymity to take a stand as a *group* (see Chapter 8). They did so, however, in the shared role of *customers*. They concentrated on values and expectations vital to that role. They did not, for example, gather a few weeks later to protest the firing of the guard, who, notwithstanding nine years of acceptable performance, was terminated for following the instructions of his boss. His firing ought to have concerned other *employees* of the mall-owning corporation. But, in our world of markets, networks, and organizations, *customers* do not consider it their business to interfere in internal affairs of organizations.

Nor did customers apply en masse to become employees of the mall-operating corporation in order to *transform that thick we's vision of the common good*. That would have been bizarre. *Yet, that is the strange step that logically flows from civil society critics who fail to recognize the world we actually live in and how the shared idea of citizen now plays out in the shared roles of customer and employee.*

In this, I am reminded of the 1970s and 1980s crisis in the U.S. automobile industry. Japanese, German, Italian, and Swedish automakers took market share from Ford, General Motors, and Chrysler because the latter resisted quality and innovation. A barrage of books, articles, TV shows, and other media hammered at American manufacturers. Many critics advised consumers to vote with their wallets. *But no one suggested that consumers become employees.* When Sandel, Putnam, and Etzioni admonish us to "Get involved!" without seeing that organizations and not places are our thick we's, they, in effect, ask us to take on the role of employee instead of customer in governmental organizations. *That is not going to happen.* That is not how we live our lives in a world of markets, networks, and organizations.

Civil society advocates probably do not like this harsh fact of contemporary life. Millions of us may not like it. And, yet, there it is. Our path forward does *not* lie directly ahead of our place-based path behind. If *we* are to take control of our best futures, it must be in the world we actually inhabit. If we are to heal violations of liberty, democracy, and civil society like that in the Albany story, we need to look to markets, networks, organizations, friends, and family for solutions.

The mall-owning corporation would have been well advised to gather employees to discuss how the arrest of the T-shirt wearing father affected *their* common good. Two other matters would have been worthy of attention as well: (1) the firing of the guard but not the boss; and (2) the failure of the security guards and police to arrest owners of stores selling the T-shirts or to ask them to throw that inventory in the trash. Why, the employees might have discussed, did the commercial liberties of tenant stores outweigh the free speech liberties of the father and son in the common good of the mall-owning corporation? How should the corporation's policy against disruptive behavior apply to shoppers and stores? How come the guard got fired and not the boss? Why was the guard terminated after nine years of good performance? What was the process involved? Was it due process?

*Issues such as these—**not civic discussion groups or time for social clubs**—cut to the heart of balancing self-interest and the common good in the mall-owning corporation*. Our challenge is not to "make room" for nongeographic professional and workplace communities. *Organizations-as-thick-we's already occupy all rooms in the house.* The action has moved. The vitality of liberty, democracy, and civil society no longer links to town or neighborhood for millions of people. It is not just that the public square has shifted to malls. Rather, it is how thoroughly shared paths, shared roles, shared ideas, and shared fates—alone and together—have reconfigured with regard to malls and the other contexts in which we actually, not theoretically, live our lives.

As Sandel rightly notes, we must engage in balancing self-interest with a substantive common good if we are to preserve the skills and judgement necessary to civil society. We cannot eviscerate the positive liberty of *groups* to attend substantively to *their* common good and expect either the negative or positive liberty of individuals to survive. But in our new world, the *common good of mid-level social formations—of our thick we's—has shifted from places to organizations*. If we are to understand how and why shared social and political values of liberty and democracy shape civil society, then we must look to our lives as *employees* in organizations.

· ·

We also must examine how our shared role of *customer* links to liberty and democracy in a civil society. A different kind of we emerges as a creature of markets and networks: *collectivities of I's*. Collectivities of I's are market segments of customers, voters, investors, or networkers who share similar interests, ideas, and preferences, but not *fates*. Collectivities of I's profoundly influence markets, networks, organizations, friends, and families. *But they are thin, we's, not thick we's, because collectivities of I's do not* **share** *responsibility for implementing the choices supported.* As customers, contributors, and voters, collectivities of I's expect others—especially organizations—to do-it-for-me (see Chapter 9).

As a consequence, individual liberty is as vulnerable to collectivities of I's as it is to extreme proceduralism. The religious right, for example, wants governmental organizations to promote substantive, content-filled versions of the good life grounded in particular interpretations of Christian morality: no abortions, public subsidies for faith-based organizations, no homosexual unions, prayer in schools, no pornography, and so on. Proceduralism does not deter them from actively participating in political markets for government control. Nor are environmentalists in, say, Ohio and Missouri deterred from battling oil company executives residing in New York or Texas over the preservation of Alaskan wildernesses. In each instance—like many others—plenty of organizations appeal to plenty of collectivities of I's to support substantive elements of the good.

Note, though, that the substantive good promoted in markets and networks by advocacy organizations **equates** *with the common good* **only** *for the organizations—the thick we's—doing the advocating.* When, for example, an organization from the religious right promotes judicial candidates in state or local markets for political control, it is accurate to say that participants in the advocacy organization—members of that thick we—subscribe to a substantive view of *their* common good equal to the substantive view they promote. Participants in the advocacy organization commit time and attention to their belief and cause—*and to one another*—in the manner of a thick we. They have a common good expressed in *their* organization's purpose.

The advocacy organization *markets* their purpose—*their ideas*—to collectivities of I's with similar perspectives and interests. As voters or contributors, however, collectivities of I's are *consumers* who expect the elected judge and the organization in which he or she participates—the court—to do-it-for-me. *As collectivities of I's, they neither anticipate nor share any responsibility in daily life for balancing their self-interest and the interests of others in some common good fostered by shared fates.* The job of implementation is handed over to other people and organizations.

This invites the possibility of tyranny. But it is a tyranny of minorities, not the tyranny of the majority of concern to de Tocqueville. When, for example, politically effective thick we's appeal to collectivities of I's to elect creationists to a state Department of Education and, through them, to substitute the shared idea of Genesis for the shared idea of evolution, the effects reach well beyond the advocating thick we's and their supporting collectivities of I's. Yet, neither the collectivities of I's nor the advocacy groups are *personally responsible* for implementing the decision. *They* do not have to show up each day in schools and interact with people who might disagree about creationism and evolution.

The winning advocacy groups and collectivities of I's can exclaim, "Yessss! We won!!" But the thick we's of the schools—teachers, students, administrators, school boards, and some parents—must implement creationism. Such thick we's quickly encounter messiness, both among themselves and from other parents who, in the shared role of customer, expect schools to do-it-for-me. Many parents become outraged that their children might be deprived of a science education critical to future success. Some, like the shoppers in Albany, might abandon anonymity and speak out as a group. If this happens, say, at a local school board meeting, parents might hear the school board intone, "It's state policy. While we board members sympathize and think it's a bit crackpot, there is nothing we can do about it." This, of course, sounds *bureaucratic and procedural*.

These tyrannies arise in markets and networks, not places. We don't get Ayatollahs or Papa Docs. We get right-to-life judges *unqualified* to do their jobs or lead their organizations, which, in turn, produces horrendous *customer* experiences in courts. Many lawyers now advise clients to avoid local and state courts because so many ideologically oriented judges pursue the rule of personality guided by Christ, not the rule of law. *Our tyrannies of minorities produce market results that expose individual and group liberty to substantive positions crafted by thick we's and collectivities of I's with regard to whom adversely affected individuals (litigants) and organizations (courts) are unrelated by day-to-day shared fates.* We get market tyrannies of *shared ideas delinked from shared fates.*

. . . .

It is a glory of markets that individuals have the option to express preferences about products, services, ideas, and issues anonymously (see Chapter 8). We need not dissent to influence our world. We can shop; we can vote; we can contribute dollars. Yet, with this option comes another: the option to isolate choice from *personal responsibility to implement the choices made.* In contrast, governing together in a thick we means a daily struggle to balance individual liberty with the common good. In thick we's, implementation is a personal responsibility—or, better said, an *interpersonal, shared* one. In shared paths and thick we's, policies adopted (hierarchically, democratically, or otherwise) are implemented by people who know one another. The job is not handed over to strangers or other organizations. In a family, for example, "No TV until homework is finished," *must* be enacted by the family. Policies, choices, and ideas modulate because implementation is interpersonal; parents adjust to objections of their children and vice versa.

As *customers* of government organizations that are subject to the whims and ideas of advocacy organizations and collectivities of I's, we get frustrated. We learn through *an experience at odds with the brand promise of democracy* to distrust the thick we's—the employees of governmental organizations—to make and deliver good things to have that are *good*. We shift our loyalties and take our business elsewhere.

But where? The two-party system does not offer much choice. Accordingly, an increasing number identify themselves as independents—a satisfying label, but one without any unifying *organizational* substance. Many others concentrate time and resources on single issues and advocacy organizations. Meanwhile, the statistics and behaviors recounted by Sandel, Putnam, and Etzioni suggest that millions of customers and *potential* customers *stop buying at all.* Voting atrophies. *And that, in turn, makes advocacy organizations and the collectivities of I's more powerful forces in our lives.* Tyrannies of minorities grow.

All of which threatens liberty, democracy, and civil society—but differently so. Berlin's two concepts of liberty still have much to teach us, as do the observations of de Tocqueville and civil society commentators, such as Sandel, Putnam, and Etzioni. We have much to learn from all of them. We cannot use their insights and wisdom to build strong shared values, however, without acknowledging and acting in the world in which we actually live. We may not like the picture staring us in the face. But we must *see* it if we—as employees, as volunteers, and as customers—are to ensure that liberty, democracy, and other values thrive along with value in markets, networks, and organizations and among friends and families.

11 Community

In the early 1990s, I traveled to an Episcopal church in Connecticut to meet a support group of managers who had lost jobs to downsizing. The group was not strictly Episcopalian, nor even strictly religious. But, as I stood to address them, it felt right to be in a church. The men and women were shaken. Their life purposes had been cold-cocked by forces they did not understand. They seemed lost and dazed, and they certainly needed faith and hope. Were they worried about money? *Of course!* But there were many other anxieties in their congregation of misery. In our world of purposes, people who do not participate in organizations are people whose purposes and values are at risk. Human beings shape and test values in association with other human beings. Families provide such a context, as do friends. But today, beyond friends and family, we most meaningfully share values in organizations.

Income-generating jobs are not required for organizational participation; we can also volunteer our time and effort to make an organization into a thick we for ourselves (see Chapter 6). Indeed, I mentioned to those at the church what seemed obvious yet unspoken. Each had lost a job; each had forfeited a connection to an organization. *But they were participating in an informal organization of their own making.*

Together, they were pursuing the *shared purpose* of assisting one another in finding new jobs. Each committed time and effort in the manner of our *shared role* of employee. They were taking *shared risks*. They were examining beliefs, behaviors, and attitudes; consequently, they were acting on meanings and purposes in their lives. Each week, they explored *shared ideas* they hoped might help them move beyond the current crisis. My invitation, for example, centered on their interest in learning more about Jon Katzenbach's and my book, *The Wisdom of Teams*. Most crucially, they were risking some of their faith and fates by participating together in a *shared path*.

Shared purposes, shared risks, shared ideas, shared roles, shared paths, shared fates—their informal organization wove together age-old sources of shared values. Place had nothing to do with it. The men and women resided in towns and cities across Connecticut and New York. But, in response to the trauma of contracting markets and downsizing organizations, they had not turned to local communities defined by place. *Instead, they instinctively found a community by doing what is normal in our new world of purposes: They organized.*

. . . .

That people could experience community in organizations was considered illogical by the influential German sociologist Ferdinand Tonnies, who published *Gemeinschaft und Geselleschaft* (translation: *Community and Society*) in 1887. Tonnies meticulously distinguished living *together* in communities from living apart as *individuals* in societies of markets and states.

Tonnies' book is a masterwork of classification; it reads like a text in botany or zoology. He lays out a strict either/or scheme in which shared values are strictly *community* affairs. *Societies* have no shared values—only what Tonnies labels as conventions and public opinions reflecting aggregate behavior of strangers. Individual values, by contrast, cannot happen in communities; they arise only in markets and states. In community, individual will is natural because it keeps thought under good regulation. In society, individual will is rational because thinking governs all else. In community, the personal virtues are sincerity, character, valor, kindness, and faith because obligations run to the group. In society, individuals have no virtues, only strategies of cleverness, greed and ambition, because obligations are to the self alone.

In community, *group* will is natural, organic, and real because it emerges out of family, custom, agriculture, art, and religion. Law, too, derives from family and custom; legal responsibilities link to role and status. Work is domestic, agricultural, or craft-based and meaningful because it is done for its inherent usefulness to all. In society, by contrast, group will is artificial. It arises from the cumulative effects of individuals contracting with one another out of self-interest. Law is based in property and contract; obligations run from person to person, including artificial persons such as corporations. There can be no spirit of unity in society because no one acts on behalf of the whole. Work is uninteresting labor performed in exchange for money according to the dictates of capitalism—that is, under mandates set by bosses and machines. There are no shared values, only monetary value established by prices in markets. The market determines everything. The state's sole function is to guide markets on behalf of the wealthy and powerful.

As Tonnies sums up, "In community, people remain essentially united in spite of all separating factors, whereas in society they are essentially separated in spite of all the uniting factors."[1]

Like any great classifier, Tonnies abhors gray areas. He imprisoned the idea of community in a world of places—a distressing prospect for those of us who live in a world where place no longer binds people together through inescapable shared fates. In Tonnies' analysis, ideas that flourish beyond the control of place-based cultures— ideas such as market, state, science, and contract—are community-destroying ideas. He book is translated *Community and Society,* but his argument is "*Either* Community *or* Society."

Tonnies' work echoes that of others who, over the centuries, have premised shared values on place. He extrapolated from the origin of humanity in nature. He deemed it impossible for people to share community values beyond the boundaries of place, and absent the kinship, agriculture, and cosmology associated with place. Based on his observations of late 19th and early 20th century states and markets, he forecast the annihilation of place-based we's—what he called *natural* we's—in favor of collectivities of selfish individuals under monopoly capitalism or totalitarian communism. He could not imagine *any* context in markets and states that would sustain the experience of community.

---

1. Ferdinand Tonnies, *Community and Society* (New Jersey: Transaction Publishers. 1996), p. 65.

Or, his logic disallowed it. In particular, he wrote that marrying the *idea* of community to the *idea* of organization was abominable. He permitted the experience of community only to people born or adopted into places with cultures dictating all of life's meaning and purpose. Unless *all* of life's many purposes were *shared together*, people could not achieve community. In Tonnies' view, organizational purposes failed on both counts. First, organizations dealt with some—not all—of life's purposes. Second, organizational purposes were not shared. Rather, they were merely mirror images of the aggregated interests of individuals transacting in markets. In Tonnies scheme, if purposes originated with individuals instead of groups, or were specified and partial instead of unstated and total, then community was impossible.

Tonnies spent his life arguing on behalf of community; he deeply believed people needed the shared values of community to live rich, full lives. Few of us disagree. But his logic is too severe. He promotes deep-seated assumptions that communities are only real and natural if they have a territorial foundation—a premise that confounds our pursuit of community in a world bereft of places. By defining the idea of community and the idea of organization as mutually exclusive, he condemned us to an either/or choice: Either fill your wallets or fill your souls. Value *or* values.

We live lives bounded by time, information, and purpose, not place. We share in the values and meanings of community *when* we make that our *shared purpose,* not because of *where* we reside. Beyond friends and family, our most compelling shared purposes arise in organizations. The downsized managers I met in church that evening did not just happen to bump into each other. They purposively sought each other out. Their purposes were many: economic, educational, crisis support, networking, friendship, and more. But their time was short and fragmented; they were not looking to live with one another 24by7—just to share the experience of navigating through one of life's most challenging phases. They were looking for community.

. . . .

Contrary to the either/or logic in Community and Society, *we—like the men and women of that support group—discover and practice the shared values of community when we participate in organizations.* Organizations come in all sizes, shapes, and forms. The support group was an organization, albeit an informal, unincorporated, and voluntary one. They had no products, services, or customers. Nor was it their purpose to generate profits. But they did share a purpose of mutual assistance that they pursued together.

We confuse ourselves if we narrow the meaning of organization to corporations or businesses. *Organizations exist when people share purposes to which they hold themselves individually and mutually accountable.* Here are some purposeful organizations in which people I know participate: a magazine, a high school, a construction crew, a group of self-employed lawyers who collaborate on cases, an entertainment business, a community development organization, a synagogue, a law firm, a medical group, a summer arts camp, an accounting firm, a Web site, a legislature, a leadership education project, an investment bank, a political campaign, a start-up company, a conservation group, a touch football team, a house cleaning service, a government regulatory agency, an energy company, a town council, a university, a technology business, a plumbing business, a school for dyslexic kids, a book publishing company, a transportation logistics concern, a literacy program for adults, a leveraged buyout firm, and a movie project.

I could go on. So could you. Hundreds of millions of us participate in one or more organizations as employees, independent contractors, students, or volunteers. Organizations might be gargantuan or tiny, for profit or nonprofit, governmental or not governmental. They can be formal or informal, incorporated, partnerships or neither. They can be temporary or open ended, defined by projects or by processes or both. They can stand alone or as part of larger, encompassing wholes. *However configured, though, organizations always reflect a blend of individual and shared purposes.*

That we bring individual and shared purposes to organizations is self-evident. We join organizations for a variety of personal reasons, ranging from income to self-fulfillment. Meanwhile, we cannot rightly describe organizations as *organized* in the absence of shared purposes. Shared purposes answer the question, "Organized for what?" Shared purposes are as essential to organizations as common interests were to place-based communities.

To be shared, organizational purposes need not be 100 percent agreed upon and subscribed to in every imaginable dimension and detail. Such perfect mutual understanding and consensus *never* happened in place-based communities. Nor does it occur in organizations. *Shared* means some minimal yet mutual recognition of purpose and direction supported by actual commitment of time and effort.

Explicitly defined purposes distinguish organizations from markets and networks. Markets shower benefits on people who pursue individual, not shared, purposes—synergistic gains come as a byproduct of the famous invisible hand. Networks, meanwhile, operate through access and connection. The greater the number of people with access and connections, the more useful the network. Beyond connection itself, however, the purposes of networks are narrow and agnostic. To the extent networks specify purposes, it is often to *proscribe* them. For example, we are prohibited from driving too fast or under the influence of alcohol. We are forbidden from selling human beings on eBay. In many colleges and universities, students are instructed not to share music files.

Organizations, by contrast, always define rich and varied purposes that are *visible* and *prescribed*. Tonnies recognized that organizations have defined purposes. Indeed, he asserted that, in defining purposes, organizations block the shared values of community. Communities, he argued, have purposes as universal as life. In the absence of unlimited and unstated purposes, he thought community was impossible. Organizations could not be communities because organizations did not have undefined and unlimited purposes.

Communities in places had no defined purposes. Instead, to paraphrase a popular bumper sticker, "purpose happened." Communities just were; they just existed; they were as natural and as extensive as life itself. People born or adopted into places lived together in communities that shaped (1) every imaginable aspect of life's purpose and meaning and (2) did so entirely for each such aspect. People shared beliefs and behaviors stretching across *every* category of values—religious, family, political, social, economic, environmental, medical, legal, and technological. Moreover, the whole spectrum of beliefs and behaviors with respect to each category (e.g., the political versus the religious) were experienced *in* the community as opposed to apart from it. There were no distinctions between, say, political values at home versus political values at work because home and work seamlessly intertwined in places people lived together.

By specifying *certain* purposes, Tonnies argued, organizations precluded the purpose-*full*-ness of community. In this, however, he confused the idea of individual economic purposes in markets with the idea of shared purposes in organizations. Tonnies argued that individuals maintained an economic focus *every moment they were at work*. He considered organizations a different form of markets. Noneconomic concerns might arise in organizations, but, to Tonnies, money occupied attention like a conquering army. People in organizations, he claimed, continuously negotiated and contracted with one another over financial self-interest.

Tonnies previewed our habit of treating value as trump card. Money ruled people in markets. Money was the root evil seducing people away from nature's Edenic communities into soulless societies without shared values. Tonnies believed in what the British jurist Henry Maine had described decades earlier as humanity's *permanent* transition from status to contract: the elimination of role and status in family, tribe, and community in favor of contractual relationships and values subject only to agreements among and between individuals.

Like Maine, Tonnies was too extreme, too draconian. In our new world of markets, networks, and organizations, money *is* a necessity. But the majority of us do not allow monetary concerns to consume every waking moment of our lives. Hundreds of millions of us spend many hours each day collaborating with other people in organizations without moment-by-moment negotiations over money and self-interest. Contrary to Maine's prediction, status and role have not vanished. Instead, they have shifted contexts. Our status and roles in organizations, for example, determine much more about our shared values than formal contracts with those organizations or informal, negotiated relationships with other employees. Tonnies failed to anticipate just how extensively our lives with other people in organizations might combine shared paths, shared roles, shared ideas, and shared fates. *He did not see that working together in organizations could sustain the beliefs and behaviors long associated with the experience of community.*

Contrary to Tonnies' observations, the purposes we bring to organizations *can be* as universal as life itself. Relationships, economics, technology, religion, family, politics—all these and more can arise in our experience with other people in organizations. In our lives together in organizations, we fall in and out of love, master skills and meaning, take individual and group risks, make political, social, and technological choices, influence the fate of the planet, exercise faith, and adhere or do not adhere to personal philosophies.

Our concerns shift and vary. But anything can, and does, happen in our lives together in organizations.

In Chapter 5, I related the story of the born-again Christian whose proselytizing challenged my friend's construction crew to think and act on a variety of religious, social, political, and economic values. Tests like this do not occur every moment we spend together in organizations. But such things did not occur every moment of every day in every life of every person who lived in places either. The experience of community was never as compacted (or exciting!) as that—either in places or in organizations.

We too often ignore, act surprised, or discredit evidence that individual purposes in organizations blend many different categories of values. One study conducted during the height of the dot-com gold rush, for example, asked managers like those I met at the church what they considered critical in joining or staying with an organization. Did their responses include money? Yes. We live in a world of markets, networks, and organizations. Our livelihoods depend on money.

*But in this and every similar survey I have **ever** read*, money ranked below interesting and challenging work, attractive organizational culture and values, effective and inspiring leadership, real opportunity for voice and participation, and sense of mutual commitment.[2] Money ranked alongside career opportunities and skill development. Value in the form of salary, bonuses, and skill development was critical. But managers deemed value a *minimum* condition. They wanted more than value from life together with other people in organizations. They sought to participate in organizations whose shared *social and political values* inspired the mutual commitment and group will historically linked to the idea of community.

Shared purposes in organizations range across life's many challenges. All organizations—whether for profit, nonprofit or governmental—blend economic and noneconomic purposes. It is mostly with respect to *formally defined* purposes that differences arise. 3M, for example, is a publicly held company whose profitability depends on how well they make and sell a wide variety of products and services. Governmental and nonprofit organizations often designate nonfinancial and noneconomic purposes. The American Red Cross focuses on disaster relief. The IRS collects taxes. Bronx Educational

---

2.   Ed Michaels et al, *The War for Talent* (Boston: Harvard Business School Press, 2001), p. 45.

Services provides literacy education to adults. The Nature Conservancy preserves open spaces. The National Rifle Association lobbies against gun control. The California Supreme Court determines legal outcomes. And so on.

Our shared purposes in organizations, however, are not artificially limited to formalizations. Just as happened in communities in places, informal and unstated purposes "happen" in organizations. Today, for example, many organizations struggle over how best to govern themselves, even though few organizations make self-governance an explicit purpose. Notwithstanding the noneconomic purposes formally defined by governmental and nonprofit organizations, each *must* pursue a *blend* of objectives that include the economic. The classic call to action, *Reinventing Government,* was not primarily a book about reinventing government; it was a manifesto for *reinventing governmental service organizations by incorporating economic and market concerns into shared purposes*. It explicitly exhorted employees in governmental organizations to act on shared ideas and shared roles such as performance, marketing, and customer. Governmental and nonprofit thick we's, then, cannot ignore economic and financial purposes any more than private sector thick we's can ignore social, environmental, political, and other noneconomic purposes. All organizations—regardless of sector—confront the necessity of integrating economic with noneconomic values in their shared purposes.

Organizations cannot ignore purposes merely because they go unstated. Yes, organizations attend to stated purposes more explicitly than unstated ones. 3M, for example, manufactures hundreds of products ranging from Post-it Notes to medical supplies. People at 3M take steps each day to achieve the stated purposes associated with marketing, selling, manufacturing, distributing, and servicing these products. Those are the purposes most in evidence at 3M most of the time. But other purposes operate at 3M even if, at any given moment, they seem hidden. 3M is an organization—*a community*—with manifold human purposes. It is surely a different kind of community than, say, ones found in ancient Athens or Tonnies' 19th century Prussia. 3M's stated purposes are configured oddly by comparison. Still, the full range of human purposes and values operate among people who work together at 3M. Like other organizations, it provides a community experience to those who make it their purpose to find it.

We do not share fates with other people 24by7 in a single community. As mentioned in Chapter 2, we do not live in a single market, single network, or single organization. We cannot, then, experience the *whole* of our social, economic, political, or religious values in organizations any more than in families or among friends. We lead crisscrossed lives. Like the adults in Chapter 6's story about development, we must integrate purposes and values across many different contexts.

The architecture Tonnies used to describe place-based communities is elegant and whole. Continuity throughout life was designed into it. People lived together in social formations whose shared relationships, shared roles, shared ideas, shared purposes, and shared fates neatly reinforced one another. There were conflicts, hypocrisies, and inconsistencies. But tensions—like harmonies—occurred in the single, all-encompassing social formation Tonnies labeled community.

The shared path of family overlapped the shared paths of friends. Shared paths at home, at work, in church, and in school were populated by the same people. Each person's several roles and status were apparent at all times. People who lived in places did not have one set of roles at home and another at work or the mall (see Chapter 6). Although wisdom and expertise varied, most of the ideas governing communities were shared. Resources were appreciated in common. Purposes were as universal as life itself. Fates were inescapably and completely shared. Everyone knew everyone else and each other's shared values very well. Tonnies' communities were very thick we's. Their relationships had high degrees of integration (see Chapter 2).

Our lives, by contrast, are jumbled and chaotic. *Continuity* is a grave challenge. We live in hundreds of markets, networks, and organizations. Millions of us have multiple families, whether as one generation unfamiliar with another or, more literally, from multiple marriages and divorces. In our new world, it is unlikely that *all* of our friends know one another and our families. Friends at work may not know friends at home or at church; neither group may know friends from "growing up." We transition from context to context, role to role, and purpose to purpose.

Our shared paths, shared roles, shared ideas, shared purposes, and shared fates are *not congruent*. But, contrary to Tonnies' argument, this lack of congruence *across the whole of our lives does not preclude a lack of congruence in any part of them.* In particular, among shared paths and thick we's in families, friends, and organizations, we experience shared paths, shared roles, shared ideas, shared purposes, and shared fates that reinforce one another. Like the men and women at the church that evening, we can find the congruent sources of shared values necessary to the community experience. Not surprisingly, then, many of the values we most strongly share with other people are those practiced in organizations.

. . . .

Thick we's in organizations of all sizes and shapes establish formidable realities about "the way we do things around here." These are not necessarily the best values; rather, they are the strongest, most predictable shared values. You would have little difficulty introducing me to the prevailing values of the organization where you work, learn, play, or pray. Such values extend across social, political, economic, legal, environmental, family, and other categories. Among other things, you could lay out your organization's purpose; the authority relationships and pecking order; how decisions are made; the degree to which open communications and opinions are welcome and by whom; the current and prospective economic health of the organization; how rewards are divided; the way people treat one another; how and why that treatment might vary depending on role, status, project, or process; and whether the organization is family friendly and helps people achieve a reasonable balance between work and nonwork.

In contrast, you would be hard-pressed to get beyond gross generalities in acquainting me with the social, political, economic, family, or other values prevailing in your town or city. Mostly, you would describe who held power ("The Democrats run this town.") and the quality of some government services ("The schools are good."). Indeed, if you could explain things more fully, I would bet you participate in local government service organizations as more than a consumer—that is, as employee or volunteer.

Strong, predictable values in organizations do not mean that organizational belief, behavior, attitude, and speech are permanent or unchangeable, or that the patterns in one organization necessarily mirror another. The established values regarding how decisions are made, who has a voice, who is considered a permanent versus temporary member, how rewards are divided, and the balance between work life and personal life differ substantially in my friend's construction crew compared to the high school where his wife teaches. Both have little in common with Merrill Lynch or the U. S. State Department or the San Francisco 49ers.

Values change in organizations. Indeed, because shared fates are at stake, organizational experiences generate the *purposes, controversy, and dynamism necessary to change*. You could point to some predictable values in your organization that you consider good and to others you deem bad or unfair (and wish would change). Most people in most organizations care (and care a lot!) about "the way we do thing around here."

Consider, for example, the social, political, and economic values sparked by the shared idea of innovation at 3M Corporation. For most of the late 20th century, 3M's brand was synonymous with innovation. By the mid-1990s, however, the pattern of actual behavior, speech, belief, and attitude at 3M revealed an organization more risk averse than innovative. Some people at 3M believed their company's claims to innovation were hypocritical; many argued that anti-innovation beliefs and behaviors, such as risk aversion and closed-mindedness, were widespread. People witnessed the squashing of inventive possibilities, the personal dangers in speaking candidly, and spreading attitudes among longer-term employees to just hold on until retirement. The buoyant confidence of an organization of innovators gave way to more self-doubting realities.

No human society is perfect. *We all know that*. Certainly, no organization is perfect. But *all* organizations have more predictable patterns of belief, behavior, attitude, and speech than towns, cities, or nations in our new world of purposes. If you had moved to the Minneapolis area and gone to work for 3M in, say, 1998, your co-workers would have initiated you into 3M's shared values—the good, the bad, and the in between regarding social, political, economic, legal, financial, health care, and family beliefs and behaviors. As for Minneapolis and its suburbs? Well, you might have spoken to real estate brokers about schools, golf clubs, and religious organizations. Beyond that, you might have subscribed to the local papers to get a feel for the place. Perhaps you would have read Zagat's to learn where to eat.

The thick we's forged by community experiences inside organizations count among them real people who share fates. Such we's and their strong shared values shape identity much more than the force of place. Two individuals meeting at an airport in, say, Cleveland or London, and discovering each work at 3M have more to discuss—have a deeper, broader shared experience—than two strangers who happen to live in Minneapolis. A Minnesotan 3Mer meeting a Canadian 3Mer at an airport in Miami would find each other's company more interesting than two otherwise disconnected Canadians or Minnesotans.

People who participate in the same organization have richer shared identities and shared values than do people who live in the same nation, city, or town because they blend individual purposes into the thick we of the organization. They simply have more at stake in a meaningfully shared way. Our fates are inescapably bound up with others in organizations. *In our world, organizations provide us with an opportunity to behave ourselves in a community of people we know and with whom we share purposes.* The great challenge we face concerns the purposes and values of organizations and how to connect them to the greater good of markets, networks, families, and friends. Our legacy depends on how we integrate value and values in the community experience *available* to us—not in glorifying or regretting lost communities of place. Like the men and women I met at church that evening, we need to look to shared purposes, not places, to find one another in community.

12 Democracy

The employee of British Petroleum is attached to his organization because it is independent and free: his co-operation in its affairs ensures his attachment to its interests; the well being it affords him secures his affection; and its welfare is the aim of his ambition and of his future exertion. He takes a part in every occurrence in the organization; he practices the art of government in the small sphere within his reach; he accustoms himself to those forms without which liberty can only advance by revolutions; he imbibes their spirit; he acquires a taste for order, comprehends the balance of powers, and collects clear practical notions on the nature of his duties and the extent of his rights.

· ·

You have just read the passage from Alexis de Tocqueville's *Democracy in America* quoted in Chapter 10—except I have substituted "employee of British Petroleum" for "native of New England," and "organization" for "township" and "place." I might have substituted the name of any organization, large or small, formal or informal, because, if we wish to explain political values today, we must look to how our experience in organizations links to the markets, networks, friends, and families in our lives.

In a world of purposes, the organization *is* our town. It is our *polis*, our primary political association. *Polis* is the word the ancient Greeks applied to city-states, and an idea used since to describe political entities at the middle level between individuals and families on one hand and league, state, nation, or empire on the other. "Political" relates to the polis and, as originally used, referenced beliefs, behaviors, attitudes, and speech regarding the "affairs of the polis." Until recently, those affairs corresponded to villages, towns, fiefs, and other places where individuals and families shared fates. Today, the affairs of the polis most essential to our lives are *the affairs of the organizations* in which we participate.

Organizations have inherited the mantle and function of polis because they are where we most extensively, actively, and inescapably share fates with other people beyond family and friends. Our lives together in the thick we's of organizations are not the 24by7 co-existence of an ancient village or town—places where people *lived* with one another. We do not live with one another because of place; rather, we *work* with one another because of purposes. There is no place in a world of purposes where people live together in the manner of the polities that dotted the planet for thousands of years. Few among us, for example, choose to live in a closed context that determines every aspect of our lives in the manner, say, of a company town or an Amish village (although *we* can make that choice—an individual freedom uncommon among hundreds of millions of people who still live in worlds of places).

Our polis—the organization—is shaped by purposes, not place. It differs in many ways from the polis of places. Organizations arise when individuals (not families) throw part (not all) of their lots together. Our polis exists where we work or volunteer, not where we reside. Our polis is not fixed, nor are we fixed in it. Instead, our polis experience depends on choices we make about which organizations we wish to participate in and our purposes in doing so.

Whatever the particular blend of work—work of the spirit, work of the mind, work of the body, work of the heart—our purposes in organizations are richer and more dimensioned than the *individual* transactions and connections that characterize markets and networks. Much of what we do in markets and networks plays out *individually*—but not in organizations. We do not spend our time and effort in organizations exchanging money, time, or votes for goods or services. We do not show up for work each day to negotiate the purchase and sale of services with other employees. Yes, there are employment *markets* and the transactions that define them. But we do not concentrate the bulk of our time and attention at work on employment market transactions. (Indeed, if we do, it signals a feeling of *disenfranchisement*, a sense that our individual purposes are disconnected from the shared purposes of the organization. For those blessed with opportunity, this may mean it is time to seek participation in a different organization.)

We bring individual and group purposes to organizations—purposes reinforced by shared paths, shared roles, and shared ideas. Beyond family and friends, our most predictable shared paths happen in organizations. The shared role of employee encompasses thousands of distinctions in expertise and assignment. Such broad categories as blue-, white-, and pink-collar, exempt and nonexempt, and manager versus worker only begin to distinguish varieties of specific jobs and titles mutually understood by people who work together in organizations. The strong, predictable shared values of shared paths and shared roles also mirror many shared ideas, such as vision, mission, performance, and strategy—each having unique meanings to thick we's in organizations. The generalities of Ford Motor Company's and British Petroleum's vision might echo. But not the highly particular beliefs, behaviors, attitudes, and speech shared among thick we's who must convert vision from aspiration into performance. Making and selling cars (Ford) and locating, extracting, refining, and distributing petroleum to fuel cars (British Petroleum) demand highly distinctive strategies and skills. The different challenges provide their respective thick we's with different paths to independence and freedom.

The congruence of shared paths, shared roles, and shared ideas yields a range of personal obligations that run *both* to individuals *and* to groups, a pattern that has characterized the polis forever. Our fates and purposes are shared in organizations. *Reciprocity* does not arise primarily from contract or exchange. Yes, we have legal relationships with the organizations that pay us (although not necessarily with those in which we volunteer). But, while important, our legal employment contract is a minimal formality. Our most compelling obligations—our practical notions about the duties we owe to others during the hours we work each day—arise from the strong predictable values of shared paths, shared roles, and shared ideas.

The popular philosophy of individualism cannot explain the beliefs, behaviors, attitudes, and speech on display in organizations like Ford or British Petroleum—or my friend's construction crew. Organizations cannot exist without *shared* purposes and *shared* values—without *both* I values *and* we values that matter to our lives together in them. Other than friends and family, organizations are our thick we's. They are where we experience what it means to share fates with other people who are not otherwise related. We can choose

to isolate ourselves in the places we reside—but not in the organizations where we work. In that polis, we *must* participate in *groups*.
We must practice *together* the arts of self-government in the small
sphere within our reach.

. . . .

Billions of people around the globe share some understanding of the
idea of democracy. Centuries of experiences have enshrined voting
as *the* cornerstone political value in liberal market democracies. The
free ballot occupies our shared idea of democracy, often to the
exclusion of *other* political beliefs and behaviors long associated with
the democratic experience of *groups*. Voting is not the sole
democratic political value passed down through the ages. Others
relate to participation, voice, and consent (especially consent to
group purposes with which individuals who are part of those groups
disagree).

In a world of places, voting blended with other values to sustain a
democratic experience in towns, neighborhoods, cities, and states.
But we don't participate in places in the manner described by de Tocqueville. For millions of us, reinserting "township" for "organization"
in the opening passage converts it into a museum piece, a diorama of
democracy. Yes, we still count votes in the towns, cities, states, and
nations where we reside. But few of us have robust democratic experiences as a result. *Instead, we are more likely to experience a blend
of democratic and other political values in organizations where we
have no right to vote than in towns and states where we do.*

Democracy has bifurcated. *Voting* has migrated to *markets and
networks*—to the *market democracies* in which we live. As discussed in Chapters 8 and 9, we vote (or don't vote) preferences in
markets of *all* types, not just political markets. The free ballot is the
legal currency of political markets. We ballot individually. If we vote
as a consequence of groups, it is because we actively participate in
organizations in political markets, or because we align with collectivities of I's (see Chapter 10). Whenever we purchase or don't purchase any product or service, and whenever we choose or don't
choose to invest in any company or donate money to any nonprofit
organization or subscribe to any idea advocated by an organization,
we likewise express individual preferences in *market democracies*.
Voting in political markets is a variant of our strong, shared roles of
consumer and investor (Chapters 6 and 7).

We experience a greater spectrum of political values regarding voice, consent, and participation in organizations and among friends and families instead of markets. Our *actual* political experience ranges from antidemocratic authoritarian and hierarchical values in some organizations and families to more participatory, democratic values in others. In an increasing number of organizations, we experience a blend of hierarchy and democracy, depending on the question, problem, or charter at hand. But, if we wish to find our most compelling, actually shared political experiences, we need to look to organizations instead of locations.

In classic democratic political experience, the idea of voting blends with the idea of personal responsibility. People who vote hold themselves accountable for implementing their share in the results of that voting. This, however, fails to describe actual and predictable beliefs and behaviors in political markets. It does not describe "the way we do things around here." Our votes are the transactions of individual consumers responding to the ideas and offerings of organizations competing in political markets, instead of one democratic means among many used by thick we's to shape and implement a common good. In our world, we expect *the officials and other employees of governmental organizations* to implement the outcomes of elections—just as we expect, say, rental car companies to provide vehicles that won't endanger us and auditing firms to apply, instead of abuse, accounting rules. Our central concern as consumers of government products and services is with quality, timeliness, and cost, not *personal responsibility* for implementing government policy and choices. When it comes to government in local, state, and federal markets, we mostly bring do-it-for-me motivations instead of do-it-with-me or do-it-myself.

We flatter ourselves that such is not the case, but illogically so. By definition, the idea of self-government is contradicted by strict do-it-for-me arrangements. We can and do purchase governmental products and services. We can consume government. But we cannot participate in self-government without taking part in self-governing thick we's who share responsibility for defining and implementing their common good.

. . . .

We find fuller, more meaningful *political* experience in the organizations where we work, learn, or volunteer instead of the political and other markets where we consume and invest. Compare, for example, the widely shared idea of organizational "buy in" to the shared idea of voting. Buy in is commonly understood by millions of people in thousands of organizations around the globe. Over the past few decades, leaders in organizations have sought buy in from employees when new directions were afoot. A few years back, for example, the CEO of British Petroleum declared his company must find additional sources of energy. Soon thereafter British Petroleum (known as "BP") tested the slogan, "BP: Beyond Petroleum." We can be sure the CEO is seeking buy in from thousands of employees whose livelihoods currently depend on petroleum products.

When, for example, we read (as we did in the spring of 2002) that the FBI sought more effective coordination among headquarters and field people to deliver on the its new brand promise of prevention (see Chapter 9), we can reasonably assume that FBI leaders sought buy in from employees. Or, when we read (as we did in late 2002) that a new U.S. Department of Homeland Security would combine scores of different agencies, we can be sure leaders in those organizations sought buy in, especially from the employees who must implement the changes. Or, when we read (as we did in 2001 through 2002) about the merger of Hewlett-Packard and Compaq, we can be certain that leaders of those companies sought buy in from the thousands of employees upon whom the fate of the new combination depended.

These illustrate buy in—a shared set of beliefs and behaviors now routinely expected as part of "the way we do things around here" in governmental, nonprofit and for-profit organizations. Executives in private sector companies seek buy in as predictably as they promote shareholder value and customer service. Employees in organizations embarking on change *expect* an effort directed at gaining their buy in. Buy in—in organizations—is a characteristic shared idea of our new age.

The phrase "buy in" connotes economic purpose. On its face, it is about value instead of values. Yet, buy in blends the social and the political with the economic. Value is inherent in buy in because organizational change affects job expectations, responsibilities, and performance. Buy in also relates to social values such as trust, integrity, candor, and patience. Buy in, for example, cannot occur without clear explanations grounded in mutually recognizable views about the circumstances and challenges facing an organization. Buy in must be *informed*. The kind of ignorance organizations might foster among consumers and investors is a far riskier proposition *inside* because employees share fates in more meaningful ways. In organizations, unlike in markets and networks, people are more likely to exert time and energy to convert ignorance into understanding. Whether formally or informally, word usually gets out. As a result, people in organizations *know* whether efforts to gain buy in are sincere.

Notwithstanding its economic and social values, however, the shared idea of buy in speaks mainly to political values—to beliefs and behaviors concerning *terms of belonging*, such as participation, voice, rights, responsibilities, and consent. In our world, jobs are livelihoods. In that sense, we *live* in the organizations where we work. Organizations are where we most meaningfully experience community (Chapter 11). It ought not surprise us, then, that political values matter tremendously in organizations and that, when organizational change is afoot, leaders seek buy in.

Employees who buy in indicate they understand, accept, and are committed to change and its implications. They expect explanations for why they should buy in to cover a spectrum of individual and group purposes ranging from job security to personal growth to group survival and prosperity. They also expect to participate in shaping new directions, as well as the implications of changes for themselves. *They expect a voice.* As a consequence of *shared political values*, employees who buy in also expect *to be held accountable for carrying out the changes at hand, whether or not they agree with those changes*. They expect to be held accountable for implementation.

In highlighting buy in as a shared idea influencing political values in organizations, I do not mean to suggest it is the acme of human political experience. Nor do I mean to detract from or disrespect voting by noting its migration to markets. It is a glory of our age that so many of us enjoy the freedoms and possibilities linked to voting in market democracies. Rather, in each case, I am describing values as they are instead of what I or others believe should be. However much anyone likes or dislikes it, and whether or not it comports with any particular political theory, buy in *is* one of our most predictably shared ideas and shared political values. Buy in exists; our opportunity is to enrich it, instead of dismissing it.

Some people sneer at buy in as trivial or conspiratorial. Others rightly point to the potentially coercive context in which employees either buy in or find themselves out on the street. Such perspectives, however, too quickly ignore the *democratic impulse* in the shared idea of buy in. In my experience in scores of organizations, buy in conveys a real (if imperfect) commitment to voice, participation, and consent—to organizational *governance by the thick we's responsible for implementing ideas and directions*. Although it is not about voting, buy in is a democratic idea. It is a widespread practice in which political and social values blend with economic value to shape the terms of belonging and participation in organizations. Buy in can be enriched and improved—a lot. But not by advocating practices more fitting to a world of places than the world of markets, networks, and organizations in which so many of us actually live today.

No written or legislated law requires buy in. If buy in has legal weight, it is the kind we associate with customary instead of judicial, legislative, or administrative law. Buy in arises from our actual beliefs, behaviors, attitudes, and speech in organizations and not from judicial chambers or legislative committee rooms. Our constitutionally guaranteed legal vehicles for democratic participation in elections are free speech and the right to vote. The right to vote emerged over centuries; it is a human right we must preserve and extend. But as a shared idea that translates into actual belief, behavior, attitude, and speech, the right to vote has shifted to markets. In markets, voting has separated from other values critical to a full democratic experience. Voting is no longer thick with beliefs and behaviors regarding participation, voice, consent, and rights and responsibilities. This helps explain why a minority of eligible voters actually register and cast ballots in most elections. *In our new world, buy in is practiced more predictably by far greater percentages of people working together in organizations than voting is by individuals acting alone in political markets.*

. . . .

What distinguishes the shared political experience of employees in organizations from the democracy-as-voting consumer experience of collectivities of I's in markets and networks? It has little to do with birthrights based on accidents of place—the legal designation as citizens of this, that, or another nation. Instead, the difference turns on *choices we make* about time, attention, commitment, and purpose. When we bring do-it-for-me consumer attitudes to markets, our democratic experience is, at best, one of voting preferences, informed or otherwise. When, on the other hand, we participate in the life of an organization—when we buy in to the shared purposes of an organization—we are likely to have a *political* experience that goes beyond voting. We throw ourselves into *the affairs of the organization*.

Consider schools. For teachers and administrative staff, the school is a polis because it is the organization employing them. But what about students, parents, and local taxpayers? *Are schools a polis for them?* It depends on whether people *work*. Because of academic and extracurricular participation, students *can* have a polis experience; by doing so, they can learn many shared values vital to thriving in a world of markets, networks, and organizations. Or, they can choose not to. Meanwhile, parents and taxpayers *through voluntary effort* can choose to put forth *real work* on behalf of schools. If they do, then the school is a polis for them. The vast majority of parents and other taxpayers, however, *do not work* (voluntarily or otherwise) within or for schools. Their shared role is *consumer* and, possibly, investor. Their activities are voting and paying taxes. The nature of our political experience in schools, then, is better understood by identifying whether we are consumers and investors in local education *markets,* or employees or volunteers in school *organizations*.

Any adult can make a school a polis through work and participation, but most do not. This is neither morally good nor morally evil—it just is. Among the strongest, most predictably shared values in our world are those of adults as consumers in education markets. But they are *consumer* values, not 18th century *citizen* values or 21st century *employee* values. We ought to bear this in mind as we contemplate challenges ranging from better education to intergenerational equity to school safety to privatization.

Our political experience reflects choices we make about roles in markets, networks, and organizations. It is acutely different from the fixed polis of place into which our ancestors were *born*. For those of us who participate through work and effort, the organization is a polis. The choice to participate conditions our shared experiences and shared values. But it is a choice. Each of us has known people who minimize effort as employees at work—ticket punchers who check their brains, hearts, and souls at the door. Such people can be purposeless, which, in our world, is analogous to being homeless in a world of places. They may have weaker, less predictable values because they miss out on the shared path, shared ideas, and shared roles at work. They flee from participating in the affairs of the organization and, consequently, ostracize themselves from a core polis of their lives. In the most extreme cases, they fail to do their jobs as most narrowly construed. Most of us choose otherwise in today's highly dynamic competitive environment because our job security and organizational participation depend upon it. Still, it is a matter of choice.

This, too, is neither good nor evil. It just is. It just is the way a world of markets, networks, organizations, friends, and families functions. The risks and rewards of working together in organizations echo the risks and rewards of living together in, say, Athens in the 5th century B.C. But it is *not* the way things work in 21st century villages, towns, cities, states, and nations. *Our places have been emptied of the shared fates that make for a polis.* In their stead have risen markets, networks, and organizations.

Centuries of governance, political theory, and practice have left plenty of machinery in and about *place*. That machinery matters. But we understand and make the best use of it when we *see* how it operates in a framework of markets, networks, and organizations, and when we get over our delusions that the machinery itself— which, after all, is just machinery—connects us to the experience of the polis. As we saw in the Florida fiasco of the U. S. presidential election of 2000 and various attempted reforms in its aftermath, the matrix of markets, organizations, and networks controls the *machinery* of voting, not the reverse.

. . . .

Consider, then, the town of Union Vale in Dutchess County, New York, where I reside. Union Vale is, to be sure, a place. It has boundaries enough. But those boundaries are archaisms: incoherent jurisdictional lines drawn for governmental service organizations providing me and my fellow residents of Union Vale (as well as visitors and nonresidents) fire protection, road maintenance, recycling services, emergency medical care, contracted cable TV services, zoning choices and enforcement, park and recreation services, local conservation services, and misdemeanor adjudication services. Sitting within these crosshatched webs is a Town Council of five members who have *some* authority to direct *some* government services. Even at this local level, the mix of executive, legislative, judicial, and administrative organizations is bewilderingly complex. (Imagine, then, New York City or London or Hong Kong!!)

Various governmental service organizations superimpose and overlap the boundaries of Union Vale. Union Vale residents are served by three different school districts, each of which also serves residents of other towns. Judicial services are provided by county, state, and federal court systems. Traffic regulation, enforcement, security, and safety protection are provided by two police organizations: one a Dutchess County organization, the other a State of New York organization. Farming and agricultural services are delivered through a county organization. Environmental protection is provided by several county, state, and federal organizations. Gas and electrical conduits that run through Union Vale to serve New York City residents are governed by the Federal Energy Regulatory Commission. Air traffic is managed by a federal organization.

As I write this, I know there are additional governmental service organizations upon whom I depend that do not spring to mind. That is the point. The constellation of governmental service organizations and the markets and networks in which they operate have morphed beyond the reach of our inherited understanding of the now *ancient* history of town-as-polis. My posture and the posture of most people in Union Vale *vis a vis* the cascade of organizations is that of *consumer* and, possibly, *investor*. Not employee, and not the voluntary form of employee described for schools. *None of the many governmental service organizations is a polis for me or most of the other 4,000 residents of Union Vale.*

In this reality, our cherished concept of citizen is threatened. It survives more as a shared idea than a shared role. It has parsed itself into separate strands that have, in turn, divided from each other. Yes, citizen still connotes an assemblage of rights and responsibilities. It permits us to vote in political markets. *But, with the exception of jury service, none of the responsibilities of citizenship include work—the basis for belonging to and participation in organizations.* Our shared understanding of the rights and responsibilities of citizenship concentrates in transactions such as voting and paying taxes, which, in our world, makes us consumers and investors (albeit, hopefully, reliable, well informed ones). If we are describing democracy as voting, we are discussing citizenship in the guise of consumers transacting in markets. But if we are describing democracy or any other political values in the more primary, interpersonal way derived from people who share fates governing themselves in thick we's, then we are necessarily looking at organizations.

I vote in Union Vale elections. But my vote is transactional, something best understood in a *market* context. My vote is the legal currency I use to gain better services from the various governmental service organizations in my life. It is not my only currency. I also pay fees for recycling and recreational services, and school taxes to one of the school districts that overlaps Union Vale. But if

I, or any of my fellow Union Vale residents—or people who do *not* reside in Union Vale (for example, developers)—wish to proactively shape local affairs, I would need to participate in governmental organizations themselves or *organize* to exert more influence on those organizations.

The 1990s introduced us to the fascinating idea of stickiness. So-called "killer apps" were technologies, products, and services that were sticky—that is, captured consumer usage in a way that promised long-term habit. *Well, work in organizations—whether for pay or voluntary—is the sticky stuff that glues together shared political experience and shared political values.* When we work in an organization, we are more likely to participate with others who share fates and, as a result, practice stronger, more predictable beliefs, behaviors, attitudes, and speech regarding terms of belonging, such as consent, voice, and responsibility. Work in organizations is sticky. Voting in markets is not sticky.

Could I work in one of the many organizations serving Union Vale and make that organization a polis of purposes for me? Yes! (And my right to do so illuminates the liberal market democracy experience that has sired our world of markets, networks, organizations, friends, and families.) But neither I nor *more than 90 percent* of other Union Vale adults do so. Once again, that is neither bad nor good. It just is. It just is an illustration of how people sort out time and attention according to individual and group purposes in markets, networks, and organizations. Most Union Vale residents do not work or volunteer in local governmental service organizations because they choose to work and volunteer in *other* organizations. Naïve idealists who hearken back to Norman Rockwell-style shared ideas of the small town cannot square this circle—one circumscribed by being consumers, investors, networkers, family members, friends, and employees in a kaleidoscope of markets, networks, and organizations.

Thank goodness there are people in Union Vale (and, indeed, people from neighboring towns) who choose to work in governmental organizations serving Union Vale. It is they who throw their lots together in a polis experience; it is they who richly and multidimensionally share political purposes and values together. We, their consumers and investors, depend on them for judgement and service. We depend on them to incorporate our concerns and needs into the good things to have they provide (see Chapter 9). We depend on them to ensure that the *brand* of local governmental organizations stands the test of ethical concerns ranging across value categories from family to economics to politics to technology. But my nominal citizenship and actual residence in Union Vale has little connection to the long tradition of the polis. That polis, the polis of place, is dead. Our concern is with the polis that has arisen in its stead: the organization. Our challenge is to blend values in ways that promise a good life for all who depend on organizations, whether as employees, volunteers, consumers, networkers, or investors. Today, we must make democracy work in two venues, not one—by being informed voters in political markets and by participating democratically in the polis most essential to our lives together with others: the organizations where we work or volunteer.

13 Governance and Problem Solving

I have not met many people who hate the idea of governance. I have met plenty who distrust government or abhor bureaucracy. Aside from politicians and journalists, nearly everyone detests politics and recoils when issues are politicized. Politicizing, it seems, is wholly negative (in part, let's admit, because those we accuse of politicizing promote positions we dislike). But among people with whom I've worked in all manner and size of organizations, the idea of governance suffers neither the jungle of politics nor the quicksand of bureaucracy. Governance is a strongly shared idea we might deploy to integrate value and values in organizations—especially by thinking differently about the we who are governing.

Similarly, I have never met anyone who thinks ill of problem solving. Oh, yes, I have encountered complaints about protracted, superficial, or disingenuous problem solving. Analysis paralysis, railroading, rubber-stamping: these speak to beliefs and behaviors antithetical to sound problem solving. Plenty of people gripe about them. But no one questions problem solving itself or the widely shared idea that problems exist to be solved. Like governance, problem solving encompasses many shared values in our new world of purposes.

But which problems should we solve? How do we work together to do so? Critically, who are the *we* who must solve them? Pro-life advocates, for example, believe legalized abortion is a problem to be solved. Pro-choice supporters believe threatening a woman's right to choose is a problem. Each group agrees on the need for problem solving, but they differ diametrically on defining the problem.

Problem definition is a wise practice in problem solving. Competent problem solvers carefully characterize the challenge at hand. I recall an effort by executives in the early 1990s to grow the American Express Travelers Cheque business ("Cheque" is that company's spelling of check). They wished to increase market share. But first, they asked, "What market?" Was it travelers checks? Was it cash and checks? Or, was it *all forms of payments* (cash, checks, money orders, credit cards, and more)? At the time, American Express held most of the travelers check market. Travelers checks, however, accounted for a sliver of total payments. By defining the problem, the executives set parameters on solutions. If they concentrated only on travelers checks, their strategies would aim at people traveling. If, at the other extreme, they selected all payments, they would need innovative strategies for delivering the benefits of travelers checks (for example, refunds if lost or stolen) to customers spending in wider circumstances, such as shopping for groceries or gas while going to or from work. They might, for example, consider rebranding their product from Travelers Cheques to Safety Cheques (or some such thing).

Problem definition can convert impasse into shared purpose. Or, it can fail. It is *possible* for *some* pro-life and *some* pro-choice advocates to come together to solve a problem defined as reducing the number of unwanted pregnancies. Neither pro-life nor pro-choice supporters favor unwanted pregnancies. Many in each camp seek to reduce abortions by curtailing unwanted pregnancies. Pro-life and pro-choice advocates organizing to reduce the number of abortions need not agree on legalized abortion. They must, however, concur on defining a problem against which they can form a *shared purpose*.

In our new world of purposes, organizations are the pivotal social formation for problem solving in support of shared purposes. Organizations arise when people articulate shared purposes about solving mutually defined problems—when they see organizing as an effective means for shared action. Organizations emerge at the intersection of shared purpose, shared belief, and shared action—the confluence distinguishing thick we's who are not necessarily friends or family from individuals interacting in markets and networks.

In choosing to define their problem closer to travelers checks than all payments, the American Express executives weighed shared purpose, belief, and action. They asked whether the people of their organization—their thick we—would believe in the defined challenge enough to take action. Competing for all forms of payments seemed too aggressive. People lose heart—fail to believe or take action—when purposes and problems are not credible. An organization of pro-life and pro-choice advocates is more likely to form around reducing unwanted pregnancies than, say, scientifically establishing when life begins or agreeing on a slate of judicial nominees.

But how do people in organizations define purposes and problems? How do they go about solving the problem once it is defined? How would a newly formed group of pro-life and pro-choice advocates establish some credible shared purpose? How did the American Express executives decide? How does any thick we in our new world of purposes use shared purpose and problem solving to convert belief into action, and shared paths, shared ideas, and shared roles into shared values?

Governance.

And politics.

. . . .

Governance could be a revitalizing word for how we go about establishing shared purposes in organizations and then use problem solving to accomplish them. Or, governance could fail as a shared idea. The prevailing response to widespread corporate scandals, for example, narrows the shared idea of governance to a battle among shareholders, government organizations, and executives over profits. This chapter argues for a broader view of governance—one vital to thick we's who participate in organizations, as opposed to participants in markets for shareholder value and corporate control. If the business press, elected officials, and shareholder value zealots kill off the possibilities in governance, then some other word will emerge to better fit a world in which organizations are the essential mid-level social formation bridging individuals, friends, and families to the largest social formations: markets, networks, and nations.

Familiar language about the governance of organizations speaks of managing and leading. Politics—always essential to governing—is a hateful word in organizations (and elsewhere). We often must look back in time to find constructive meaning for politics. As intended by the Greeks, for example, politics were beliefs and behaviors—shared values—pertaining to *the affairs of the polis* (see Chapter 12). In that sense, politics *was* governance.

Updating this meaning requires applying it to *the affairs of the organization* because organizations are the *polis* in our lives. The affairs of the organization include how organizations set shared purposes, define problems to be solved, and do purposeful work. We need not abandon the language of management. We need not repeat the mistake of the past quarter-century when executives, pundits, and gurus got carried away with either/or distinctions between leadership and management. Our world of purposes operates effectively through a both/and philosophy. We benefit from both leadership and management. Similarly, we can blend value and values through appeals to many shared ideas: governance, politics, leadership, and management.

Our inherited ideas about organizational governance are twofold: (1) hierarchical management of the internal affairs of organizations; and, (2) formal, mostly legal constraints imposed on organizations by external forces. The bulk of this chapter concerns the first idea, especially why and how inherited assumptions about hierarchical governance and management fail the test of reality. In contrast, popular ideas about how and why external forces impose (or do not impose) constraints on organizations come closer to the mark.

The encyclopedic laws, rules, and regulations constraining organizations (whether fair or unfair, good or bad) seek desired outcomes from markets, networks, and nations. Broadly, the constraints set parameters of permitted behavior, rather than reaching in and running the daily operations of organizations. Antidiscrimination, workplace safety, environmental protection, lemon laws, truth-in-advertising—these and a zillion other rules and regulations advance or protect the interests of employees, customers, investors, networkers, and families (and, of course, organizations themselves) in markets and networks for employment, capital, and goods and services. *For the most part, though, how organizations govern and manage themselves to comply with rules and regulations is left up to organizations.*

If organizations transgress rules or regulations, formal redress happens in legal and governmental markets and networks, not in the offending organizations (the main exceptions being formal procedures set by collective bargaining agreements and voluntary processes established by organizations). From lawsuits to new or amended laws and regulations, grievances and initiatives play out in markets and networks.

As a consumer, if you seek to correct potential or actual harm from products or services (toys, guns, cars, the Internet), you can sue, you can seek legislation, you can campaign for candidates, you can boycott, and you can provide information to others in markets and networks. You can also seek media attention. As an employee or investor, if you believe you have suffered from the actions of an organization (discrimination, workplace safety, misleading financial information, and so on), you can sue, you can seek legislation, you can campaign for candidates, you can boycott or strike, and you can provide information to others in markets and networks. You can also seek media attention.

Markets and networks, in this sense, are social formations of last resort. Yet, as we know from experience, this safety net—the option of suing, legislating, campaigning, and so forth—is *extraordinarily expensive, time-consuming, and erratic*. Among other things, *organizations* have greater power and resources than individuals in markets and networks. Organizations hold more and better cards regardless of venue, grievance, or initiative. Courts? Organizations have access to better lawyers and can fund more careful and protracted legal work. Legislature and agencies? Again, more resources, better lawyers, and more highly placed lobbyists. Elections? More influence and access to political parties, advocacy organizations, and lobbyists, as well as larger resources for funding campaigns, advertising, and so forth. Of course, when organizations battle other organizations, the field levels. But, in our market democracies, individuals contending with organizations are Davids against Goliaths. Indeed, when individuals prevail, we almost always find *organizations* have come to their aid. Individuals rarely succeed solely *as* individuals.

In design and conduct, our strong shared values of looking to markets and networks to constrain organizations are intended to be exceptional. Our rule is that *organizations ought to govern themselves*. This philosophy underpins the central *legal and formal* aspect of *internal* corporate governance that, importantly, is democratic and role-based: *shareholders elect directors who oversee management on behalf of shareholders*.

Directors, however, are expected to oversee management—*not manage*. As long as directors toe this line, they and the shareholders they represent are protected from legal liabilities arising from the actions of organizations. As long as shareholders stay clear of the *day-to-day affairs* of the organization, we do not pierce the corporate veil—the flip side of which is that internal organizational governance and management is *not* the province of directors or shareholders. We must, at least, permit ourselves a smile at this: Shareholder *democracy* directed at corporate governance is designed to stay clear of the main action of governance—that is, the core, everyday affairs of shared purposes, problem solving, and purposeful work. It is, by design, a democracy that envelops organizations with the demands of one role-based group (shareholders) who have no *responsibility* for how another role-based group (employees) actually governs the affairs of the organization.

External forces that constrain organizations, then, arise *in markets and networks in order to promote the operation of markets and networks*. When transgressions occur, *redress comes in markets and networks*. We celebrate, attack, or ignore various role-based rights and responsibilities threaded through all this. As consumers, nearly all of us applaud lemon laws. On the other hand, there is less unanimity among us as employees, family members, and friends regarding antidiscrimination laws in employment markets. Like so much in our new world of purposes, our instinctive conception of governance—*the rule of law in market democracies built on a public philosophy of individualism*—speaks most directly to *the interplay of individual rights and responsibilities in markets and networks, as opposed to self-governance in organizations, our most critical thick we's.*

If something is broken, we cry for reform in markets and networks. If pundits or scholars claim some need for new policies and strategies, they, too, run to markets and networks, or to appeals for individual responsibility. The mid-level social formation most evident in our lives—the organization—*is* constrained by all this. But, for the most part, how we govern ourselves in organizations day-to-day is left up to us in organizations. Indeed, many people outraged by corporate scandals now think management has too much freedom and too little responsibility. The call goes out to legal and capital *markets* for more rules and more regulations to protect shareholders who, by and large, are strangers, instead of fellow participants in the thick we's in question. We overlook an additional option: *demanding that thick we's in organizations take responsibility for governing themselves toward a better blend of value and values.*

In part, the focus on executives traces to our inherited assumption that *internal* organizational governance is hierarchical and bureaucratic instead of democratic. Complaints about greed and the assignment of responsibility to do something to correct it get leveled at top management instead of *all employees in the thick we.* We assume those at the apex of a hierarchy have an iron grip on how value and values get blended in organizations. According to shared ideas, we look to markets, not organizations, for democratic experiences. As a result, we repeatedly fail to see, understand, or build on the most formative experiences of self-governance in our world of purposes: *how we **actually** work together to solve problems in organizations, and toward what shared purposes.*

. . . .

For the past 15 years or so, I have engaged people in conversations about democracy and self-government. I begin by asking, "Do you live in a democracy?" The instant answer is "Yes." I ask what makes for the democracy in which they live. Responses detail the right to vote; freedoms of speech, assembly, and faith; the rule of law; jury trials; a free press; and individual freedom and liberty. When I probe for where this democracy in which they live *is*, the answers are familiar: town, state, and nation.

At this point, I suggest they equate where they live with time, purpose, attention, and shared fates. Most people agree that, under this view, they *live* among friends and family, and in organizations. With regard to the organization in which they work or volunteer, I then repeat the first question, "Do you live in a democracy?" With the exception of some who work in nonprofits, the instant answer is "No." When I seek an explanation, they point to the absence of the right to vote, freedom of speech, assembly and faith, rule of law, jury trials, free press, and individual freedom and liberty.

It turns out, though, that with further discussion, most people recognize that the "No" to the question about democracy in organizations was as ill-considered as the earlier "Yes." Our *actual* political experience in organizations is richer and more interesting than inherited assumptions about hierarchy suggest. Popular, but erroneous, myths about organizational governance and management can be traced to centuries of experience with the division of labor, bureaucracy, hierarchy, and command and control. But the most telling word in all this—the one that should tip us off to our profoundly altered reality—is *bureaucracy.*

If politics and politicizing appall all but politicians and journalists, bureaucracy numbs everyone, including bureaucrats. I do not know a soul who defends bureaucracy *or an organization that wishes to be more bureaucratic.* Yet, less than a century ago, bureaucracy was respected for its power and effectiveness in governing and managing organizations—even as it was feared for its initially symbiotic, then parasitical, relationship to the democratization of nations.

Here are some advantages of bureaucracy noted by the sociologist Max Weber: efficiency, impartiality, speed, objectivity, clarity, and meritocracy. The rise of bureaucracy initially advanced democracy in nations by overturning what Weber called honorific arrangements—leadership positions granted because of birth and class. Bureaucracies subsequently threatened democracy through the rule of experts. This double-edged sword aside, bureaucracy rose rapidly in private sector companies, as well as in states, nations, towns, cities, and markets. The advantages flowed from the bureaucratic design:

- Fixed and stable distribution of tasks
- Hierarchy of authority
- Decision making and management based on rules
- Objective, disinterested, and impersonal exercise of authority
- Established qualifications for decision-making positions supported by training, education, and slow progression up a career ladder
- Lifetime employment

Our inherited managerial practices—hierarchy, and command and control—trace to this design. Among the elements of bureaucracy, the distribution of tasks and the hierarchy of authority still contribute to effective organizational governance and management (though they are insufficient by themselves). But the rest of the bureaucratic superstructure is worse than useless. It impedes the purposeful work and problem solving on which organizations rely to achieve shared purposes and the common good. *Efficiency, fairness, speed, objectivity, clarity, meritocracy*: None are advanced in bureaucratic organizations. Bureaucracy solves no problems; it generates and compounds them.

Bureaucracy rode 19th and 20th century social and political forces—democratic, socialist, and communist. It responded well to economic and market forces. Large-scale, industrial oligopoly and monopoly capitalism directed at producing and distributing commodity products and services operated effectively enough under bureaucratic management. (Henry Ford, again: "I don't care what color car they want as long as it is black.") Producers and shareholders profited, while consumers benefited and labor suffered. Characteristically, though, even those who hoped to lighten labor's load—

progressives, unionists, management experts—looked to bureaucracy as the favored form of governance.

Today, formal and informal organizations of all sizes and across all sectors (private, nonprofit, governmental) confront radically different forces that have been set loose by markets, networks, and organizations. Weber lived in a world of places; we don't. We know the forces in *our* new world: technology, globalization, governmental deregulation and reregulation, demographics, media, worldwide financial markets, reflexive markets and networks, and so forth. We also know the myriad ways these forces have pushed organizations to abandon bureaucracy: total quality, customer service, innovation, speed, re-engineering, horizontal organization, globalization, core competencies, teams, continuous improvement, benchmarking, outsourcing, downsizing, strategic alliances, systems integration, and eCommerce.

All this has happened. It has transformed how purposeful work *actually happens* in organizations. *It has permanently altered the governance of the affairs of the organization*. Before discussing how, though, let's clear away another shared misunderstanding. Whereas markets divide labor and expertise, organizations have always been mostly about *reintegrating* labor and expertise. We sometimes confuse these two points, in part because we know organizations first divide up work into tasks and jobs before reintegrating them. But the magic of organizations—their essential point—is in how they *reintegrate* tasks and jobs in pursuit of shared purposes.

Weber's bureaucrats reintegrated labor through *rules*. Throughout most of the 19th and 20th centuries, bureaucracy succeeded because (1) production was divided into individual-by-individual jobs, (2) labor was mostly unskilled or monoskilled with threadbare information needs other than instructions from bosses, and (3) products and services were commodities. Reintegration happened primarily through machinery and the rule-driven designs and decisions set at the top of the hierarchy. Reintegration occurred in *organization time*, not real time—that is, the time it took for designs and decisions to wend their way through the hierarchy. Shifts in approach to purposeful work were slow and deliberate, in part because, relative to today, the environment was stable, and decisions to change the status quo required costly capital investments or reorganizations.

Classic organization design separated work into functions, functions into departments, and departments into jobs. At the apex sat the general manager and his or her direct line reports (functional heads of research, manufacturing, operations, marketing, distribution, sales, service, and so forth). Also reporting to the general manager were experts who served as staff: lawyers, accountants, human resources, and administrators. Each group—line and staff—made the critical reintegrating decisions by establishing rules and policy. They operated hierarchically, staff served as a check and balance on the line, and the general manager was boss.

Strong, predictable patterns of actual beliefs, behaviors, attitudes, and speech—shared values, whether for good or ill—arise when shared ideas (Chapters 8 and 9) blend with shared roles (Chapters 6 and 7) and shared paths (Chapter 5). The shared ideas and shared roles in the bureaucratic design, for example, fostered shared political and governance values regarding hierarchy, command and control, rules-as-fairness, individual accountability, cautious administration, and antagonisms between workers and management. All of this helps explain inherited assumptions. Job distinctions and decision-making hierarchy still contribute to effective organizational governance and performance *under certain conditions.* Beyond these, however, the only robust remnants from the wreckage of bureaucracy are questionable tendencies toward top management privilege and secrecy—values much in evidence in corporate scandals.

Today, shared ideas, shared roles, and shared paths in organizations produce a wider range of political and social values: hierarchical and democratic, open and secret; more performance driven than rules-based; dynamic instead of rigid. Read carefully, for example, some widely *shared ideas* inside effective organizations: vision, mission, town hall meetings, buy in, and taking ownership of problems. *Shared roles*? Yes, we continue to distinguish employees, managers, and executives. But millions of people in organizations have experience with shared leadership and fluid membership in projects and teams. Today, the governance of organizations encourages explicit concern for customers, employees, shareholders, and alliance partners. *Shared paths*? Today's prevailing organizational building block is twofold: the individual and the small group. How small groups govern themselves in thousands of organizations would freak Weber.

Unlike Weber, I am not advocating an ideal form of governance. Nor am I claiming every organization in our new world of purposes is fully democratic or the pinnacle of humankind's social, political, and economic experience. I am saying, "Let's take a close look at actual experience in organizations—*our most pivotal mid-level social for-*

mation, our polis. They are more dynamic and richer in political, social, and economic values than we acknowledge or respect."

. . . .

The reintegration of purposeful work happens differently now than 20 or 30 years ago. First, expertise has spread from top to bottom and all across organizations. Indeed, it has spread beyond formal organizational boundaries—many organizations today must reintegrate work with expert labor provided by *other* organizations. Second, expertise is exercised as much by those who do work as by those who mostly make decisions. The demarcation between decision-making and work is no longer absolute. Third, decisions are not made primarily by rules; they emerge from the dictates of continuously shifting performance demands. Fourth, labor increasingly is multiskilled, instead of unskilled or monoskilled, and reliant on real-time, rich information. Fifth, the building block of work is not the individual under command of a boss: It is both the individual and the small group. Sixth, organization design concentrates on integrating work processes, information, and technology rather than job descriptions and reporting relationships. Organization experts worry more about the span of communication than the span of control. Seventh, products and services are customized, not commodities. Organizations aspire to provide good things to have to "markets of one" (see Chapter 9).

I recently flew to Los Angeles, where I picked up a rental car at the airport. A bus shuttled renters from the airport to the car lot. Here are some skills I observed in the bus driver: driving; knowledge of airport security checkpoints and procedures; logistics, communications, and accounting for checking in renters; baggage handling; mastery of video and audio information and bus technologies; knowledge of local conditions, roads, and travel information; and differentiated customer service (#1 club and so forth).

The driver was a multiskilled professional. He was an expert. Why? Because *he* must deliver his company's brand promise of customer service, timeliness, and continuous improvement. *He* is the face of his company's brand—the key point at which labor, capital, technology, and information are *reintegrated* to serve customers. Individual performance is necessary, but not sufficient. The driver's performance—and his fate in the company—depends on *other people* as well as technology. He would fail if critical reintegration decisions had to migrate up and down a bureaucracy of rules-based decision makers. The driver is as much a decision-maker as a doer.

The driver is increasingly the rule, not the exception, among thick we's who compete effectively. Our new world of purposes depends on tens of thousands of multiskilled positions in organizations of all sizes and shapes. From my friend's construction crew (Chapter 5) to megaenterprises like Siemens or Disney, organizations rely on skills and expertise to make reintegration happen—not just senior decision makers who sit atop the hierarchy. The sociopolitical and technical reality of organizations has altered. Instead of Weber's bureaucracies, in which unskilled labor was reintegrated by high-placed experts making and applying rules to people and machines, today's organizations rely on expertise from top to bottom and ask those *as close to the real work as possible to do the bulk of reintegration in as close to real time as possible*. Organization time—bureaucratic time—is too slow.

Weber's bureaucracies operated in the imagery of Charlie Chaplin's *Modern Times*—the film in which the boss eats lunch at an empty desk while gazing on the factory and dialing up or down the speed of machine-like operations in which workers were cogs. In our world, that kind of management is archaic—a point made by Canon copier commercials in 2002 and 2003 that poked fun at managers portrayed as dunces in mid-20th century black-and-white films and TV. The tag line: "If business were that easy... ."

As Shoshana Zuboff asserted in her pivotal 1988 book, we live *In the Age of the Smart Machine*. She warned that technology would transform front-line workers from unskilled and monoskilled laborers into experts, and from machinery cogs into knowledge and information workers. Yet, in addition to expanding expertise, our new sociotechnical regime also dumbs down jobs. Cash register clerks punch pictograms. We ought not ignore this. Too many either/or critics, however, fail to look beyond the pictograms to the more complete reality, one that acknowledges dumbing down while *seeing more*.

Seeing, for example, that fast food restaurant work groups are impressive to behold during busy meal times. The mix of skills related to technology, cooking, logistics, customer service, and teamwork ought not be dismissed lightly. *We need to see the mix of hierarchy and democracy observable in such groups*. Like other small groups, the folks behind the fast food counter reflect a characteristic pattern of shared values. In today's organizations, the reintegration of work happens *in small groups doing purposeful work and problem solving together*, as well as in individual, task-by-task jobs in functions and departments. With the spread of expertise, the shift in reintegrating from top to bottom, and the rise of small groups, organizational governance and management has become more interesting—*and more democratic.*

. . . .

In Weber's bureaucracy, design foretold behavior and belief. Like Jeremy Bentham's *Panopticon*, a prison planned so wardens could see simultaneously into every prison cell, the command-and-control hierarchies of yesteryear enabled general managers to see directly into each individual's job. If we understood the bureaucratic design, we understood governance and management values. Today, by contrast, design is less reliable as a guide to values. No executive can see so well or so comprehensively. Organizations govern and manage themselves dynamically. In a real sense (though one not fully appreciated, developed, or evolved), the people of the organization govern the reintegration of work. They make it happen. They govern themselves. And, most often, they do so in small groups—*in shared paths*.

Our strongest, most predictable patterns of belief, behavior, attitude, and speech—of values of all sorts, good, bad, and otherwise—arise in shared paths, contexts in which a small number of people known to one another persistently interact (see Chapter 5). Families and friends are shared paths. But beyond family and friends, shared paths crop up mostly in organizations. By looking at shared paths at work, we can explore the actual political values used to solve problems and to govern the affairs of the organization. (We must, of course, also look beyond small groups to grasp the complete picture of hierarchy and democracy at work.)

Importantly, small groups exist throughout the organization from top to bottom and all across. This may be too subtle or too obvious. It is obvious, for example, that the smallest organizations, like my friend's construction crew, *are* shared paths. Still, many observers miss how pervasive the small group experience is in organizations. Front-line employees participate in small groups; so do senior executives. Unlike even a decade ago, *the elemental governing experience* **shared** *by people throughout organizations*—the one they can discuss and recognize as shared—has shifted from *only* bosses issuing orders to individuals to *both* that *and* small group participation.

Whether at the top or the bottom, small groups increasingly govern and manage themselves in two ways, not one. Does the hierarchy of a boss managing through command and control happen? Yes. But, so does teaming. Like so much else in our world of purposes, we find a better explanation of organization governance by avoiding either/or in favor of both/and. The most fundamental units of purposeful work—small groups—are increasingly both hierarchical and democratic. But they are not bureaucratic.

Why? Performance demands it. In *The Wisdom of Teams*, Jon Katzenbach and I stress that small groups must use *two* disciplines: single leader and team. We emphasize that the *choice* is dynamic instead of rule-based. It varies with the shifting and multiple performance challenges confronting small groups. If performance against a particular challenge is achievable through individual tasks, command and control can work. But if performance requires the real-time integration of multiple skills and perspectives, the hierarchical option of the single leader falls short. *In that case, small groups must apply the more democratic team discipline*. Small group governance and management, like all organizational governance and management, responds best to the demands of performance instead of bureaucratic rules.

People often recall participating in high-performing teams as among their most cherished experiences. And why not? The blend of political, social, and economic values is inspiring. Yet, perhaps contrary to intuition, *the least likely way to experience effective teaming is to set out to be a team*. Down the path of team for the sake of team lies turmoil *because it is a rule-based approach ill suited to our performance-driven world of purposeful work*. It is bureaucratic. It perpetuates either/or contentions that suggest hierarchy is *always* bad.

Hierarchy can have ill effects; it can be used poorly. But, then, so can teaming. Purposeful work demands that we integrate value and values: It demands governance in small groups who think and work together. That means struggle and conflict as well as efficiency. It means both hierarchy and democracy, as performance requires. When small groups adopt teaming for its own sake or because they consider hierarchy naturally bad, they ignore performance in favor of feelings and rules. They give preference to certain political and social values out of, at best, a weak understanding of how those values relate to or promote value and the reverse. When, on the other hand, small groups apply the more democratic team discipline because performance demands it, they inevitably experience the constructive conflicts and struggles through which value and values blend well.

Meanwhile, managers who rule small groups strictly hierarchically also fail. Perhaps oddly and blindly, they too believe teaming is about feelings and rules, instead of a hardheaded discipline for small group *performance*. They don't get it—often because they exemplify a macho, single-minded focus on value and are dismissive of all but individualistic values. They are dinosaurs.

The failure to understand teaming as a performance discipline integrating value and values reaches into scholarly ranks, too. For example, in *The Corrosion of Character*, Richard Sennett writes about many adverse effects on values of modern work/life arrangements. His essay invites us to integrate value and values at work. But Sennett writes himself into a trap. He excoriates teaming as cynical, as a put-on foisted on workers by management in search of new forms of exploitation. Like dinosaur managers, Sennett fails to grasp that governance in organizations happens mostly in small groups who work *together* to perform. Ours is no longer an either/or world of places featuring pitched battles between management and labor over power. *We*—employees of all types—govern organizations for better or worse. All of us, in all positions. *We govern ourselves*.

Yes, formal authority and extraordinary power concentrate at the top. Too many top managers presumptively reserve to themselves matters essential to the common good of the thick we of organizations. They encourage team-based, democratic problem solving regarding customer service or product innovation, then exclude social and political democratic values in favor of strict hierarchy on matters of core strategy, brand, mergers and acquisitions, shareholder relations, executive pay, health care, pension management, work/life balance, and information sharing. In my experience, all of these challenges yield well to democratic problem solving and governance by thick we's in organizations. Not to the exclusion of hierarchy. But, as corporate scandals attest, strict either/or adherence to hierarchy corrodes instead of sustains good organizational performance. In our new world of purposes, we must remember that top managers *are employees*—part of the thick we, not apart from it.

Top managers are well advised to open up the common good of organizations to a healthy blend of democratic and hierarchical social and political values. This won't happen, however, by retreating to political, social, or bureaucratic approaches better suited to 19th century democratizing nations than 21st century democratizing organizations. Sennett doesn't get this. Like others out of touch with contemporary organizational reality, he invokes we's coincident with place-based communities—we's whose central shared purpose, he argues, should be to resist capitalism *instead of taking shared responsibility for it*. It's all "To the barricades!" and, I think, light-headed.

My dialogues with people about their actual experiences of democracy get interesting when we discuss *small groups who solve problems* in organizations. Inevitably, the blend of values reported includes hierarchy and teaming. Effective small groups rely on free speech (brainstorming, no sacred cows, facts are friendly), free assembly (team meetings, both physical and virtual), free press (investigative, analytical efforts to think outside the box), and agreed upon behavioral and problem solving norms (a kind of *law* of small groups). Small groups are their own juries for dealing with norm-breaking individuals (sometimes fairly; some-times not). From time to time, teams vote. None of this suggests that hierarchical command and control has disappeared in small groups. It has not. *Nor should we expect it to, unless performance and problem solving requires it.*

In shared paths in organizations, then, we find strong, predict-able blends of hierarchical and democratic political, governance, and management values. The democratic political experiences of teams (real teams, not put-ons) incorporate voice, participation, consent, rights, and responsibilities—the richer, nonvoting part of the bifur-cated democratic experience described in Chapter 12. Experience shapes habit. The choice to govern organizations through hierarchy is not as automatic as a decade ago. A decade from now, I think, it will be less so. The political and governance experiences in organiza-tions have eclipsed *Modern Times*.

. . . .

Organizational performance—not ideology or feelings—demands that we extend the hierarchical and democratic values in small groups to organizations as a whole. I do not mean performance confined to shareholder value (see Chapter 7). Rather, I mean *sustainable* organization performance that serves customers, employees, and shareholders, each as means and ends to one another. In the private sector, *sustainable* performance happens in organizations in which the people of the enterprise deliver value to customers, who generate returns for shareholders, who provide opportunities for the people of the enterprise to deliver value to customers, who generate returns for shareholders, who provide opportunities for the people of the enterprise to.... and so on, ad infinitum. Governmental and not-for-profit organizations have analogous narratives for sustainable performance (see the Ethical Scorecard, Illustrative Suggestion #1, in Chapter 17).

This reinforcing, iterative and never-ending cycle of performance benefits *all* constituencies. Each shared role vital to a world of purposes—employee, customer, investor—is both a means and end to one another in a force field blending value and values. The thick we of organizations—*employees*—must solve problems and govern toward the multiple and reinforcing ends of their common good (see Chapter 14).

Employees ought to participate with voice, responsibility, right, and consent in defining the blend of value and values promised and delivered to *customers* by organization brands, products, and services (see Chapter 9). Employees ought to work together to educate financial and other analysts about how values and value inter-relate in delivering sustainable performance to *shareholders* (see Chapter 7). Employees need to participate in shaping and evaluating the learning and performance opportunities necessary to individual and shared success for themselve as *employees*.

Organizations cannot sustain performance without integrating value and values. Maniacal, single-minded concern for shareholder value always—*always*—produces unsustainable performance. This is as accurate for the infamous (Enron, WorldCom, and so forth) as for run-of-the-mill, never-heard-about organizations. Down this path lies value without values, or values unethically subordinated to value. As corporate scandals show, shareholder value fundamentalism destroys shareholder value.

All values, no value fails just as surely. Over decades of work with not-for-profit organizations, I have at times observed well-intended employees and volunteers dismiss concern for financial value as too commercial or somehow impure. It is, I think, another form of higher-calling, either/or fundamentalism that defeats instead of advances sustainable organization performance. In such organizations, shared social and political values called democratic in name become bureaucratic in fact. The worst of consensus management emerges; every participant has veto power over the group. Neither democracy nor hierarchy operates to solve problems or govern toward the common good.

We no longer inhabit Weber's bureaucratic world of places. In our world of purposes, the real-time integration of multiple skills and perspectives critical to small group performance increasingly determines if organizations successfully respond to unrelenting performance demands from *role-based stakeholders*: shareholders, contributors, taxpayers, and customers; voters; beneficiaries; partnering organizations; and employees. Continuous improvement, customer service, speed, core competencies, knowledge work, and real time enterprise are but some of the shared ideas describing organizational performance today. *None are possible in the absence of employees who know how to solve problems—to govern—together.*

Please reread the last sentence. A 19th or early 20th century Dickensian, Marxist, or Weberian organization in which barely literate, unskilled laborers dumbly used muscle energy to carry out commands from bosses would not thrive in our new world of purposes. Yet, such organizations still dot the globe, especially in worlds of places. Too often, those organizations are exploited by organizations from our world of purposes in exchange for all-too-paltry infusions of hard currency (which, in the event, flow corruptly to the despots and elites running such places). Such organizations *cannot* compete in our world of purposes: They move too slowly, add too little value, and fail to attract or retain highly skilled, problem-solving employees. They fail to foster and sustain thick we's who deliver organizational performance for the benefit of all.

Increasingly, I think, such exploitative organizations set themselves up for defeat. Worlds of purposes and worlds of places permeate one another. Organizations in a world of purposes cannot sustain performance through atrocious values, however strongly shared or predictable. A *brand* that exalts value over values and condemns people who still live in places to poverty, disease, and corruption is a brand likely to engender hatred and terrorism. The common good of thick we's must count *all* who are affected.

Corporate scandals evidence an ascendancy of greed and value that ill serve the *brand* of our world of purposes. But we will solve little if we look only for redress in markets and networks, including markets for government control. Self-governance is a best part of our past; giving organizations wide scope—and responsibility—for governing themselves is a best part of our future. We must look to ourselves as employees—as thick we's—in organizations to take charge of shared futures by practicing the shared values of governance, politics, and problem solving required for good lives in a world of purposes.

We are responsible. In our shared role as employees, we have no choice but to hold *ourselves* accountable for how the common good of our organizations serves ourselves as well as others. We must govern our common good in the best interests of customers, investors, networkers, fellow employees, friends, and families—who, not unimportantly, *are also ourselves.* Market and network constraints on organizations are also a best part of our past. But to reform, improve, and sustain the shared values needed to ensure that good things to have are *good,* we must rely on thick we's in organizations to govern themselves toward solving the problems about which they most care and are best positioned to take on.

14 The Greatest Good and the Common Good

Figure 14.1 on the following page illustrates the both/and nature of human happiness. Happiness rises with money to a point. Beyond some material base, however, happiness does not reliably mirror money or wealth. Money counts; it is one factor. But, above some foundation, money no longer serves as *the* North Star of happiness. Happiness is a both/and phenomenon. We pursue it with both monetary and nonmonetary resources and experiences. Value is necessary but not sufficient.

. . . .

Figure 14.2 depicts the bedrock shared idea among value fundamentalists, that happiness rises with money alone. Their influence pervades markets, networks, organizations, friends, and families.

Perhaps only belief in God and individualism are as ardently preached in market democracies. But Figure 14.2 is an illusion. Money can't buy you love. People need love—companionship—to be happy. It is accurate to assert that we cannot live happily without money in a world of markets, networks, and organizations. It is also fair to conclude that happiness depends on individual rights, dignity, and opportunity. But neither individualism nor money is enough for happiness.

From the first utilitarian thinkers centuries ago to economists, business executives, and market-enthralled politicians today, true believers of Figure 14.2 have popularized money as the touchstone of

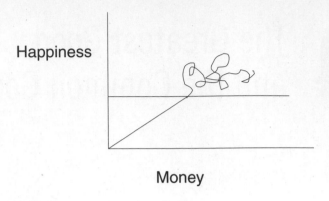

FIGURE 14-1
A both/and view of human happiness.

individual happiness. Their commandment puts value at the center of strategy and policy in market democracies. What gets measured, as the saying goes, gets done. Liberal market democracies measure value with great passion, and they outstrip other societal arrangements in producing wealth. Compared to communism, fascism, theocracy, and socialism, liberal market democracies perform brilliantly as engines of *value*. According to Figure 14.2, then, all the increased wealth should mean that people in liberal market democracies are the happiest of men and women in the best of all possible worlds.

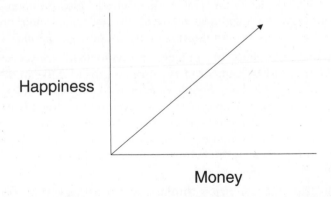

FIGURE 14-2
A value fundamentalist view of human happiness.

They are not. Here are some of their ills, as recounted by Robert Lane in *The Loss of Happiness in Market Democracies*:

- Major depression
- Feelings of hopelessness and insecurity
- Lack of trust in people and institutions
- Adolescent suicide
- Unhappy marriages

In chart after chart, Lane shows that misery indicators other than insufficient food and shelter are *higher* in market democracies. Food and shelter matter; he is not arguing to abolish markets or democracies. He is not promoting, say, Castro's Cuba. He is contending, however, that Figure 14.1—not Figure 14.2—captures the relationship between money and human happiness. Both/and, not either/or.

Lane makes a scholarly case for what most of us intuitively grasp: Companionship is key to happiness. Happy people have stable, caring relationships. Lane also includes human development and justice as nonmonetary sources of happiness. By human development, he means skills, mastery, and meaning—that is, being in control of one's destiny and deriving meaning from purpose. With justice, Lane incorporates other concerns such as fairness.[1]

According to Lane, prescriptions from orthodox economists come in one bottle: *value.* He calls this the *economistic fallacy—the conviction that happiness is proportionate to income.* Among people mesmerized by value fundamentalism, this fallacy is, interestingly, not considered ignorance. Rather, it is trumpeted as wisdom among those who look out onto the world and see only *value-creating markets battling value-destroying governments over the pursuit by individuals of value-denominated happiness.*

The economistic fallacy produces serious ills. Rarely, though, does it trigger flashbulb memories. People do not have to be evil to do evil, especially in our highly complex, interconnected world of markets, networks, organizations, friends, and families. I do not believe Ken Lay or Jeff Skilling of Enron were evil. Yet, their pursuit of shareholder value in the name of the economistic fallacy inspired strategies that robbed millions of families and friends of financial security and put millions through a traumatic energy crisis. People lost jobs because of Enron. Stress, insecurity, hopelessness, and

---

1. Robert Lane, *The Loss of Happiness in Market Democracies* (New Haven, CT: Yale Press, 2000), p. 6.

depression multiplied. So did mistrust in people and institutions. Marriages were tested; some failed.

Because business leaders like Skilling and Lay are not evil in the manner of Sadaam Hussein or Osama bin Ladin, their self-assured rectitude makes their value fundamentalism more insidious. Along with others who promote the economistic fallacy, they wield gross domestic product instead of weapons of mass destruction. They do not deal in violence. Quite the opposite. Value fundamentalists pipe sweet music into markets, networks, and organizations besotted with money and individualism. They promise happiness.

. . . .

Utilitarian doctrine seeks the greatest good for the greatest number. The founding principle is about good, not evil. Note, however, that the good equates with money, and the beneficiaries are individuals transacting in markets instead of thick we's who share fates. Here's how:

- Confronted with a choice between A and B, we are to select the one producing the greatest good for the greatest number of individuals.
- We must put A and B on a common footing.
- The common denominator is monetary value.
- We sum the monetary value possible in A versus B by establishing a value on the pros and cons of each choice across the individuals affected.
- We choose the winner.
- Individual happiness is maximized.

From Jeremy Bentham's 19th century felicific calculus forward, the exercise has toted up the positive value of individual pleasures, subtracted the negative value of individual pains, and summed both over the number of individuals affected. The great thing is putting value on all considerations, a value tuned to individuals seeking value-equated happiness in markets.

Utilitarianism and the economistic fallacy reinforce predictable beliefs and behaviors linked to shared roles in a world of purposes (see Chapters 6 and 7):

- *Customers seek value for money while ignoring how values of all kinds explain whether good things to have are good.* As did Enron customers, the Albany, New York mall shoppers described in Chapter 10 learned that negative differences between a brand promise and a brand experience trace to political, social, and other values baked into products, service, and ideas. Value packaged and delivered with questionable values tarnishes the market experiences of customers caught unaware. Energy promised for delivery vanishes. A T-shirt bought for self-expression also purchases arrest and incarceration.

■ *Investors seek shareholder value that belittles the human values explaining risk and return.* The dogma of shareholder value elevates the shared role of investor above customer and employee even as it deflects investor concern away from values. Under its dictates, "making a killing in the market" takes on literal possibilities: The Enron energy crisis, for example, jeopardized hospital operations. Concerns for the shareholder value of pharmaceutical companies and automobile manufacturers have risked the deaths of actual or potential customers. Value fundamentalism also isolates the role of investor to the private sector. Contributions to charity, for example, are not considered investments because they cannot build shareholder value (see Chapter 15).

■ *Employees work for money alone.* Utilitarianism took root in an industrializing England that brutally divorced labor from leisure. Bentham crafted his felicific calculus to respond to ills caused when work got stripped of stable, caring relationships, human development, and justice. But value fundamentalists ignore these origins and purposes. They see work merely as a means to get money in employment markets in which the greatest good for the greatest number is measured by salaries and wages, as opposed to participation in thick we's.

■ *Friends and family flee from values-less value.* Like the Colorado audience of Chapter 6, human beings obsessed with value as customers, investors, and employees divide up and balkanize their lives. The single, moneyed dimension of Figure 14.2 happiness leaves them no choice. According to the individualistic dictates of value fundamentalism and the economistic fallacy, people find companionship, mastery, meaning, justice, and fairness *only* in friends and family.

Utilitarianism does not devalue values. To the contrary, it *explicitly requires* the valuation of values. For example, around the same time the security guard and police officer jailed the T-shirt-wearing shopper in Albany, the White House Office of Management and Budget asked experts to put monetary values on civil liberties likely to suffer from the Administration's implementation of domestic security rules and regulations. Ethnic profiling, invasions of privacy, security checks, information gathering, expanded police authority—these and other policy choices affecting liberty, mobility, justice, and fairness were to undergo the cost/benefit examination of the greatest good for the greatest number. The analysis weighed the *value* of *individual* liberties lost against the *value* of *individual* security gained.

Voices from the libertarian right and the egalitarian left applauded, illustrating how thoroughly utilitarianism now pervades a public philosophy of individualism, value, and markets.[2] The main criticism was apprehension that the exercise might become bogged down in bureaucracy and slow the rush to lock down borders, tap into reams of personal information, and arrest Middle Eastern–looking people—as opposed, say, to any argument that political liberties are priceless and beyond the scale of value.

The exercise was not evil; that is not my point. My point is about the primacy of single answers in dangerous fundamentalism. Markets generate and distribute value. If we seek wise policy in the markets in which we live, we must weigh choices. We can usefully review from time to time, for example, whether the costs of airport procedures merit the benefits of security against terrorism. But value fundamentalists insist on answering *all* questions on the scale of money and monetary equivalence. All values—from political liberties to environmental protection to education to family—find *meaning* in value.

The metric is the objective. This is perhaps subtle as theory and logic, but not in everyday experience. In the White House scheme, abuses like that of the Albany security guard are lamentable costs assigned monetary value in calculating the greatest good for the greatest number. To the father and son, however, that experience—that abuse—was not abstract. Nor was it confined to money or things equivalent to money. It was not a commodity on which they would put a price.

Contemporary moral relativism worsens when values get weighed on *any* relative scale, including a scale of value. *We* in the thick sense thins into so many collectivities of I's focused on value. Customers and investors seek value. Employees go to work only to fund value-equated happiness. The thick we of organization is over-

---

2. *New York Times*, March 11, 2003.

looked; the thick we of family and friends is driven into either/or thinking. We wake up one day to see that the greatest good for the greatest number has evicted the common good from happiness.

. . . .

The common good of a thick we is not the same as the greatest good of a market, nation, or network. Consider family. Families are shared paths bound up by inescapable shared fates. The common good of family cannot reduce to the calculus of a single variable. Members of family consider family—*we*—a player in their pursuit of happiness. Families do not ignore individuals. But families do not atomize their thick we into a collectivity of I's. Families shape a common good—a shared happiness—through concern for *both* the I's of individual family members *and* the thick we of family.

Value counts in family. So do social, religious, political, and other values. Love, faith, learning, sacrifice, dignity, justice, and fairness pervade family, along with worries about money. A few years back, for example, a family member of a friend was threatened with homelessness. Others in the family pitched in to help. Cost mattered. They had to blend it with other values. But financial support was neither articulated nor attacked as a *tax,* as an unfair, *impersonal* transfer of value from some I's in the family to another I. That would have signaled deterioration in *family values*.

If happy families are all alike, the similarity comes from blending value and values together in the common good. Families are not markets. Individuals in families are not anonymous actors whose market preferences emerge without reference to, or interplay with, their thick we. Dissent is gritty and interpersonal in families (see Chapter 8). Yes, family members act from self-interest. Yes, they sometimes act surreptitiously or disconnectedly. Like Gyges in Chapter 5, they can disappear into markets, networks, and organizations to contradict or subvert family values. But, as long as people participate in families, they cannot escape the shared values, shared purposes, and shared fates of family—*of we as we.*

A single value like money corrodes the common good of families. So might religious belief, or the absolute rule of a parent, or any single answer. This happens. *But single-answer families are not happy families.* Fundamentalism destroys companionship, human development, justice, and, yes, financial value contributing to multidimensional happiness in families—just as surely as single answers wreak havoc in markets, networks, and organizations, or among friends.

There is no elegant single scale along which all family decisions are weighed. Thick we's are less artificial, more human affairs. Health care, spirituality, education, environmental awareness, entertainment, right and wrong, adventure—the issues in families are as infinite as life together in a thick we. Most involve money. But money is not the common denominator. Family is. *In the thick we's of families, friends, and organizations, "we" is the common denominator of the common good.*

. . . .

Like friends and family, thick we's of organizations pursue shared happiness in *their* common good. This includes, but goes beyond, money and value. Participating in thick we's of organizations (large and small, formal and informal) is essential to companionship, human development, mastery, meaning, justice, and fairness—to the pursuit of happiness depicted in Figure 14.1.

Companionship happens in shared paths (see Chapter 5). Other than friends and family, our shared paths arise in organizations. The men and women I met who had been downsized by early '90s market forces, for example, gathered in shared paths to help one another find jobs (see Chapter 11). They worried about money. But they also sought companionship. Employees, too, worry about money. We know this. But, as Lane notes, *companionship* is more important than pay in explaining happiness at work.

Organizations provide people the skills, judgement, mastery, and meaning necessary for happiness in a world of purposes. As discussed in Chapters 10 through 12, individuals must participate in thick we's to learn the skills and judgements of balancing self-interest with the common good that are necessary for liberty, democracy, and civil society. People also must participate in organizations to learn the technical, functional, problem-solving, decision-making and interpersonal skills demanded by mastery and meaning in a world framed by markets, networks, and organizations. Human development, mastery, and meaning is an organizational phenomenon—as much for rental car shuttle bus drivers and fast food service teams as executives running American Express Travelers Cheques or any other business. Even independent contractors, so-called free agents unaligned with any company, learn skills and attain mastery and meaning through collaborating with others in organized work.

Justice and fairness are normally thick we affairs, but not exclusively. Popularly shared ideas inordinately link justice and fairness to markets. We see and talk much about, say, the O.J. Simpson trial or the influence of money in markets for legal adjudication. We debate the fairness of markets that distribute unimaginably large portions of wealth to the top one percent of the population. As customers of organizations competing in legal markets, we experience justice and fairness personally. We experience right-to-life or other ideological, but not professional, judges who make decisions on personal or religious instead of legal grounds. When this happens, we shake our heads over injustice and unfairness.

Still, all these markets experiences explain less about our actual, everyday experience of justice and fairness than our participation in organizations. Balancing self-interest and the common good in thick we's is neither theoretical nor impersonal. Justice and fairness permeated the actions of my friend's construction crew with respect to the proselytizing born-again Christian (see Chapter 5). Teachers, administrators, and students alike gain first-hand, everyday exposure to justice and fairness when schools add cops to their thick we's (see Chapter 5). The downsized men and women I met in the early '90s asked themselves repeatedly about the justice and fairness of being terminated by their respective thick we's. Justice and fairness thread through a rich tapestry of life *together* in organizations—from project assignments, problem solving, work/life balance, and career advancement to performance reviews, training opportunities, and the reigning dogma of shareholder value.

Participating in thick we's is necessary to the individual pursuit of happiness. For this reason, governments should count all forms of organizational participation and not just jobs alone (see Census Tracking, Illustrative Suggestion #15, in Chapter 17). But, *the common good of a thick we is **not** merely the arithmetic sum of individual happiness.* Thick we's are not another form of market in which individuals maximize Figure 14.2 happiness through transactions with one another. Thick we's pursue *shared* purposes linked to shared fates. They seek *shared* happiness beyond the reach of atomization into a collectivity of I's.

. . . .

Organizations are the mid-level social formation bridging the happiness of individuals, friends, and families to the greater good of markets, networks, and nations. In our new world of purposes, the common good of thick we's in organizations is **the** glue thickening shared paths, shared roles, shared ideas, shared purposes, and shared fates into strong, predictable shared values in markets, networks, and nations—for good or ill or anything in between.

Organizations are crucibles within which the interests of customers, investors, networkers, family members, and friends blend into the common good of employees. Organizations provide thick we's the chance *to care about themselves through serving others*—a best part of enlightened self-interest for centuries. Organizations pursue shared purposes and shared success in these terms, and use shared roles along with shared paths and shared ideas to blend value and values in pursuit of their common good.

Today, *no organization on the planet can survive or thrive without blending value and values that ensure that the good in their common good supports sustainable and ethical performance.* As set forth in the Ethical Scorecard (see Illustrative Suggestion #1 in Chapter 17), organizations perform best when employees deliver value and values to customers, who generate returns for funders/shareholders/supporters, who provide opportunities for employees to deliver value and values to customers…, and so on, ad infinitum.

Sustainable success requires (1) the companionship, skills, and mastery necessary to make, sell, distribute, or service the good things to have that the organization provides; (2) being sufficiently accurate about the number and nature of customers and their needs; and (3) governing and solving problems *together* to blend value and values in a manner that justly and fairly balances self-interest with the common good. When organizations stumble, the failure *always* traces to insufficiencies in fellow-feeling, skills, strategies, and shared values—to either/or pursuits unduly favoring one constituency over others, one value over others, I over we.

Enron chased a common good dominated by concern for executive wealth and shareholder value. Their thick we enjoyed unsustainable short-term success, then stumbled and spread unhappiness through markets, networks, organizations, friends, and families. For decades, we recently learned, the FBI pursued a common good favoring prosecution, which was more accomplishable by its employees alone, over prevention, which demanded collaboration with other organizations. According to some in the FBI, this blend of value and values unduly increased vulnerability to terrorists. Toward the end of the '90s bubble years, we read repeatedly about dot-com organizations whose thick we's pursued a common good in which customers were given good things to have for free. From file-sharing teenagers to information-hungry investors, customers learned strong, predictable beliefs and behaviors that made the common good of such dot-coms unsustainable.

This balancing act is both the beauty and the bane of pursuing happiness in organizations. It reflects the tougher, half-full, half-empty reality of Figure 14.1 happiness: *How can people who live together in thick we's shaped by purposes rather than places pursue and achieve their common good?*

The greatest good and the common good differ much less for people who live together because of place—for example, in a remote village having no intercourse with the rest of the planet. Scholars, for example, might debate how well Jeremy Bentham's felicific calculus equated the common good of 19th century English shared paths, shared ideas, and shared roles into the greater good of an English nation in which place still prevailed over purpose as a force shaping thick we's. But we must think differently about we. Our thick we's are not place-based; they do not link to towns, villages, and nations. They do not have the lowest common denominator required for calculating the greatest good.

"We" is the common denominator of the common good. It is the highest, not lowest, denominator. While the thick we's of organizations reflect common patterns and concerns—for example, balancing and blending the interests of customers, shareholders/funders, and employees each has a unique version of their own common good. How Saab shapes and pursues its common good differs from the FBI or The Nature Conservancy or my friend's construction crew. There is no single dimension along which we can equate these and other unique versions of the common good in order to calculate a greatest good.

We can, however, ask if the common good of any organization contributes to the greatest good of markets, networks, and nations. We can ask if the blend of value and values in the brand promise and brand experience of the organization's common good is good. We—both as thick we's who pursue the common good and collectivities of I's who, as customers, shareholders, networkers, friends, and families, are served by that common good—can hold organizations to a higher standard than the value-obsessed happiness of individuals. When we do, we will enrich the common good of our thick we's with all the dimensions of human happiness on which the greater good depends. We will restore "we" to a sustainable partnership with "I" in pursuit of both the common good and the greater good.

15 Capital and Caring

Many years ago, a friend of mine joined a leveraged buy out firm. Leveraged buy out firms provide capital to management groups who purchase the companies they work for. The managers hope to get rich; they pay close attention to financial performance. Shareholder value, however, is not fundamentalist dogma to my friend. He believes the pursuit of shareholder value for its own sake destroys the dreams that inspire managers and those who work with them. The financial performance of the thick we's in whom my friend invests both flows from and contributes to organizational skills, strategies, and shared values advancing the interests of investors, customers, and employees. My friend is a capitalist. He believes he succeeds, however, *only* when he invests capital in a thick we who care about themselves and others.

I thought of my friend in 2002 when I read Charles Handy's article, "What's a Business For?"[1] Handy opens with a second question, "Could capitalists actually bring down capitalism?" He answers by warning against a shareholder value fundamentalism that estranges capital from caring—a capitalism that butchers the human ties connecting an organization's common good with the greater good of

---

1. Charles Handy, "What's a Business For?" *Harvard Business Review* (December 2002).

markets, networks, and nations. In this uncaring capitalism, "all businesses become cash flow generators" (see Chapter 7).

Handy explains that ancient laws of property and contract combine with shareholder value fundamentalism to elevate the role of shareholder above the roles of customer and, especially, employee. Legally, he notes, shareholders own a company's assets. Meanwhile, according to a widely shared idea, *employees are a company's most important assets*. The logic here is punishing. Shareholders own employees, or at least, the person-hours of people at work—positions more in line with 18th through 20th century capitalism than our 21st century world of purposes.

Business leaders, however, do not intend to promote wage slavery when they exclaim, "People are our most important assets!" They wish to inspire people, not dehumanize them. The widely shared idea and the senseless logic it implies beg examination. On closer view, we see that *people* increasingly explain the difference between organization success and failure. As discussed in Chapter 13, today's competitive environment yields best to thick we's who use skills, knowledge, and shared values to define and solve problems. Machinery and equipment matter. But, contrary to the dictates of capitalism from the 18th through most of the 20th century, success in 21st century organizations demands marrying capital to thick we's who care instead of capitalizing on machinery and workers who, in the manner of *Modern Times*, are cogs in that machinery (see Chapter 13).

Capital markets and their supporting legal framework emerged in a world of places where owners normally participated in the businesses they owned. This was not always true, of course. The idea of providing capital to a business without participating in that business is centuries old. But, in our world of purposes, the rule and the exception are reversed. *This reversal is inevitable in a world of markets, networks, and organizations.* Tens of millions of individual and institutional shareholders residing across the globe currently have financial interests in companies in which they otherwise do not participate. This is our reality—a reality that signals great opportunity because the more impersonal the connection between *most* shareholders and the thick we's they have capitalized, the more likely capital markets raise and redistribute money efficiently and effectively.

Note, though, the italicized *most*. In capital markets that effectively fund thick we's who care, *most* shareholders do not participate in the thick we's of the organizations whose financial instruments they hold. Capital markets, though, like many markets, gain from intermediary organizations ("middlemen") like my friend's leveraged buy out firm. These organizations—these thick we's—make it their common good to gather capital and oversee investments. Our world benefits when those thick we's take an active interest in the affairs of the thick we's—the organizations—they fund. The benefits, though, depend mightily on the investment philosophy of the thick we gathering and redistributing capital. Some active investors pursue both value and values. Others seek only shareholder value.

We cannot increase the capital available to thick we's who care if we restrict capital investment to people who participate in the thick we's they capitalize. The relationship between employees and *most* shareholders *must* differ from the owner/worker relationship in a world of places. Handy challenges us to reform legal arrangements to better line up with this new reality. He believes we must square the legal and financial ownership interest of shareholders with the ethical ownership interest of employees.

Thick we's *own* the common good of their companies. *They* define and implement it. According to another widely shared idea, employees must *take ownership* of the problems and purposes they tackle. The rest of us as investors, customers, networkers, friends, and families *must* hold employees accountable for whether the good things they promise *are* good. As illustrated by stories from Enron to the FBI, from the American Red Cross to WorldCom, we suffer when thick we's pursue narrow value alone. Our ability to find sustainable blends of value and values, however, is threatened by shareholder value fundamentalists who manipulate the legal and financial interests of shareholders to split off and subordinate the ethical ownership interests of employees. Instead of marrying capital to caring, active investors obsessed with value open the door to a single answer to Handy's first question:

What's a business for?

Shareholder value.

Shareholder value fundamentalism is a failure of capital markets. To understand it, though, we must begin with what is obvious: *All markets succeed and fail.* The root causes of success often explain failure too. All markets, for example, innovate, differentiate, and segment. One of the spectacular successes of capital markets over the past quarter-century came from an innovation that packaged up home mortgages to create securities that attracted a huge pool of investors. By standardizing credit qualifications and putting together mortgages with similar characteristics, financial intermediaries fostered an enormous market in mortgage-backed securities. As a consequence, billions of dollars of capital flowed to housing markets that otherwise might have remained idle, or even nonexistent.

Mortgage-backed securities illustrate a broader innovation in capital markets called derivatives. Derivatives are financial instruments (e.g., securities) that derive from other instruments (e.g., home mortgages). Derivatives have multiplied in number and nature beyond comprehension. They have inspired additional innovations (for example, so-called synthetic securities). Sometimes, these innovations effectively marry capital to caring. Other times, they do not. Some of our most spectacular capital market failures in recent years have traced to derivatives that dangerously divided value from values. Enron, for example, irresponsibly traded in derivatives linked to energy contracts—which my leveraged buy out friend once characterized as converting energy markets into casinos.

Innovation, differentiation, and segmentation explain success and failure in most markets. Handy, for example, notes that stock options differentiated and attracted talent in employment markets in the '90s. In 1980, two percent of executives had stock options; by 2002, 60 percent did.[2] Stock options are not inherently evil. They triggered success as well as failure in employment markets. Markets powered by innovation, differentiation, and segmentation subdivide across a spectrum serving high-end to low-end customer segments, where high and low link to price. Some people shop at Tiffany's; many more shop at Wal-Mart.

But, in every market, differentiation and segmentation also leave some people and some potentially new good things to have out of the equation. Pharmaceutical companies fail to distribute drugs to people falling below the low-end of the market. Notwithstanding mortgage-backed securities, housing markets exclude millions who cannot afford low-end offerings. Meanwhile, customers who can afford potential products and services—for example, new drugs or medical tools and procedures—go without them because companies choose not to make them part of the good things to have they provide. Drivers who could afford low- to high-end vehicles

2.   Ibid., p. 50.

went years without airbags and other safety equipment. Today, tens of millions of potential customers go without good things to have because (1) existing thick we's choose not to provide them, and (2) potential thick we's who care enough to try to do so lack access to capital.

No organization can do everything. Thick we's who care *must* choose what they will and will not do and who they will and will not serve. They must have a strategy that matches their skills and shared values to market opportunities in a manner than can achieve sustainable success. Gaps are inevitable. Sometimes gaps stretch across industries to foster huge market failures. Those, too, however, can explain market success. When businesses choose against offering good things to have to some customers or ignore potential new products and services, other businesses gain opportunities. Xerox chose not to invest in personal distributed computing. Apple, IBM, Compaq, Dell, and Gateway chose differently. A market failure turned into a market success.

That success in computing, in turn, has produced a market failure. Today, millions of children fall below the low end of the personal computer market. They lack access to the digital technology embedded in our world of markets, networks, organizations, friends, and families. Such children live on the wrong side of the *digital divide*. Excluding them is a potentially tragic failure of markets. But, as always, it also represents a spectacular opportunity—if only enough thick we's *with access to capital* care enough to convert strategies for closing the digital divide into reality. Both market success and market failure, then, trace to thick we's who care about serving others and who have access to the capital they need to succeed.

. . . .

Tens of millions of people in market democracies live in poverty. Estimates suggest *more than 50 percent of children in the United States are poor.* Up to 40 million Americans go without health insurance. As of this writing, more than 10 million adults cannot find work in employment markets, and millions of them have quit looking. Millions more are homeless or cannot find affordable housing, including a surprising number who once could. A friend who runs a community development organization, for example, recently told me about an accountant hired to do the company audit. A few days into the effort, the accountant came into my friend's office, closed the door from embarrassment, and asked if, by any chance, *he* might qualify for assistance. According to widely shared ideas, only the very poor need housing subsidies. That is a mistake, a widely shared misunderstanding that reinforces certain strong shared values now at odds with increasing the number of people who lead good lives in a world of markets, networks, and organizations.

All these statistics reflect market failures. So, too, do any number of *potential* innovations currently not funded by capital markets. I am aware, for example, of thick we's with ideas from new cooking technologies to new forms of education and entertainment, from financial instruments to put affordable housing within reach to customer feedback technologies to assist governmental service organizations. Both opportunity and failure, then, sit at the margin of markets—at the edge beyond which existing or new good things promise satisfaction to customers with unmet needs.

Neither new nor existing good things reach potential customers, however, without marrying capital to caring thick we's. Unless some thick we who cares, like my friend's leveraged buy out firm, gathers capital and invests in another thick we who cares, like my other friend's community development organization, market failure does not give way to market success. The particular pairing just mentioned, though, is unlikely. Leveraged buy out firms participate in private-sector capital markets. They invest in for-profit, instead of nonprofit or governmental, organizations.

This makes sense. Yet, it is a blight of shareholder value and other prevailing single answers that combine to narrow instead of enlarge the vision of capital markets. In our understandable excitement over private sector innovations, such as cell phones, laser eye surgery, graphite skis, the Atkins diet, instant messaging, and new cooking technologies, we *ignore* how reliant the greater good of our world of purposes is on the common good of governmental and not-for-profit organizations too. In the '90s, for example, private sector housing and financial markets failed to serve a growing number of single women who had the wherewithal to borrow money. Working with governmental organizations, many nonprofit thick we's cared enough to meet their needs. As a consequence, market failure turned into market success. Tens of thousands of women found housing for themselves and their children.

Private sector financial institutions eventually learned how to serve these women profitably. Once that occurred, private sector capital markets invested in for-profit thick we's who cared. But, such investments transpired *only after* governmental and nonprofit thick we's made it part of their common good to serve a segment of the market theretofore left out. Governmental and nonprofit thick we's, then, also play an essential role in converting market failure into market success. *They, too, need capital to convert caring into good things to have.* Yet, notwithstanding the success of this and other innovations, capital markets do not rush to invest in governmental and nonprofit thick we's.

. . . .

Organizations need capital to provide good things to have. Some need more, and some need less. A community development organization cannot help families find affordable housing without a great deal of capital. The volunteer fire company a mile from my house needs less capital. Still, fire trucks cost a lot more than automobiles. In North America, hundreds of thousands of nonprofit thick we's need capital. But, the markets supplying that capital are so horrendously antiquated that many people are startled when they hear or read "capital markets" and "nonprofit organizations" in the same sentence.

I first experienced the adverse effects of broken not-for-profit capital markets as a board member of Bronx Educational Services, a literacy organization in New York City. BES was crystal clear about their common good: They helped adults move from zero literacy to second- or third-grade levels before referring them to other, more numerous nonprofits specializing in assisting adults reach sixth-grade literacy. (Many experts agree that sixth-grade literacy assures reasonable functionality for getting and holding a job, raising kids, serving on a jury, voting, and so forth.)

Every year, finding the money to fund BES was a patchwork drama that consumed the Executive Director, his staff, and the Board. At the time I joined, BES had a 15-year track record of success. Yet, unlike executives in established private sector organizations, the Executive Director of BES spent a quarter to a third of his time, attention, and energy raising money. Moreover, he and others at BES had to raise money in retail instead of wholesale ways—that is, by asking individuals, foundations, government organizations, and corporations separately and directly instead of approaching "middlemen" organizations such as my friend's leveraged buy out firm.

In contrast, private sector executives can tap into wholesale capital markets. Leaders of start-ups aside, private sector executives do not spend huge portions of their energy searching for money to fund each year's operations. Do they pay attention to financial markets? Do they speak to analysts and track their company stock? Of course. Unlike the Executive Director of BES, though, private sector CEOs and presidents concentrate on vision, strategy, talent, joint ventures, outsourcing, technology, change management, and other critical factors determining company performance. They worry about budgets, but they don't spend the better part of *every week* raising money.

In my years with BES, the good news was that a number of individual contributors reliably gave a small percentage of annually required funds. But the bad news—the news characteristic of life in nonprofit organizations—was that the lion's share of each year's budget inevitably depended on a shifting hodgepodge of funding from:

- *Government Organizations*: Various local, state, and federal government organizations invested money, conditioned on BES meeting a variety of requirements regarding who got served and how. While some grants extended beyond one year, all were subject to shifts in the policies and priorities of those who administered the grants, as well as elected legislatures and executives.

- *Foundations*: Tens of thousands of foundations in the United States are required by law to give away a small percentage of capital each year. Like any thick we who cares, foundations establish missions and strategies that define focus. Over the years, BES grew knowledgeable about foundations with missions that, at least arguably, covered adult literacy. Rarely, however, do foundations provide commitments of capital in the manner of my friend's leveraged buy out firm. Many deploy funds primarily to assist nonprofits in proving that new ideas, products, and services work. Once the new concept is proven, the foundation moves on to other organizations with other new ideas.

- *Corporations*: A long tradition from worlds of places encourages corporations to fund local nonprofits. As markets, networks, and organizations have dissolved the bonds of place, however, corporate funding patterns have shifted. Shareholder value fundamentalism has driven many corporations to reduce or eliminate funding for nonprofits. Other corporations seek to connect the purposes of the nonprofit to the brand of the corporation. IBM, for example, provided funds for BES to experiment with technology.

The strings attached to investments by government organizations, foundations, and corporations often crisscross one another and make the operations of nonprofits like BES far more complex than their size would normally suggest. A nonprofit organization with an annual budget of a few million dollars, for example, often must provide a greater number of products and services to a wider range of customers than comparably sized for-profit organizations. In addition, nonprofits routinely face information and record keeping requirements that far outstrip what for-profit organizations of similar size would consider sane.

In addition to complexity, nonprofits struggle against built-in frustration. "Proof of concept" grants, for example, *design in fiscal failure as a likely consequence of innovative success*. Ideas that prove useful to customers generate demand that, perversely, must garner different funding to remain operational. Innovative responses to market failures die from lack of ongoing support. Each year, BES obtained some "proof of concept" grants. One I remember sought to demonstrate the effectiveness of software applications. Many adults benefited from the applications. But computers, software, and associated teaching and support skills cost money *every year*. Moreover, the funds needed *increase* with growth in customer demand. Like most nonprofits, BES knew, even as it took the original money, that success would not ensure continuation.

Similar travails happen in the private sector. Mostly, though, they bedevil start-up enterprises whose CEOs devote significant effort to raising capital. They, however, have access to private sector capital markets. While securities laws impose constraints, start-ups do not contend with confusing restrictions about who they wish to serve and how they wish to serve them. Those choices are left up to the thick we's who govern the day-to-day affairs of their organizations. Moreover, having raised sufficient capital to prove innovations, companies can return to efficient capital markets for funds needed to widen and commercialize success. *Start-ups have a chance to evolve beyond the start-up stage.* Nonprofit thick we's, in contrast, *regularly* succeed with innovation only to remain stuck in start-up mode.

The inefficiency and ineffectiveness of nonprofit capital markets begets inefficiency and ineffectiveness in nonprofit industries:

- Only a sliver of the hundreds of thousands of nonprofit organizations in North America have annual budgets in the *tens* of millions of dollars. In contrast, the annual resources of thousands of private sector organizations exceed a *billion* dollars.

- The top 200 nonprofit organizations providing products and services explain *less than one-tenth of one percent* of the world's economic activity; the top 200 private sector organizations account for more than a *quarter* of it.
- The largest two to five organizations in many private sector industries hold 30 to 70 percent of the market. It is rare for a handful of nonprofit organizations to account for more than 10 percent of any market.

Industry concentration explains market success as well as market failure. We know, for example, that we must avoid the evils of monopoly and oligopoly. But concentrated industry structure helps to establish best practices. Over the past few decades, concentrated industry structures have facilitated the spread of brand, outsourcing, strategic alliances, information technology, quality, reengineering, and other *democratic* approaches to good performance.

Innovation *is* a tough challenge in large enterprises. As Clayton Christensen writes in *The Innovator's Dilemma*, people with new ideas to offer large organizations must overcome established profit streams and entrenched skills, strategies, and shared values. Such hurdles went a long way to explain the failure of Xerox to take advantage of personal distributed computing. Still, many innovations do wend their way through large organizations. Meanwhile, *concentrated industry structures facilitate the spread of successful innovations first done in smaller organizations*. Big industry players often excel at what's called *fast following*—that is, adopting the innovations of others. Many banks, for example, were fast followers of the governmental and nonprofit thick we's who figured out how to serve single women looking for affordable housing.

This example of fast following, however, is exceptional. Unlike their for-profit counterparts, nonprofit thick we's who successfully innovate encounter frustration more often than of excellence. There are extremely few large nonprofit "fast followers." Instead, too many market failures *stay market failures* because nonprofit thick we's who care lack access to efficient and effective capital markets and remain stuck in equally inefficient and ineffective industries.

. . . .

One reason people stumble over joining "capital markets" to "nonprofit organizations" lies in the adjective *nonprofit*. How, we ask, can capital markets operate in the absence of profits?

Actually, millions of shareholders trade in capital markets every day without attending to the profitability of companies whose financial instruments they hold. Millions decide to buy, sell, or hold securities every day on indicators other than profitability, including revenues, hits to a Web site, number of customers, entry into new markets, market share, innovation, technology, government regulations, lawsuits, and geopolitical events. Hundreds of investment theories ignore even these indicators in favor of analyzing movements in capital markets that have nothing whatsoever to do with organization performance.

We must distinguish capital provided to organizations by *active investors*, like my friend's leveraged buy out firm, versus capital provided by shareholders seeking gains *in markets*. Capital market effectiveness depends on both individuals and institutions who trade in capital markets, and active investors who capitalize thick we's. Active investors are concerned with profitability. But, as reviewed in Chapter 7, the *sustainable performance* of companies reflects a zillion factors in addition to profitability. Today, for example, many active investors pay more attention to the strength and predictability of an organization's cash position than to accounting-based profits. But, take note: *All* organizations, *including nonprofits*, have cash flows; all *can* build sustainable and predictable cash positions. Bond markets, for example, already provide capital to nonprofits whose balance sheets and cash flows merit the risks taken.

Efficient and effective capital markets, then, are not beholden to profits. They do, however, rely on (1) gathering capital from millions of shareholders who seek to gain in markets, (2) active investors who provide capital to thick we's who care, and (3) thick we's who combine strategies, skills, and shared values to deliver sustainable performance, both financial and otherwise. Current not-for-profit capital markets are deficient in the first two conditions—and that, in turn, causes too many organizations to fail to satisfy the third.

I recommend two possible approaches to improve these conditions (see Illustrative Suggestions #12 and #13 in Chapter 17). Through legalizing *dynamic deductability*, we can build large pools of not-for-profit capital supplied by investors who buy and trade instruments whose price at the time of sale, not the time of purchase, sets the amount of taxes saved through charitable deductions. In addition, foundations, corporations, and wealthy individuals can form leagues (somewhat analogous to professional sports leagues) whose members agree to provide capital over sustained periods to nonprofit organizations who meet certain performance criteria. Whether through these or other innovations, however, the growth and effectiveness of nonprofit thick we's who care in converting market failures into market successes depends mightily on reforming today's ineffective and inefficient nonprofit capital markets.

. . . .

Enacting laws to foster a capital market in dynamically deductible units requires government action. Government action also shapes how capital markets fund governmental organizations who might respond to market failures. Currently in the United States, for example, the federal government uses tax and other policies to invest capital in governmental, as well as nongovernmental, organizations focused on homeland security. The September 11, 2001, terrorist attacks revealed a serious failure in the markets, networks, and organizations responsible for security. The federal government chose to respond to this failure; it chose to use governmental resources and authority instead of trusting exclusively to private sector capital markets and private sector thick we's to get the job done.

All of us know that such choices—from the War on Poverty to the War on Terrorism—emerge from organizations and political parties that compete in markets and networks for political control of government policy. There are, of course, many market failures in addition to homeland security. Each offers opportunities for government organizations—working alone or together with not-for-profit and for-profit thick we's—to convert failure into success through innovation, differentiation, and segmentation. One leader of an affordable housing nonprofit, for example, wryly suggested in early 2002 that his and other organizations combine to promote a new policy in markets for political control: "No homeland security without a home."

Were such an alliance to try, however, their success would turn on defeating single-answer fundamentalists who promote shareholder value, utilitarianism, the economistic fallacy, and the cult of individualism to narrow instead of widen the capital invested in governmental and not-for-profit thick we's who care. These men and women—and the advocacy and other organizations they lead—have highly recognizable and predictable shared values including:

- *Market idolatry*: Markets are superior to governments. Governments can neither command nor otherwise manage markets. Governments can encourage or induce lower costs. Governments can reward innovation. But governments must stay out of markets if individuals are to reap the greatest good for the greatest number.
- *Individual responsibility and opportunity*: Markets provide opportunities for individual happiness. Governments guarantee individual liberty and opportunity to participate in markets. But governments must avoid policies that stifle individualism. Yes, some individuals fail. That is too bad. But it is the price paid for individual liberty and market value. We must look to markets, not governments, to show compassion to such people. Volunteers arise, who—in the self-interested pursuit of happiness—put a value on charity and lend a hand. A thousand points of light shine in markets powered by individualism.
- *Value-denominated unfairness, inefficiency, and insult*: Governments cannot afford to care for individuals who must care for themselves. Governments might help the *neediest*—but, really, governments should reject that option because it insults the dignity of the individuals aided. It also unfairly transfers value from individuals who take care of themselves to individuals who do not. Government is an inefficient, morally bad actor in markets. *Government has no value*. Its only purposes are procedural fairness, content neutrality, and security. The government that governs best governs least—or, actually, not at all. The best government would be no government—an ideal condition for maximizing individual pursuits of value-denominated happiness in markets.

"No homeland security without a home" contradicts these shared values. Were an alliance of organizations to float this policy, we can be certain that single-answer politicians, advocacy organizations, parties, lobbyists, talk radio hosts, and various media celebrities would attack it as big government, socialist, left wing, liberal, anti-individual, anti-market, and anti-family.

They also would trot out another widely shared idea: *the small town*. According to this popular illusion, people share values because they live together in small towns and neighborhoods. People reach out to neighbors in need. Government—especially big government—destroys neighborliness. Governments frustrate individual pursuits of happiness and corrode the shared values of *place*—of school, church, social club, and picnics in the park.

Government housing programs do not fit this imagery. Nor do any government programs directed at market failures other than security. According to the orthodoxy's dreamscape, happiness exists in neighborly, faith-based volunteerism and a thousand points of light. Those who promote the orthodoxy ask us to *see* houses being raised for those in need by their friends and neighbors—*just like in the 19th century of legend*.

There is a catch to all this: reality. Not the reality of reality TV, though. *We do not live in a world of places*. Nor, indeed, does the sweet imagery being marketed match up well with the *actual* experiences of people who still *do* live in places. It all makes for a powerful brand, however. It sells values and *imaginary we's*. It appeals to various collectivities of I's (see Chapter 10)—thin, not thick, we's who like to believe there is some world of places they can move *back to* if only they find the right job, get that raise, make a killing in the stock market, and use their money to move next door to *those* neighbors.

. . . .

Toward the conclusion of his article, Charles Handy cites logic, law, and common sense to remind us that businesses exist for purposes beyond making money. Businesses, from the inception of capitalism on, have sought to make some difference to society—both through avoiding harm and caring enough to provide good things to have to selected customers. That, Handy argues, answers "What's a business for?"

His question is essential. Nonetheless, I think we must expand it. In a world of markets, networks, organizations, friends, and families, we must not only ask, "What's a business for?" We must ask, "What's an organization for?" This book offers many responses. Organizations provide us the opportunity to participate in thick we's who inescapably share fates. Organizations are our "towns," our mid-level political formations in which we balance individual self-interest with a common good shaped in substantive, as well as procedural, ways. Organizations are communities in which we pursue many of life's purposes. Organizations sustain and promote shared social, political, and economic values critical to democracy and civil society.

Organizations also give us the chance to participate in a thick we who cares. Some thick we's, like my friend's leveraged buy out organization, care about gathering and investing capital. Others, like Xerox, care about helping individuals and organizations with documents. Others care about making and selling Beanie Babies. Others care about preschool kids. And still others care about helping people find affordable housing.

I mention Beanie Babies to remind us that innovation, segmentation, and differentiation produce infinite variety. As mentioned in Chapter 9, our world of purposes can talk about pursuing an aspiration for "a market of one"; a world in which each and every one of *your* particular needs from the trivial to the profound is met in highly customized ways. That may be impossible to achieve. But the aspiration speaks to—indeed, it drives—how markets, networks, and organizations can convert market failures into market successes *as long as capital finds thick we's who care.*

Among the tragedies of our reigning orthodoxy is the widely shared misunderstanding that the *ideas* of markets, networks, and organizations refer *only* to the for-profit sector. The orthodoxy answers, "What's a governmental organization for?" with, "Nothing except proceduralism and security." The orthodoxy answers, "What's a nonprofit organization for?" with nostalgic, place-based shared ideas about small towns and neighbors, and a thousand points of light forever cut off from the power of efficient and effective capital markets.

The orthodoxy answers, "What's a business for?" with, "Shareholder value." Those who promote value, markets, and extreme individualism succeed in building great value for themselves. They condemn the rest of us, however—including many people in collectivities of I's who unwittingly support such single answers—to unnecessary and hurtful market failures. There is no market failure that thick we's cannot solve if they care enough and gain access to capital. That is a glory of our new world of purposes. It is, however, a vision of value and values that *sees* real instead of imaginary we's who care enough to help themselves by helping others.

16 So What?

This chapter sets forth a strategy for reintegrating value and values in our world of purposes. The strategy asks thick we's in organizations to hold themselves accountable for connecting how their common good contributes to the greater good of markets, nations, networks, organizations, friends, and families. It also asks consumers, voters, investors, networkers, friends, and families to reward those organizations that take that initiative. A number of illustrative suggestions follow this chapter. We might or might not act on any of them. We *must*, however, pursue some strategy like the one described here. The future of the planet now depends on it.

Act in markets, networks, organizations, friends, and family.

In *The Prince*, Machiavelli trashed philosophers who promoted imaginary instead of real republics. He exhorted princes to gain, hold, and use power in the real world. He advised a ruler he hoped would retain power in the chaos of 16th century Florence. This book, in contrast, is neither solely for rulers nor strictly about virtue, vice, and power. I write for people who lead and follow, and who act as I's in addition to we's. My first "So What?", though, comes straight from *The Prince*: As I's and we's, when we lead and when we follow, we *must act in our real world of purposes instead of imaginary worlds of places that have passed us by.*

Hundreds of millions of us now live in markets, networks, organizations, friends, and families, constellations of social formations that have defused the power of place to bind us together with shared fates and shared values. Billions of other people continue to live—and share fates—in a world of place. Millions of them still populate particular places in mostly developed nations, such as the United States and Germany, as well as not yet fully developed ones, like Congo, Indonesia, and Brazil. For them, but not for us, place-based social formations of village, town, and neighborhood remain real—not imaginary—thick we's.

Markets, networks, and organizations give structure to our world more than towns and neighborhoods. *This has happened*. We experience neither community nor polis in places (see Chapters 11 and 12). If we wish to make the places we reside more conducive to good lives, we must act in and through markets, networks, and organizations. When, with Machiavelli, we ask "So what should we do about our circumstances?", our first answer acknowledges the real—not imaginary—social formations in which we actually live the whole or major parts of our lives. *We must get real.*

Chapter 2 provides one guide for choosing the balance of purpose and place in *your* life. It helps solve a critical, initial question: *What world do you live in?* Without knowing the answer, you cannot solve problems caused by the split between value and values. It is a mistake to assume that solutions fitting a world of places will solve problems dictated by a world of purposes. Chapter 2 helps you see your world as it is so that you and others can act in it.

Ours is not a tidy world. It cannot be analogized to nesting Chinese boxes or Russian dolls. I recall a college professor with whom I served on a commission to reform university governance 30 years ago. He eulogized college as a microcosm of the greater world. The professor believed young men and women chosen to lead took positions atop collegiate pyramids that nested neatly within other collegiate pyramids that, in turn, sat within yet larger, more encompassing pyramids. The recommendations of the Governance Commission, he stressed, ought to preserve this structure to best prepare leaders for responsibilities in cities and towns neatly nesting within counties and states and, ultimately, nations and the world.

Even then a discordant nostalgia sounded in his song. Nesting boxes and collegiate pyramids were fragmenting under demographic, financial, technological, environmental, and political forces, spawning a messier world of markets, networks, organizations, friends, and families. The jurisdictional boundaries that gave skeletal form to a world of places were disintegrating. By the '90s, all comprehensibility as bone structure was gone. Spaghetti, worms, miasmic webs, Jackson Pollock paintings—plenty of images portray the kaleidoscopic world of markets, networks, organizations, friends, and families. But none depict neat, nesting places.

Place-based proximity no longer dictates shared fates for millions of people. Centrifugal forces have isolated age-old sources of shared values from one another, sources previously blended by the power of place. Shared paths at home bear no relation to those at work (see Chapter 5). Other than family member and friend, shared roles have mutated from neighbor and citizen to consumer, investor, networker, and employee (see Chapters 6 and 7). These strong shared roles yield strong shared values, but differentially across shifting contexts. Value prevails over values among consumers and investors; values govern shared ideas of the hearth. Balancing work and family captures only one part of our age's characteristic contest: how best—and pragmatically—to integrate value and values in good lives so differently constructed?

Dizzying forces in markets, networks, and organizations have made cancerous growth rates seem, if anything, too measured a description for the pace at which information, ideas, and knowledge has exploded. Ignorance has jumped yardsticks. In the Information Age, ignorance scales to a lack of information and the use of disinformation rather than an absence of ideas or expertise. As Anthony Giddens notes, abundant expertise is a consequence of a modernity built on markets, networks, and organizations.[1] Instead of unavailable answers, our dilemma orbits around trust and reliability: *Will the experts to whom consumers and investors must bring do-it-for-me motivations act in the best interests of all? Will experts and the organizations in which they participate provide good things to have where good means more than value for money and financial return on investment?*

Like Machiavelli's audience, today's leaders tangle over power. But our age has reconstituted who are the princes, where are their principalities, and what are the limits of their power. Our leaders are

---

1. Anthony Giddens, *The Consequences of Modernity* (Stanford: Stanford University Press, 1990), p. 27.

executives, not royalty. They rule *organizations* competing in governmental, not-for-profit, and private markets and networks. Organizations are the principalities in which leaders blend virtue and vice in pursuit of power. In a world where virtually all the material and immaterial basis of life is mediated through products, services, and ideas provided by organizations, organizations hold the *essential* answers to what good means, and how it is developed, deployed, and experienced (see Chapter 9).

Our princes, too, have tremendous power over the good. Yet, unlike princes in the 16th century, our leaders have but partial and selective power over us. Leaders of organizations—like everyone else—live in a kaleidoscopic world of markets, networks, organizations, friends, and families. Individuals are not wholly ruled by any single leader. We have been liberated from the imprisoning effects of place and rulers of places. In lives spread across markets, networks, organizations, families, and friends, individuals must *self-consciously choose* to submit the whole of their life purposes to single leaders—or to single answers. We have words for those who do: cultists and fundamentalists.

Most of us do not make that choice. Most of us choose to rule ourselves. The fate of the planet, though, now depends on how well we succeed individually and together. With individual freedom comes individual risk and individual responsibility. In the language of the '60s, *we must get it together.* Neither place nor the rulers of places, however, assist as they once did. People do not get it together—individually or with others—because of place. In our real world, individuals have great opportunity, but have lost the stabilizing anchor of place-based conformity—again, for good and ill. As Kenneth Gergen writes in *The Saturated Self,* people struggle to make sense of individual lives beset by a crazy quilt of relationships, roles, and ideas no longer harmonized by place. Nor does place dictate the shared fates required for individuals to get it together *with others*. Places have emptied of thick we values.

"No man is an island entire of itself," John Donne cautioned a century after Machiavelli wrote *The Prince.* "Every man is a piece of the continent." Donne, like Machiavelli, spoke to people who shared fates in places. That was their world. It is not ours. We live as pieces not of continents but of markets, networks, and organizations. Our lives benefit and suffer each day by how well tens of millions of us blend value and values in *these* social formations. The bells we ring toll for humanity in *this* reality. As a Red Cross volunteer described in the summer of 2000 (see Chapter 3), the globe now sits on the front porch. There is no place to hide. Nor, however, are there *places* we can look for answers. *We must find solutions for the problems and opportunities created by markets, networks, and organizations in markets, networks, and organizations, instead of imaginary republics of places that have passed us by.*

Do not confuse collectivities of I's with thick we's.

We can heal the rift between value and values in our new world of purposes. But we must first acknowledge who "we" are. Or, rather, we must learn when we are a thick we, and when we are a thin we, a collectivity of I's. Shared paths are thick we's. When we persistently interact with a consistent set of people known to us by name, shared beliefs and behaviors wax in strength (whether good, bad, or in between). Shared paths, however, never encompass large numbers. Above 10 to 20 people, the conditions of persistency and consistency break down.

Nor can shared paths alone explain the shared values of larger societies. For that, we must consult shared roles, shared ideas, shared resources, shared purposes, and shared fates in addition to shared paths. In worlds where people share ideas, roles, resources, purposes, and fates because of places, shared paths weave into the larger we's of town and neighborhood, city, and state. Place blends religious, ethnic, national, political, and other values to forge thick we's who, as Avishai Margolit writes, care about and hate one another. In a world of purposes, by contrast, the inescapable shared fates necessary to thick we's occur among friends and families, and in organizations. Our cares and animosities arise in them. We are more familiar with Coke versus Pepsi than the Hutu versus the Tutsi. We know that Germany and France were mortal enemies many times—*in the olden days*. But we do not expect them to go to war *ever* again. In a world of purposes, we do not *hate* people in the thick we's of other organizations. We compete against them.

Nor can we explain shared values by referring only to individuals, small groups, markets, networks, and nations. Such descriptions are at once too small and too large for completeness. They fail to account for *inevitable* mid-level social formations that weave small and large together. De Tocqueville, for example, considered towns and associations vital to 19th century American democracy (see Chapter 12). Similar observations apply to oligarchies, monarchies, tyrannies, and theocracies. The immense Soviet Union was just that: a union of mid-level social formations called soviets. Large societies are unsustainable without mid-level formations. *If they disappear, societies de-stabilize until new ones emerge.*

This has happened. Mid-level social formations grounded in place have atomized. Structures that once made sense—local government, neighborhood, community—destabilized. Individuals began bowling alone in markets. An extreme cult of individualism took hold. Powerful shared ideas promoted collectivities of I's and nostalgic, but imaginary, places as the social formations linking us together. But neither succeed because neither binds us with inescapable shared fates. Small town and neighborhood are shared ideas disconnected from actual shared lives. Collectivities of I's are thin we's that number people with similar interests but not shared fates.

This instability will persist until we recognize that organizations, not collectivities of I's, are the thick we's in which we share fates with others not necessarily friends or family. Worlds of places have given way to worlds of purposes. *Organizations are the mid-level social formations in a world of purposes.* Community experiences are inescapable in organizations (see Chapter 11). So are politics and governance (see Chapter 13). We do bring self-interest to organizations. But we cannot avoid the *common good*. We cannot go it alone and thrive. Organizations are thick we's in which individuals *must* balance self-interest with the common good. *In organizations, we are stuck with one another.*

Liberty has richer *interpersonal* meaning in organizations than in markets or nations. In organizations, the freedom of I clashes *personally* with the freedom of we. Dissent is gritty—whether those who dissent object to longstanding assumptions blocking innovation or, scarier, blow whistles on unethical or criminal activity. When any of us dissent in organizations, *we do so as individuals who participate in groups of people we know and who know us* (see Chapter 8).

Free speech in markets need not be interpersonal. Individuals can express themselves anonymously in markets. We have secret ballots. Oddly, but surely, individuals can speak to nobody in particular yet influence the largest social formations in our lives: markets, networks, and nations. Shopping, voting, and investing beg for the integration of value and values. *But none of those activities **require** dissent, consent, voice, participation, risk, or responsibility for the common good of a thick we.*

Individuals, of course, can choose to dissent publicly in markets, nations, and networks. We can sacrifice anonymity. Tellingly, though, people who seize that option typically join with others to form organizations to influence the value and values of strangers in markets and networks. Sacrificing anonymity in markets, networks, and nations is difficult. Individuals and organizations often **must** advertise, use public relations, or otherwise create stirs to convert anonymity into publicity. They have to work at it.

The individual actions of consumers, investors, and networkers make a huge difference. Their influence, however, is better explained as collectivities of I's than as thick we's. Collectivities of I's do not pursue a common good. Collectivities of I's have similar interests, purposes, and preferences about which they might or might not feel passionately. *But, shared ideas—not shared fates and shared paths—define collectivities of I's.* The consumer preferences of adults who are "DINCs" ("dual income, no children"), for example, shape markets ranging from travel and leisure to political control of government. DINCs, though, are not a thick we. They share ideas and roles, but DINCs do not inescapably share fates. They need not reckon with any common good *they must implement together.*

In contrast, employees and volunteers in organizations **must** implement their common good. Whether Enron or Kellogg's, the AARP or Bronx Educational Services, the Environmental Protection Agency or the Union Vale Town Board, people who throw in their lots with one another in thick we's cannot escape responsibility for defining and delivering the good in the good things to have they bring to markets, networks, nations, organizations, friends, and families.

Consumers, voters, and investors in collectivities of I's, mostly worry about consequences for themselves, their friends, and their families. They seek value for money. Collectivities of I's, for example, have fueled dramatic growth in the share of automobile markets held by SUVs. Consumers enjoy SUVs; they believe they receive sufficient value for their money. Still, the adverse consequences of SUVs range from diminished highway safety and environmental damage to heroin-like oil addiction undercutting Middle East reform. Many consumers are aware of these. One recent bumper sticker, for example, asks, "How come they've got *our* oil under *their* sand?"

Mostly, though, the uneasiness reinforces the strong, predictable shared belief among consumers, voters, investors, and networkers that *other people and organizations* must respond. That, after all, is *how* our world of markets, networks, organizations, friends and families works. *That is our system.* Through preferences and behavior, collectivities of I's generate opportunities for problem solving—for bringing more and different good things to have to the world. Collectivities of I's seek solutions from others, especially other organizations whose thick we's care enough to answer the call.

Solutions emerge *only* when one or more thick we's include them in *their* common good. Markets and networks are sense and response social formations that rely on organizations to combine power, resources, and motivations to bring good things to have to individuals and their friends and families. In this sense, collectivities of I's foster market failures that thick we's turn into market successes.

We play many roles in our world of purposes. But we must not confuse collectivities of I's that emerge among consumers and investors with thick we's forged by shared fates in families, friends, and organizations. That confusion perpetuates instability in markets, networks, and nations; it engenders unhappiness at home and among friends. By clarifying how thin we's and thick we's interrelate, each of us takes responsibility for ensuring that mid-level social formations—organizations—blend value and values to stabilize our world of purposes.

Link the common good of thick we's to the greater good of markets, nations, networks, friends, and families.

Autarky is a Greek-derived word for self-sufficiency. An autarky is a place free of dependency on other places. It is difficult to imagine autarkies in the 21st century. There may be autarkic villages in remote places whose oil, water, minerals, or eco-tourist attractions have yet to be discovered by markets, networks, and organizations. But autarky is unsustainable as national policy. Sadaam's Iraq, for example, *had* to sell oil. Iraq could not escape interdependency with others.

The improbability of autarky is not new; international military, religious, and commercial connections date back a long time. Still, over the past quarter-century or so, powerful forces have reconstituted the entangling alliances on which nations depend. Today, autarky is not just a question of nations keeping clear of other nations. *Nations cannot escape markets, networks, and organiza-*

tions, or vice versa. Sadaam sold oil not only to, say, France or Korea, but to and through petroleum markets, networks, and organizations to other organizations and their customers. His regime acquired arms, food, medicine, and technology through markets, networks, and organizations.

The question was not merely, "Would France or the United States or Russia do business with Iraq?" The equally compelling, *everyday* question also was, "Would BP or Halliburton or Deutsche Bank—or any other organization—do business with Sadaam Hussein and Iraq?" In our new world of purposes, this question compounds on itself to become, "*Would any of **us** participate as consumers, investors, or employees of organizations doing business with organizations doing business with organizations doing business...with Sadaam?*"

Organizations cannot be autarkies *even in theory.* Pure self-sufficiency contradicts their reason for being: to provide good things to have to *other people and organizations.* Plenty of executives try to minimize external dependencies in favor of insularity and control. Roger Smith of General Motors, for example, ignored many forces in the world beyond his company (see Chapter 3). But Roger Smith never renounced *all* contact with customers, investors, and suppliers. He did not pursue autarky. That is nonsensical for organizations.

*Organizations **must** link their common good to the greater good of the planet.* In a world of purposes, this is what organizations do *this is what they are for.* Employees and volunteers *must* take responsibility for blending value and values in the good things to have they provide to others on whom, in turn, they depend for their livelihoods. *To ignore or abuse that responsibility is to fail to lead a good life in our new world of purposes.*

This ethical imperative is inescapable. It *must* inform the many, shared ideas crucial to organizational purposes: brand, strategy, vision, mission, and so forth. I believe we know this. Tens of millions of employees and volunteers in organizations have more than a mere inkling about their responsibilities as thick we's to ensure that good things to have are *good.* We are not brain dead. We understand that the common good of our organizations *must* incorporate concerns ranging from work/family balance to customer satisfaction to returns for those who invest or otherwise support our thick we's. The Ethical Scorecard proposed in Illustrative Suggestion #1 in Chapter 17 should not astonish anyone. It is common sense.

Nonetheless, value subordinates values in the common good of too many organizations today. From shareholder value to extreme individualism to the economistic fallacy confining happiness to money, powerful shared ideas grip too many leaders, too many organizations, and too many strategies. These shared ideas have long since become variants of single-answer fundamentalism. They instill fear. They thin out our thick we's and divide us from one another and from the world we actually live in. They are replete with an either/or mentality exalting me over we.

Either let value, markets, and individualism trump all choices, or watch out!! Either let millions of people go uninsured in health care markets, or watch your organization lose its cost-based competitive edge and you lose your job! Either continue misinforming markets, networks, and nations regarding accurate costs of new drugs or tax cuts or SUV safety, or watch your organization lose market share and you lose your job!! Either accept environmental damage as an externality of market economics or embark on "save the world" strategies that diminish shareholder value and, along with it, take *your job*!! Either rely on individual volunteers and a thousand points of light to help tens of millions of people left behind by markets, networks, and nations, or watch your government pick your pocket and give your money to "them"—*to people who cannot make it as individuals and must suffer the consequences of their own failures*.

These fear-inspired, hate-filled threats are profoundly antithetical to our strong shared values of problem solving and tolerance—beliefs and behaviors essential to good lives in a world of markets, networks, organizations, friends, and families. As consumers, voters, networkers, investors, family members, and friends, we worry about a world gone mad for value. We want a healthy, sustainable blend of value and values restored to some center of gravity that can better life on this planet for ourselves and our children. We want to do our part, to make a difference. *But, we live in a world in which autarky is impossible.* Autarky is nonsensical for organizations. It is ridiculous for individuals too. Most of us cannot and would not choose to move ourselves and our families to some remote world of places. We *choose* to live in a world requiring us to rely on organizations to do-it-for-me. We *must* count on thick we's to ensure that their common good contributes to the greater good of all.

Shareholder value, economistic fallacies and cults of individualism obscure what stares us in the face. In relying on organizations, we rely on ourselves. *We are them! They are us!* By explicitly and thoughtfully linking the common good of our thick we's to the greater good of markets, networks, nations, organizations, friends, and families, we can break the cycle of fear and hopelessness inspired by value unblended with values and I's bereft of thick we's. We also carry a best part of our past into our best future: *We do unto others what we would have others do unto us*.

Embrace the democratic values essential to organization performance.

Today, achieving the common good of organizations requires both democratic and hierarchical social and political values. This is, I think, one of the best-kept secrets of our age. A democracy so vulnerable in markets for political control is resurgent in organizations. Why? *Because performance demands it*. Hierarchy is not enough.

The same forces that have driven mid-level social formations out of places into organizations have transformed those organizations. Hierarchies flattened because strict individualism and hierarchical authorities failed to deliver performance. In more than a quarter-century of working with organizations large and small, formal and informal, and governmental, for profit, and nonprofit, I have not—repeat, *not*—observed *anyone* find solutions to pressing problems of performance through hierarchy alone.

Both/and. Not either/or. Hierarchy contributes to performance. It still promotes efficiency and effectiveness by ordering relationships and roles. No organization would succeed if employees showed up each morning and took a vote on what to do that day. That silly image, however, is an either/or view trotted out by managers and leaders still smitten with individualistic values and the power of hierarchy. They are dinosaurs. *They never deliver sustainable performance.*

They never advance the common good of their thick we's because their policies cannot solve problems demanding a blend of hierarchy and democracy. Customer service, innovation, quality, reengineering, strategic alliances, eCommerce, shareholder relations, governmental compliance, work/family balance, pension reform and management, flex time scheduling, hiring, retention, firing, continuous improvement, performance management, strategy, managing change, information technology, purchasing, public relations, marketing, and distribution channel management—none yield to hierarchy alone.

None of this is new news to millions of employees in organizations. It is old news. It is "the way we do things around here." Overly hierarchical leaders fail. As one management writer proclaimed years ago, the days of the divine right of managers are finished.[2] This new reality extends to followers, too. People who refuse to act in the absence of moment-by-moment commands and permissions from bosses also fail. They do not learn to think for themselves or to take responsibility for participating in shaping and delivering the common good of their thick we's. Increasingly, they wake up one day out of a job or otherwise tarnished by secretive, hierarchical choices made at the top.

The common good of organizations demands that we *weave together* hierarchical and democratic social and political values. *This is promising because strong, predictable shared values practiced in organizations bridge to the values shared among friends and families in markets, networks, nations, and the world*. People who experience robust democracy in organizations are more likely to respect dissent, free speech, consent, participation, and responsibility in markets, networks, and nations. They are less likely to violate the liberty and freedoms of others.

Is the resurgent democracy in organizations complete? *Of course not*. Any number of organizations continue to operate in strict hierarchies. Hundreds of organizations, from sweat shops to steel mills to state agencies, have yet to embrace *democratic* performance practices, perhaps because we have narrowed the shared idea of democracy to mean voting alone. Meanwhile, other organizations that have adopted democratic shared values for *some* performance challenges revert to hierarchy and secrecy for others. Questions arise about environmental responsibility, living wages, the need for downsizing, the intended uses of charitable donations, or the costs of new drugs or tax cuts or military interventions. Instead of expanding on the democratic social and political values so obviously linked to performance in matters of continuous improvement, innovation, quality, and customer service, executives and officials act secretively and hierarchically. They reserve voice, dissent, and consent to themselves. They seek buy in *only after* decisions get made.

---

2.   Edgar H. Schein, "Reassessing the 'Divine Rights' of Managers." *Sloan Management Review* (Winter, 1989).

Irrationality clouds thinking. Too many leaders and followers alike fail to connect the dots of actual experience. *We fail to ask why and how participation, voice, dissent, consent, rights, and responsibility, which all contribute so powerfully to quality, innovation, and continuous improvement, somehow threaten the common good on matters of environmental prudence, work/life balance, information disclosure, executive pay, or shareholder relations.* We fail to see that unalloyed hierarchy and secrecy produce failure instead of performance. When this happens, we subordinate values to value. We tarnish the brands of our thick we's. *The time has come for us— leaders and followers—to embrace the social and political values that got us here; namely, performance-driven blends of democracy and hierarchy in pursuit of our common good as thick we's.*

Use purposes to blend value and values in a world of purposes.

In the late winter of 2001, I shared coffee and conversation with an executive from the International Chamber of Commerce who was deeply troubled by media coverage of globalization. She explained to me that gatherings ranging from International Monetary Fund meetings to the annual assembly of the rich, powerful, and famous at Davos, Switzerland included debates about serious challenges, such as sustainable economic development, global warming, biodiversity, poverty, terrorism, and North/South fairness. She also explained that those sessions inevitably attracted fringe ideologues who, she despaired, gained more media attention than the problems discussed. Instead of enlightening customers, she charged, popular media chose to entertain. Media reduced globalization to a sound bite: *"Anarchists take battle against multinational corporations and governments to the streets."*

Six months later, terrorists armed with box cutters took down the two World Trade Center towers in New York and a wing of the Pentagon in Washington D.C. Globalization suddenly meant more than Bill Gates getting a pie in the face. No one—and no place—was safe. The immediate victims of September 11th hailed from scores of nations and every continent. Neither place nor nation, however, thickly described their lives. Those who died pursued many life purposes in markets, networks, organizations, and among friends and family.

September 11th is now a flashbulb memory. Soon, we will have to remind ourselves and our children about how we *felt*—and about the full range of all too real hopes and fears triggered by the attacks. People around the globe were touched *personally* by the tragedy. According to the extravagant math of six degrees of separation (see Chapter 2), all 6 billion people on the planet knew someone who knew someone who knew someone who knew someone who knew someone who knew someone who died. Hatred did not dissolve. But animosities born in place-based cultures stepped to the shadows as billions of people imagined themselves for a brief, stunning moment as part of a "September 11th we"—a we that had nothing to do with place. It was born in a fiery event and burnished by shared ideas. Generosity of spirit—not malevolence—swelled the briefly *shared purposes* of the "September 11th we."

In that all-too-transitory moment, many thick we's in the media dropped news-as-entertainment in favor of problem solving, questioning, understanding, communication, and responsibility. Media organizations, at least momentarily, shifted how their common good contributed to the greater good. Coverage blended value and values in delivering complicated yet critical information that people needed to help victims, take security precautions, learn about Islam, and reflect on life together on this planet. Reporters, newscasters, editors, and writers acted as if *they were involved*—as if they, too, were part of the "September 11th we." They suspended their shared practice of reducing viewers, readers, and listeners to spectators at a blood sport. "Me" and undiluted value deferred, however briefly, to "we" and shared values of all kinds.

Many of the shared ideas inspiring the "September 11th we"— freedom, opportunity, problem solving, tolerance, good will, and justice for all—spoke to the American Dream that, by the 21st century, had been marketed across the globe. Billions of people in and beyond the United States took a breath to recommit themselves to this best part of the past. For the first time in a half-century, the American Dream gained moral strength from vulnerability. *People the world over did not want that dream to die*.

Not all 6 billion, mind you. Plenty of terrorists hungered to turn the American Dream into a fiery nightmare. As events showed, there also were men and women who thirsted for a different legacy from America's past—one associated with intolerance, self interest, value, extreme individualism, and isolation. Hundreds of millions of us, however, wished to take the best part of the American Dream into the best part of the *world's* future. We wished to globalize the American Dream by making it *Humanity's Dream*—a worldwide embrace of what Abraham Lincoln once called "the last best hope for earth."

That special moment faded. *It had to.* No billion-fold "we" can last long. However traumatic the flashbulb event, such immense we's are thin, not thick. They grow from shared ideas instead of everyday, inescapable shared fates. They are collectivities of I's who, even when reminded that the resources of this planet must be shared, lack the wherewithal to move forward *as thick we's.*

Shortly after September 11th, big media declared, "This changes everything forever!" But what eventually does change—and how permanently—now depends on the *purposes* that hundreds of millions of us bring to markets, networks, organizations, friends, and family. Early signs are ambiguous. The value and values melted together in the burning World Trade Center towers caused millions of people to rebalance their purposes in families and among friends. Value and values, however, still diverge in too many markets, networks, nations, and organizations.

Airlines, for example, responded to crushing cash drains by immediately firing people. The accounting gimmickry that gutted '90s prosperity shifted from the private to the public sector, as political leaders loaded budgets with accounting tricks to cover over red ink. Organizations in capital markets flipped the switch from always on to always off, from anything goes to nothing doing. Market failures spread; market successes were harder to come by.

The falling economic tide grounded tens of millions of boats. Jobs evaporated, unemployed people stopped looking for work, the number of uninsured families skyrocketed, consumer debt exploded, and business executives lost their nerve. For the first time in more than a decade, the vast majority of consumers, employees, and investors felt personally at risk. Value-obsessed stories shifted from headlines about "How high is up?" to "How bad can this get?" Had the economy been the center ring in big media's daily briefing to the rest of us, the political leadership in the United States and elsewhere would have been in disarray. Approval ratings would, I think, have run at historic lows.

Instead, approval ratings soared because the daily update was about values instead of value. It was about the United States of America at War Against Terrorism. It was about a red-white-and-blue American September 11th built on the shared ideas of individualism and small towns. It perpetuated a strong and distinctive *brand* that, notwithstanding Michael Sandel's warnings about proceduralism (see Chapter 10), embraced substantive positions on the good.

Thick we's linked to this brand appealed to collectivities of I's by declaring, "You are with us or against us." Various American political celebrities and governmental organizations chose unilateral might as right over the multilateral rule of international law. Many of America's Republican political leaders and their talk radio lieutenants appropriated the flag as their property, failed to protect, let alone encourage, dissent, deployed disinformation to gain market share, embraced "my way or the highway" hierarchy, and enacted laws making liberty, opportunity, and justice for *some*, not all. Within 18 months of September 11, 2001, the *brand* of the American Dream so many wished to make Humanity's Dream had given way to a different, less inclusive Americanism that exchanged respect-from-shared-aspirations for respect-from-fear.

This happened. Really. Still, before you get too hot under the collar *fur 'em or agin 'em*, let me reiterate: We must look at actual beliefs and behaviors—actual values—before we condemn or celebrate what is good or bad. Millions in and beyond the United States *sincerely* believe many of the steps taken were necessary—were a heroic example of ends justifying means. Lincoln, let us remember, violated the Constitution to preserve the Union.

The writing of this book wraps up in early 2004. Just what long-term effects September 11th and the twin forces of globalization and terrorism will have on future events is beyond my crystal ball. Whatever happens, however, is our responsibility. It will reflect *our purposes* and the actions we take as consumers, investors, networkers, employees, family members, and friends to pursue those purposes. We must look to ourselves—both as I's and as thick we's—to bring the best parts of our past forward to life together on this planet. We cannot find any best part of our past in value-less values or values-free value. Winning is not everything. The *shared values* won for ourselves and our children matter, too. *We* matter. But *we* are different. Our world is different. We live in a world of purposes—a world whose value and values reflect *the purposes we live for* instead of *the places we live in*.

17 Illustrative Suggestions

This chapter offers a number of specific suggestions (outlined in Table 17.1) for improving our new world of purposes. I hope readers will consider them for their merit. As much as anything, however, I offer them as illustrations of how to think in terms of markets, networks, organizations, friends, and families in developing responses to the challenges now confronting us.

1. The Ethical Scorecard

All organizations have the following constituencies: customers, funders/supporters, and employees. Some organizations also have partners, who might be other organizations or individuals engaged by the organization. We find these constituencies in the for-profit, non-profit and governmental sectors, in large and small organizations, in informal and formal organizations.

Today, most organizations emphasize one constituency above others. Advocates of shareholder value, for example, argue that shareholders, as legal owners of organizations, deserve primary consideration. Even *The Balanced Scorecard* is unbalanced in favor of shareholders (see Chapters 3 and 7). We hear echoes of "first among equals" in shareholder value or "the customer as king" or "employees as our most important assets."

TABLE 17.1   Illustrative Suggestions

	Suggestions
1	The Ethical Scorecard
2	Annual Report to People of the Enterprise
3	Brand Values Committee of Board of Directors/Trustees
4	Corporate Purchasing on Behalf of Employees and Their Families
5	Jury Trials of Fact Inside Organizations
6	Employee Based Participation in Selection and Guidance of Lobbyists
7	Customer and Employee Membership on Board of Directors/Trustees
8	Minimum Values Standards in Qualifying Vendors
9	Forward Auditing
10	Employee Participation in Organization Charity
11	From Organizational Newsletter to Free Press
12	Dynamic Deductibility: Creating an Efficient Capital Market for Nonprofits
13	Private Capital Leagues for Nonprofits
14	Establishing a Third Legislative House: Lobbyists
15	Census Tracking: Counting Organizational Membership in Addition to Jobs
16	Founding a "Problem Solvers" Party
17	Require Government Organizations to Have and Report Against Vision, Strategy, and Values
18	Selective Knowledge Testing of Voters for Information Only
19	TV Show: "Brand Values"
20	TV/Web Show: "Brand Trials"
21	TV/Radio Show: "Civil Disagreement"
22	TV/Web Show: "What Works"
23	Reality Show: "Congress of Organizations"
24	Abolish Political Party Affiliations for State and Local Judges
25	360 Degree Feedback on Local Officials Just-in-time to Vote
26	Opt-in State and Local Purchasing Efforts
27	New Media: Trusted Infomediaries

The logic of such claims is linear. It might recognize and respect the interests of other stakeholders. But it subordinates those interests to the favored stakeholder. The interests of the preferred stakeholder serve as primary objective and tiebreaker. While more promising than a bald obsession with only one constituency, these "first among equals" approaches nonetheless suffer from either/or thinking. They provide a single answer to conflicts.

In contrast, the Ethical Scorecard depicted in Figures 17.1 through 17.3 locates *the common good* of an organization in an iterative, both/and logic making all constituencies both means and ends to the others. In the Ethical Scorecard, organizations with purposes, problem solutions, and goals create a narrative or story of performance that respects all constituencies equivalently. No constituency is ignored or subordinated to any other. One consequence is enhanced sustainability because the thick we of the organization commit themselves to achieving good performance that is fully good.

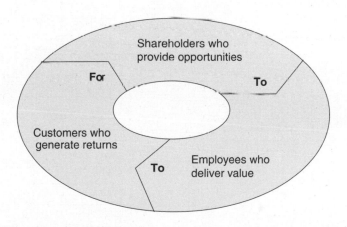

FIGURE 17.1
Ethical Scorecard—For-Profit

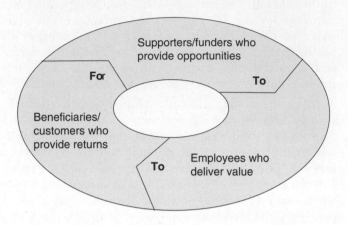

FIGURE 17.2
Ethical Scorecard—Nonprofit

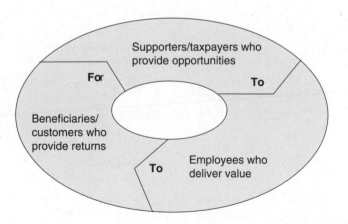

FIGURE 17.3
Ethical Scorecard—Government

2. Annual Report to the People of the Enterprise

We are familiar with annual reports to shareholders that pay homage to the hard work, great skill, and inspiring purposes of employees. Rarely, however, do sections in annual reports to shareholders report on the full range of concerns that matter to the people of the enterprise—the thick we responsible for the common good and performance of organization.

A report to the shareholders is intended for that audience. That makes sense. Still, authors of annual reports to shareholders often present exaggerated pictures. I recall one executive who sighed and said that he hoped the descriptions of employees in his company's annual reports to shareholders might someday be accurate. Annual reports to shareholders sometimes incline toward rosier pictures about competitive and financial performance, too. But it is considered poor practice—not to mention illegal—to mislead shareholders.

An annual report to the people of the enterprise would provide thick we's the chance to review direction and performance against the many interests and concerns employees have at work. Such a report need not obsess over warts. But it ought to portray a fair, objective, and balanced picture of how effectively the thick we use shared political, social, financial, technological, family, and other values together to achieve their common good.

3. Brand Values Committee of Board of Directors/Trustees

A Committee on Brand Values established by Boards of Directors or Trustees would monitor promises made and delivered by an organization's brand. The focus would be on *all values:* economic and financial along with social, political, family, environmental, technological and others. The committee could lead discussions and reviews in the full Board that evaluate and shape brand promises, brand delivery, and brand experience.

In doing their work, the Committee on Brand Values might distinguish between minimum requirements of brand versus those values that help differentiate the brand from competition. Illustrative minimum requirements might include complying with laws, avoiding endangering people, disclosing risks to safety, providing whistleblower protection, and setting standards for balancing work and family/personal life. Differentiating brand values might promise and deliver extraordinary customer service, a ban on disinformaton, or environmental protection standards well above legal requirements.

The Committee on Brand Values should set and monitor policies and principles to ensure the organization delivers the brand values it promises. The Committee might step in to investigate or review instances of significant failure or success. For example, a Committee on Brand Values in any number of American companies might have stepped in to make sure that the advertising use of flag imagery following the September 11th tragedies was consistent with their company's practices regarding paying federal taxes, complying with security measures, and so forth.

4. Corporate Purchasing on Behalf of Employees and Their Families

Large and medium size organizations have purchasing power. Small organizations can attain purchasing power through alliances, outsourcing, or participating in programs sponsored by credit card companies. Corporate purchasing efforts focus, appropriately enough, on gaining volume and quality advantages for products and services the organization requires. But volume and quality advantages also matter to employees and their families. Organizations offering employees the chance to gain from purchasing power—whether on a mandated or opt-in basis—enhance the benefits of participation.

Corporate purchasing programs often set minimum requirements on vendors who wish to qualify. Purchasing programs for employees and their families might do likewise. A value-focus might be benefit enough. But a purchasing program might move beyond value to all values. Such programs might establish minimum standards regarding social, family, technological, environmental, and political values with which vendors would need to comply to qualify for participation.

Purchasing programs offer another advantage: political participation. Employees can oversee and implement such programs. Employee participation might be voluntary. Or, it might be mandatory. Or, it might be done on a rotational basis so that (1) no set of employees is obligated more than others, and (2) all employees have the opportunity to participate. All employees could exercise voice, participation, consent, and responsibility. By setting standards, selecting vendors, negotiating offerings, and converting offerings into purchases by employees and their families, employees would win access to superior goods and services as well as personal experience at governing themselves in a thick we.

5. Jury Trials of Fact Inside Organizations

Jury trials are among the most honored and cherished of democratic institutions. In submitting ourselves to the judgement of a jury of our peers, we seek adjudication grounded in the common sense of people charged with serving both justice and the best interests of a community. Today, as noted in Chapter 11, organizations are our communities. Yet, we do not have jury trials in organizations. Alleged wrongdoing—whether major or minor—is investigated and adjudicated by executives and managers, often with the involvement or oversight of Human Resources experts and lawyers. Rarely is a jury of peers established to investigate or adjudicate wrongdoing.

Jury trials in organizations would benefit the thick we. Such trials need not determine punishment as well as fact. There are precedents for separating the punishment phase from the fact-finding phase. The consequences of wrongdoing, if proved, could be determined by a different person or set of people. For example, executive wrongdoing might go to the Board for punishment, while union member wrongdoing might go to a body with union representation.

But there is no status or role in any organization that, on its face, precludes participation in fact-finding. Expert testimony, of course, will be required occasionally—just as in public jury trials. The basic question of factual wrongdoing is eminently a question for peers—people who, like the accused, have thrown their lots together in an organization of their choosing.

6. Employee Oversight/Review of Lobbyists

Organizations that hire lobbyists can establish employee oversight and review processes to ensure fuller employee participation and voice in the direction given, and performance of, lobbyists. The nature and number of such processes would vary by size and complexity of organization and number of lobbyists. In the case of reasonably extensive lobbying efforts, an organization might establish a committee of employees to regularly meet with and review the objectives, approaches, and impact of lobbyists. The committee's charter could range from information gathering and communication to mandatory restrictions on lobbyists. This committee could publish their information and findings and, say, hold an all-employee meeting to discuss lobbying once or twice a year. Like other employee governance processes, this one can be done on a rotational basis in order to build the number of employees who directly participate over time.

In adopting such procedures, organizations would build democratic participation and governance processes for employees. Lobbying is among the most powerful means deployed in markets for governmental control. Today, a narrow band of executives set the agenda for lobbyists, and value tends to trump values. Organizations increase the likelihood of a better blend of value and values by increasing the number of voices speaking to the lobbyists. Employees, for example, may be more likely than executives to bring concerns about family, technology, the environment, and other values to lobbyists, especially when executive job descriptions are narrowly focused on ensuring competitive advantage and shareholder value.

Yes, there is a risk of renegade employees who shift the balance toward one or more nonfinancial concerns. But that is unlikely: Employees care deeply about their own jobs. Such processes put employees in positions of responsibility to all constituencies. Employees who oversee and review the work of lobbyists must keep an eye on the common good of their thick we.

7. Customer and Employee Participation in the Board of Directors/Trustees

Boards of Directors or Trustees who invite formal or informal participation of customers and employees are more likely to blend value and values in the common good of all stakeholders. Today, however, Boards of Directors or Trustees speak and listen too often with the narrow voices of shareholders alone. In theory, management represents the thick we of the organization: all of the employees and the most critical strategic partners. In practice, the voice of management reflects the core concerns of executives. Not always, of course. In particular, those who adhere to an Ethical Scorecard better represent all voices.

Customer and employee participation could range from membership itself to committee activities to information and review processes. There is no one best way. Mistakes will be made; lessons will be learned. But, today's organizations are our *polis*, our mid-level social formation straddling families and individuals on one side and markets, networks, and nations on the other. Boards of Directors or Trustees stand atop the formal structure of organizational governance. We need to ensure that all voices critical to the common good of an organization find ways to participate at the highest levels of governance.

8. Minimum Values Standards in Qualifying Vendors

Thousands of large organizations have seized on the power of purchasing to improve quality, speed, and cost. Efforts include, but go beyond, volume discounts. By establishing standards for things like minimum errors or defects, speed of delivery, coordination between buyer and seller, and information sharing, organizations exercise control over vendors for the benefit of customers, shareholders, and employees.

Some vendor quality efforts are more aggressive than others—for good and ill. From time to time, for example, we read that a powerful player has abused the employees of vendor organizations or destroyed the profitability of suppliers. Meanwhile, other organizations expand their qualifying standards to demand compliance with anti-discrimination or environmental laws. Like all organizational efforts, then, the use of purchasing provides opportunity for good and ill and everything in between.

Large organizations have had more success than small ones. Still, there is a rise among small and medium size organizations in coordinating with one another. Sometimes such coordination is done explicitly and directly. Sometimes—for example, through eCommerce auction sites or credit card companies—the coordination is done by a third party in return for a small charge.

Any organization can use purchasing to ensure minimum standards regarding family, environmental, social, technological, and other values. The more who do, the more likely that networks of organizations crisscrossing industries will subscribe to shared values of all sorts. The standards might be set by specific employees. Or, organizations might establish explicit employee participation processes. However accomplished, vendor qualification programs put organizations in a position to influence the ethics of other organizations. They reduce the odds of tarnishing brands through doing business with others who run afoul of shared standards of conduct. Employees are less likely, for example, to awaken one day and learn that their company has supported an organization that manipulated energy markets, failed to pay taxes, defrauded its investors, endangered workers, used child labor, misinformed consumers, or purchased oil from tyrants.

---

9. Forward Auditing of Risks

Shareholders, customers, and employees all gain when organizations audit their performance by looking both backward and forward against both rules and risks and do so continuously instead of periodically. Today, however, auditing is backward looking, rules based, and periodic.

Auditing principles were established in the late 19th and early 20th centuries when markets were far more stable than today. In that world of places, a company's past financial performance—so long as it was accurately reported—gave reasonable assurance of future performance. Accounting and auditing rules and principles effectively ferreted out problems in annual audits.

Today, however, markets and networks are wildly dynamic. Organization performance—past and future—turns more on understanding and managing against risks than complying with rules about financial books and records. Several corporate scandals revealed abuse of rules. Yet, the auditors involved—even the honest and diligent ones—were late in discovering the abuses because of their narrow, backward-looking, and rules-constricted focus. The morass of accounting rules combine with the narrow professionalism of accountants to put horse blinders on those most responsible for objective, outside assessments of organization performance.

Auditors *must* ask more than, "Were the rules followed?" That question matters. But, organization performance today depends much more on asking, "What are the most critical performance risks facing this organization, and how well does the organization control those risks?" Among the many critical risks facing Enron, for example, were those linked to how that company financed its energy deals. Enron used risky techniques that pinned success to the price of its own stock. An auditor asking risk-based questions would have discovered this risk quickly and questioned Enron management about what, if anything, they were doing to manage and control the risk. The answer would have been, "Little or nothing." The ensuing audit report could have highlighted the imbalance between the risk and the efforts to control it. That kind of report—as opposed to short statements regarding compliance with narrow bookkeeping rules— would have put an earlier, perhaps less damaging, end to Enron's dangerous pursuit of shareholder value.

Organizations face a rainbow of risks as differentiated as human values themselves (see Chapter 7). By continuously reviewing and reporting on the balance between performance risks and efforts to control those risks, auditors can help shareholders and their advisors make better choices. They also can help employees and customers understand the implications of an organization's performance.

10. Employee Participation in Organization Charity

Many organizations give to charity. Beginning in the 1980s, several larger organizations recognized the chance to link philanthropy to their brands. Other organizations are less focused. Their charitable choices might reflect the whims of chief executives, the social and personal networks of Board members, random calls from charities, or historical ties to charities located in roughly the same place as the organization.

Organizational charity, however, is not limited to money and services provided to nonprofits. Indeed, a much wider, more everyday and informal aspect of charity involves employees who help fellow employees. Because organizations are thick we's, people jump to each other's aid in many ways—from pitching in with one another's kids to helping in times of acute crisis.

Charity—both formal and informal—provides thick we's with a critical opportunity for participation, voice, consent, dissent, and implementation. Through establishing various charitable structures and processes, thick we's can take the initiative and direct their organization's assistance—both to nonprofit thick we's who care and to themselves. They can enrich the shared values of their community and take responsibility for how their common good contributes to the greater good of markets, networks, nations, friends, and families.

---

11. From Organizational Newsletter to Free Press

Many organizations have newsletters; few have a free press. Few organizations invite openly critical and controversial voices in the dissemination of information and news *inside* their thick we's. Doing so would be risky. From the disclosure of sensitive competitive information to the ugliness of personal attacks—an unbridled free press inside organizations could wreak havoc. Or, it might not. A free press might act responsibly. It might add a healthy channel to debate and opinion *otherwise confined to hall talk*.

Leaders delude themselves if they believe controversy goes unnoticed when unpublished. Organizations are our polis—our mid-level social formation in which we throw in our lots and fates with others who are not necessarily friends or family. We depend on organizations for our livelihoods. Organizations are hotbeds of controversy. *The risks of unwanted disclosures and personal attacks already exist.* The question facing organizational leaders is not how to avoid such phenomena. Rather, it is how to turn the energies and interests of employees in knowing what's going on to best advantage for all involved.

In inviting a responsible internal free press, organizations put the onus on thick we's to act in the best interests of customers, shareholders, partners, and themselves. Might they do a bad job? Yes. Just like employees and executives might do a bad job putting together budgets, installing new technology, or improving customer service. Governance and political values reflect the reality of shared beliefs, behaviors, attitudes, and speech—good, bad, and in between. Values of hierarchy and secrecy serve certain ends; so do values of broader participation and openness. Today's organizations increasingly depend on integrating the expertise and skills of their employees and partnering organizations in the real-time service of performance. Integration, in turn, requires democratic political values of voice, consent, problem solving, and tolerance. A responsible free press could enhance those values to the benefit of all.

12. Dynamic Deductibility: Creating Efficient Capital Markets for Nonprofits

Today's capital markets for nonprofits resemble 18th century private sector capital markets. They are grossly inefficient and whimsical. Nonprofit organizations and the markets and networks in which they compete mirror that inefficiency and ineffectiveness (see Chapter 15).

Nonprofit thick we's who care enough to convert market failures into market successes gain when they have access to effective capital markets. We can build more effective nonprofit capital markets through legislation creating dynamic deductibility. This legislation would give nonprofit organizations and their contributors a choice to raise capital in equity markets that trade in dynamically deductible units (DDUs). Nonprofits would establish an offering price for dynamically deductible units. Contributors would then have the option: immediate deduction or hold. If they hold, they can sell their DDUs later in the market. They will be permitted to deduct the sale price of their units in the year they sell (with adjustments for gains or losses similar to today's capital gain/loss rules).

The market price of DDUs will rise and fall because of organization performance and how investors, analysts, and advisers evaluate it. Nonprofit organizations have a wide array of robust performance indicators, including operating sustainability, innovation, technology, market share, and customer service. Once we have an attractive and efficient capital market in DDUs, we will see nonprofits take better advantage of many strategies and approaches that enable for-profit organizations to balance and integrate the concerns of customers, funds providers, employees, and strategic partners.

13. Private Capital Leagues for Nonprofits

Those who provide capital to nonprofits can create private leagues to reward sustainable performance and growth. In some respects, these leagues would mirror professional sports leagues:

- A number of capital providers commit to funding a minimum amount over a set period of time. For example, 30 capital providers might commit to contributing $5 million each over a five-year period. The 30 might include organizations that draw on smaller contributors.

- The capital providers concentrate their efforts in one nonprofit industry—for example community development, family counseling, or adult literacy.
- The league then invite nonprofit organizations in the chosen field to join.
- League admission requires commitment to specified aspects of performance—for example, innovation, extending success, outsourcing, and openness to consolidation.
- Performance periods ("seasons") are set. "Standings" are tracked throughout these periods. The capital providers establish rules by which those "ahead in the standings" gain a larger share of the next season's capital contributions.
- The best-performing nonprofits win more capital.

Private capital leagues would foster greater sustainability and continuity in performance, consolidation in the selected industries, and better dissemination of ideas and best practices. Chief executives could be liberated from fundraising to concentrate more on vision, strategy, innovation, and the common good of their thick we.

14. Establish a Third Legislative House: Lobbyists

We know that lobbyists are a powerful, yet shadowy, force in political markets for government control. Let's take lobbying out of the shadows by establishing a House of Lobbyists. We will need to solve many issues regarding membership, rules, nature of participation, and so forth. For example, given the zillions of lobbyists, there may need to be a minimum qualification based on size or sponsorship to have full membership in such a House.

Whatever rules get established, however, we gain transparency and understanding when we formalize the purposes and participation of lobbying. The news media is more likely to monitor the issues and affairs of a formalized institution than the miasma of activities so easily hidden from public view. Top lobbyists will become celebrities, with all the upside and downside of that status. More attention will go to interactions among a House of Lobbyists and the other institutions of government (Executive, Legislative, Judicial, Administrative—at federal, state, and local levels). Lobbyists and those who pay them will discover good and powerful reasons to hold themselves accountable to larger concerns, and thus will be more likely (albeit not certain) to blend value and values.

15. Census Tracking: Count Organizational Participation in Addition to Jobs

What gets measured gets done. Today, we closely monitor jobs. This makes sense, of course. But jobs are only one form of participation in the thick we's of organizations. We also participate as volunteers, students, members, and so forth. We should count such participation. We also should use a census and other efforts to measure the shared values of those participating.

By doing so, we gather the data needed to monitor who is and who is not participating in organizations, and with what effects. We encourage a broader array of policy options. We will learn, for example, that people who have jobs are not necessarily full, active participants in their organizations. We will discover that some people who do not have jobs nonetheless participate vitally in organizations. We will seek out opportunities to build thick we's as a means for solving challenges. For example, uninsured Americans might gain financial support and insurance in exchange for agreeing as thick we's to adopt certain health care best practices ranging from not smoking to exercise to prenatal care. We will find opportunities to experiment and learn, and disseminate best practices for building both jobs and organization participation.

16. Found a Problem Solvers Party

A Problem Solvers Party would commit itself to identifying and making progress against specific challenges. It would eschew ideology in favor of performance. Membership in this party—and especially leadership of this party—would demand an open mind, a generous heart, and rigorous guts.

The Problem Solvers Party would go beyond experimentation and piloting to dissemination. In particular, it would understand and rely on markets and networks, as opposed to legal fiat. Yes, of course, laws and regulations must be utilized. But a Problem Solvers Party would distinguish itself through commitment to *always* working "two or more answers" instead of merely "one answer."

A Problem Solvers Party would respond to the realities of a world of markets, networks, organizations, friends, and families. Markets never—*never*—operate well with only one commodity offering or one answer. Instead, markets and networks endlessly subdivide into segments that each seek different solutions.

Such a party would have faith in the dynamism of our new world of purposes. Its first instinct would be, "let's try that," instead of, "let's kill it unless it wins us elections." Accordingly, a Problem Solvers Party would confront symbolism and "litmus tests" head-on. It would be agnostic with regard to ideology and aggressive with respect to performance.

Progress would be measured against particular problems. A Problem Solvers Party would recognize and accept that no problem is ever likely to be solved completely. It would acknowledge that most problems worth solving are more like conditions—states of affairs that we work hard to continuously improve. A Problem Solvers Party would commit itself to as many approaches as might work against at least some meaningful segment of the problem itself.

---

17. Require Government Organizations to Report on Vision, Strategy, and Values

Over the past quarter century, we have learned a ton about what makes for an effective organization. Cynical punditry aside, organizations that care about performance use vision, strategy, quality, reengineering, outsourcing, joint venturing, teams, process management, enterprise technology, and much more. The best practices followed by organizations in the private and nonprofit sectors apply equally well to governmental organizations. Yet, governmental organizations too often fail to use them and hide behind, "we're different" as an excuse.

The governmental sector is different, but not so different as to negate best practices of organization performance. Today, for example, many state and local governments in the United States face severe budget crises. The zillions of organizations involved are battling over funding, headcount, and expenses. All of that makes sense. Yet, too few state and local governments are embracing the challenges with fundamental looks built on a both/and perspective. For example, they are not taking advantage of budget crises to challenge themselves to both restructure costs and *simultaneously improve benefits and services*. Yet, that both/and result has occurred in many private sector organizations who committed themselves to quality, continuous improvement, and reengineering, as opposed, say, to expense and headcount control.

State and local governmental organizations that fail to get beyond expense control and service cuts will not emerge from the crisis as stronger, better-performing thick we's. We need to demand that governmental organizations apply the best practices of other organizations. The demand, however, is not enough. We also must demand that governmental organizations report about their efforts and progress. Our new world of purposes has an abundance of proven ideas. More often than not, ignorance arises from a lack of information instead of a lack of ideas. Governmental organizations have access to ideas that have worked in the private and nonprofit sectors. They need to use them.

18. Knowledge Surveys of Voters for Information Only

Markets and networks operate best when all involved are educated and informed. As one New York clothier advertised a few decades back, "An educated consumer is our best customer." This is just as true for political markets and networks, whose effectiveness depends on Thomas Jefferson's famous advice that an educated populace was necessary to democracy. His dictum now runs to market democracies: market-based voting and market-based consumption of government policy, goods, and services.

Missing, inaccurate, or purposely distorted information bedevils markets. Ronald Coase, for one, identified information failures as dangerous to markets. We all know this. *We also know that poor information and weak education currently characterize our political markets for governmental control.* In part, our ignorance arises from structural complexity. Governmental markets span as many separate industries as private sector and nonprofit markets. But we have far less opportunity to influence governmental markets, networks, and organizations as consumers and taxpayers than we do as consumers, investors, employees, and networkers in the private and not-for-profit sectors. As consumers, shareholders, and employees in private and nonprofit industries, we actively transact in industries as numerous and varied as the colors of the rainbow: automotive, clothing, health care, family planning, homeless shelters, and on and on and on. In contrast, as taxpayers and customers, we have little power of or opportunity for choice in political markets for governmental control. We can vote for executive, legislative, and judicial officials. But we cannot otherwise distinguish our concerns and preferences through our transactional behavior across the unbelievable array of government activities.

In the end, we are reduced to voting for human beings instead of transacting in markets. Meanwhile, candidates and the organizations promoting them must advertise—they must compete in markets. This produces exaggeration and disinformation. It is inevitable, perhaps, for even the best-informed voter to find him or herself ignorant of many issues. That is our reality. Because we have so little opportunity to influence governmental industries on a transaction-by-transaction basis, we must rely on other organizations to correct against information disorders that, in turn, produce inefficiency and ineffectiveness, making *market democracies* vulnerable.

Put differently, when democracies shift from towns or organizations—from thick we's—to the larger social formations of markets, networks, and nations, democracy itself encounters severe structural difficulties. We must act now to begin understanding the nature and consequences of these endemic problems. We can begin by selectively surveying voters about their knowledge of issues shortly after they vote. We will discover widespread ignorance. The discovery will shock us. But, armed with a better understanding of our ignorance, we will have better positioned ourselves to do something about it.

---

19. TV/Webcast Show: "Brand Values"

The top 200 corporations in the world account for more than 25 percent of the world's gross domestic product. In addition, various large, influential governmental and nonprofit organizations have real clout—for example, the SEC, IRS, and FBI, Planned Parenthood, the Sierra Club, and the AARP. The largest organizations in all sectors exert tremendous influence on our new world of markets, networks, organizations, friends, and families. We depend on them to do-it-for-me; we look to their brands to guide many of our most critical choices.

A television show about brand values would review and evaluate the performance of organizations against the full spectrum of values that interest us: social, political, economic, family, religious, technological, and environmental. Such a show would ask and answer, for example, "What does Wal-Mart stand for?" and "What does the FBI Stand for?" and "What does the Federalist Society stand for?"

Through investigative journalism, public polling, and discussions with shareholders, employees, customers, and partner organizations, the TV show can present a richer assessment of the value and values promoted by the brands of organizations now in control of the destiny of our planet.

Neither we nor the organizations should expect the profiles to be all good or all bad. Because of our "gotcha"-besotted media, I realize this suggestion could lead to tabloid productions. That, of course, is not the intent. We must be guided by common sense and common concern. The thick we who put together the TV show must stand accountable for their own brand—for their own vision of how their common good contributes to the greater good.

Hundreds of millions of people the world over rely on the value and values of brands. I believe millions of viewers would appreciate efforts to explore the shared values of the organizations, brands, products, and services so thoroughly woven into the fabric of our lives.

20. TV/Webcast Show: "Brand Trials"

This is a variation on the previous suggestion. Its title plays off the widespread practice of organizations, who conduct new product and service trials. When an orange juice maker, for example, wishes to learn more about a new flavoring or packaging approach, it conducts trials.

Most of us, of course, also associate the idea of a trial with the legal process. This TV show joins together these two shared ideas. The show would explicitly raise a challenge regarding some critical aspect of a brand—importantly, an aspect that demanded the blending of value and values. For example, such a show might ask, "Does Merck balance its concern for health with its concern for profits?" or "Does Ford Motor Company protect the great outdoors that its SUVs give consumers access to?" or "Does Nike encourage sportsmanship?" or "Does the SEC protect investors?"

The TV show should present evidence on many sides of such questions while also soliciting viewer response and opinion. The trial might mirror traditional advocacy; there might be a "pro" and a "con." Or, the trial might sound more like a discussion or conversation. Whatever approaches are used, the intent is to provide viewers the information and ideas they need to reach their own conclusions—and to build broader, more widely shared values regarding the implications and consequences of what we purchase and how we use brands to guide us.

21. TV/Radio Show: "Civil Disagreement"

Civil Disagreement would ask each side of a disagreement to articulate to the other side's satisfaction the other side's point of view. The idea behind the TV/radio show is to convert a lack of understanding into shared understanding.

The show would invite two or more conflicting parties to attend. In the beginning, it would probably be easier to keep it at two. Each party would present its point of view. Instead of proceeding to scream at each other, however, the show would require opposing parties to sincerely explain their opponent's point of view. A moderator might help out, or serve as judge for whether such attempts succeed. Or, panels or audiences might assess the quality of efforts to build shared understanding— even if not shared agreement.

To illustrate: Imagine that an advocate of school vouchers joined an opponent of that idea. This show would demand good-faith dialogue. The point is not to establish agreement. (Although, I have found agreement often happens, in whole or part, through this exercise.) Rather, the objective is to reach shared understanding when the voucher supporter satisfactorily makes the case against vouchers, and the voucher opponent for vouchers. We all win when each side can articulate to the other's satisfaction the other's point of view.

22. TV/Web Show: "What Works"

"What Works" (or, perhaps "Best Practices") would be a three-part reality TV show that seeks to celebrate, explain, and spread ideas and solutions that achieve demonstrable results against challenges and problems of interest to viewers. Each week, "What Works" would focus on the success of an organization tackling challenges in fields such as education, health care, environment, and government.

The show will have several dimensions. People in the "best practice organization" would join people from one or two other "learning organizations" in the same field to discuss what has worked and why. The viewing audience can be invited to use 800 numbers or Web connections to pose questions. Employees from the learning organizations would declare what they aspire to achieve with what they have learned. Over time, the show could serve as a node in a growing network of participating organizations committed to identifying and achieving what works.

The test for What Works is progress not perfection. The show's producers, staff, and visitors will focus on products, services, solutions, and ideas that make a difference. The show will not be primarily about advocacy or public policy. Rather, its focus should be on performance.

23. TV Show: "Congress of Organizations"

Each television year, a group of 20 to 30 people would form a "Congress of Organizations." In the best case, actual organizations (Coke, Microsoft, GM, the FBI, Planned Parenthood, et al) would send representatives. Alternatively, the organizations would be fictional but represent real industries (e.g. "CarCo," "ComputerCo," "PharmaCo," "Crime Prevention and Prosecution Agency," "Affordable Housing and Neighborhood Revitalization Nonprofit" et al).

If participants are not from actual organizations, they would receive sufficient briefings regarding the interests of their industries as well as the full variety of concerns related to each issue/question. Participants would be instructed to be themselves—to be "real" in the sense of representing their organization and industry while simultaneously representing the public as a whole.

The Congress of Organizations will have an agenda of issues tailored to reflect actual challenges of great concern: tax policy, regulation, family leave, and so forth. Representatives would work full time for, say, eight to fourteen weeks, during which the cameras run. The footage of their efforts would then get edited and televised—as close to concurrently as possible.

During the filming, the show would invite lobbyists and other people from the various industries, as well as interested organizations, to interact and influence the participants. The intent is to create a congress of organizations that sits for a brief time and deliberates on matters of great importance—and to see what happens and learn from it.

24. Abolish Political Party Affiliations for State and Local Judges and Reward Judicial Efficiency

The rule of law is vulnerable to market forces in a world of markets, networks, and organizations. That holds as a matter of logic and experience. Today, for example, political organizations have succeeded in establishing unqualified, ideological men and women as judges in many federal, state, and local jurisdictions. Their ideologies, of course, might be trouble us. But their incompetence is frightening.

The quality of legal adjudication suffers badly when going to court approximates going to the racetrack. Yet, this kind of gambling characterizes courts run by men and women who rule by personality and ideology instead of principle and law.

Meanwhile, extreme politics are but one of the powerful market forces now distorting the rule of law. As an employment market, state and local adjudication woefully trails other legal pursuits in compensation and reward. Even federal judges barely earn as much as first-year associates of major law firms. At least however, federal judges have honorific sources of reward and better (if still not fully effective) qualification processes. State and local judges, by contrast, too often are hardly esteemed at all—in part, because, while many are dedicated and hard working, too many others flout the law and deserve condemnation instead of respect. They do not earn it.

Even these market forces are insufficient to explain the dilemma. Like other fields of expertise, the law has metastasized in complexity. Today's state and local jurists confront specialization that demands the highest levels of competence, will, and effort. The variety of issues and challenges beg for greater professionalism and for a court system that innovates in order to ensure that it provides good things to have.

The rule of law is a linchpin of market democracies. But our markets for state and local adjudication are as bad as any described by Dickens. Somehow, we must break the cycle of bad quality delivered by poor judges. One way—and it is only one way—is to abolish political party affiliations for state and local jurists while simultaneously establishing bonus compensation systems that reward efficiency (as opposed to judicial results). Many states already use bar associations in the process of selecting judges. This recommendation goes further. It demands that we recognize markets for state and local adjudication as *markets* and work to make them efficient and effective.

---

25. 360 Degree Feedback Just in Time to Vote

Tens of millions of us confront a serious ethical dilemma at the polls: choosing whether and how to vote for candidates about whom we know nothing other than party affiliation. In markets where huge majorities of voters cannot even name standing officials other than the President and their state's Governor, party affiliation—party brands and the values of those brands—take on tremendous importance. Indeed, party affiliation becomes the only information provided "just in time" for voting. Let's improve on that.

In the past decade, organizations have discovered how "360 Degree" feedback provides useful information about personal performance. The method takes its name from a circle of perspectives. It seeks feedback from bosses, subordinates, and peers—from all directions. Some organizations extend the logic to include feedback from joint venture partners, customers, vendors, and others.

Markets for government control suffer badly from poor information. State and local markets for government control could benefit, for example, if those organizations gathered "360 Degree" feedback *and published the information just in time for voting*. The voice of customers would be particularly critical in such efforts. In all likelihood, rating or grading systems would be required, in addition to permitting more specific feedback. Perhaps only the ratings or grades would get published.

At the most radical end of this suggestion, we might require voters to have read and understood this feedback as a condition of casting ballots. In any event, we assist ourselves in being more ethical voters if we find ways to inform ourselves about the performance of state and local officials prior to casting our ballots.

---

26. Opt-in State and Local Purchasing Efforts

Like corporations, several states have recognized the power of purchasing. It is a promising movement. By offering vendors the opportunity to do business with state organizations—and hundreds of thousands to millions of consumers in states—state governments position themselves to spread quality and cost advantages. They also can use purchasing power to influence how organizations blend value and values.

State purchasing efforts can establish minimum standards of ethical behavior in addition to value concerns about quality, speed, and cost. State purchasing arms can insist on some combination of information disclosure and outside audit to confirm that vendors are maintaining and improving minimum standards. States might publish the results of such disclosures and audits to consumers. States can adopt a continuous improvement philosophy regarding value and values. The minimum standards might rise over time; those vendors that go beyond the minimum might gain preferred positions.

States ought not require consumer participation; that contradicts the logic of markets. Rather, consumers should be invited to opt into such programs. States need to learn how to use marketing, advertising, and other approaches to brand their purchasing programs. States need to deliver satisfactory experiences with such programs in order to attract growing numbers of consumers.

In adopting purchasing efforts, state (and local) governments can explore new, beneficial purposes for themselves. In a world where we are consumers, investors, employees, and networkers, a state or local government that explicitly identifies and meets our needs as consumers is likely to rise in esteem and worthwhileness.

---

27. New Media: Trusted Infomediaries

Ignorance arises more from failures of information than failures of ideas. Most of the time, we must resort to a do-it-for-me approach as consumers. We have no choice but to rely on the character of organizations that provide us the material and subjective basis for life.

Our primary means for making choices is information-poor. We rely on brands, habit, and word of mouth. We trust those who sell us goods and services. We must do so. As a consequence, we too often discover failures after the fact instead of before. To some extent, this is inevitable. But, I think, it accentuates the need for what network gurus call "trusted infomediaries."

A trusted informediary is just that: an organization, network or individual who (1) is trusted and (2) provides information. *Consumer Reports* is an example of an infomediary trusted by thousands of people seeking to understand before buying.

Trusted infomediaries have certain characteristics in common other than the fact that they are trusted. Through their brand promises and brand experiences, they prove themselves objective and disinterested. It is not that they limit information "just to facts." They also provide opinions. Nevertheless, their opinions are respected because they are unbiased. For example, many trusted infomediaries explicitly list the criteria consumers might use to make choices, and then report information against those criteria.

In its best moments, the news media is a trusted infomediary. During the immediate aftermath of the September 11th terrorist attacks, for example, local news media in New York worked hard to provide viewers information they could trust and rely on. But, for a variety of reasons, the news media has few "best moments." We need trusted infomediaries, and we need them urgently in our new world of markets, networks, organizations, friends, and families.

Index

A

Active investors, 229
The Adventures of Huckleberry Finn
  (Twain), 134, 135
Advertising
  exaggeration in, 117–18
  and ideas, 117
Alcohol, drinking and driving, 52–53
American Dream, 248–50
American Express, 188–89
American Red Cross, 103
Annual report to people of enterprise, 255
Antidiscrimination laws, 192
Anti-drug campaigns, 54–57
Areopagitica (Milton), 112, 113
Aristotle, 72, 114
Arthur Andersen, 138
St. Augustine, 30
Autarky, 242–45
Automobile industry, 117, 153
Automobile insurance industry, 98–99
Automobiles, drinking and driving, 52–53

B

The Balanced Scorecard (Kaplan &
  Norton), 38–39, 41
Beanie Babies, 134–35, 233
Bentham, Jeremy, 199, 210, 217
Berlin, Isaiah, 144–45
Biotechnology industry, 99
Bowling Alone (Putnam), 141–42, 145
Brain capacity, increase in, 129–30

Brands, 132–39
  governance in organizations and, 204
  values committee of board of directors/
    trustees, 255–56
British Petroleum (BP), 178
Bronx Education Services (BES), 225–27
Budweiser, 107
Bureaucracy and governance in organiza-
  tions, 193–97
Bush, George, 44
Bush, George W., 45, 53
Buy in, 178–80

C

Capital markets, 98
  derivatives, 222
  failure of, 221–25
  government action in, 230–32
  success of, 221–25
Catholic Church
  and Galileo, 51
  sex abuse scandals, 30–31, 53
Celebrity, 135–39
Censorship, 112–14
Census tracking, 265
Character, 132
Cheney, Dick, 53
Children, anti-drug campaigns geared
  towards, 54–57
Christensen, Clayton, 228
Citizen, role of, 86–88
Citizenship, 28
The City of God (St. Augustine), 30

Civil society
  collectivities of I's, 146–47, 155–56
  customer, role of, 155
  individual liberties, 142–44
  minorities, tyranny of, 156–57
  proceduralism, 147, 152
  shared fate and, 150–55
  thick we's, 145–46, 148–49, 151–54
  war protests, 141–42
Clinton, Bill, 44, 53
Clinton, Hillary, 136
Cloning, 128–29
Coase, Ronald, 267
Collaborative filtering, 115–16
Collectivities of I's
  in civil society, 146–47, 155–56
  defined, 6
  thick we's compared, 239–42
Commodities, 116
Common good
  defined, 6
  in family, 213–14
Community
  continuity, challenge of, 168–69
  natural we's, 161
  organizations as, 162–65
  overview, 159–62
  shared paths in, 168–69
Community and Society (Tonnies), 160–62
Companionship, 214
Compaq, 178
Connectors (in relationships), 23
Consumers
  choices as, 88–89
  harm to, correction of, 191
  role of, 78
Corporate purchasing on behalf of employees and their families, 256–57
Corporations, 226
The Corrosion of Character (Sennett), 201
Customer
  participation in board of directors/trustees, 258–59
  role of, 155
Cybernia, 19–20

D

Declaration of Independence, 94
Democracy, 8–9
  market democracies, 176
  overview, 176–77
  voting, 57–60, 176–77, 179–80
Democracy in America (de Tocqueville), 148–49, 173
Democracy's Discontent (Sandel), 142, 145
Democratic values essential to performance of organization, 245–47
Derivatives, 222
De Tocqueville, Alexis, 148–49, 151, 173, 176, 239
Deutsch, David, 51
Digital divide, 223
Directors and governance in organizations, 191–92
The Discipline of Market Leaders (Treacy & Wiersema), 37
Disenfranchisement, 174–75
Dissent, 113–14, 118–19, 241
Division in value and values, 35–39
Donne, John, 238
Drinking and driving, 52–53
Drucker, Peter, 41
Dynamic deductibility, 229–30, 263

E

Economic values, 11
Education
  public high schools with full-time policemen, 72
  schools, 181
Employees, 180
  governance in organizations and, 203
  harm to, correction of, 191
  oversight/review of lobbyists, 257–58
  overview, 85–86
  participation in board of directors/trustees, 258–59
  participation in organization charity, 261–62
  role of, 78
Enron, 84–85, 209–10, 216
Environmental values, 11

Ethical challenges, 4
Ethical scorecard, 251–54
The Ethics of Memory (Margalit), 6–7, 12
Etzioni, Amitai, 150–51, 153
Exaggeration in advertising, 117–18
Exhortation, 54
External forces in governance in organizations, 192
Exxon, 138

F

The Fabric of Reality (Deutsch), 51
Families
 common good in, 213–14
 individual liberties and, 142–43
 role sets, 83–84
 shared paths in, 66–67
 shared roles and, 80
 shared values in, 11, 88
Fast cycle time, 127
Fast food industry, 198–99
FBI (Federal Bureau of Investigation), 134, 138–39, 178, 216
The Fifth Discipline (Senge), 37
Flash bulb memories, 8
Ford, Henry, 116, 194
Forward auditing of risks, 260–61
Found a Problem Solvers Party, 265–66
Foundations, 226
14th amendment, 143
Free press, from organizational newsletter to, 262
Friends/friendships
 shared paths and, 66–67
 shared roles and, 80
 shared values in, 88
 six degrees of integration, 23–27
Fundamentalists, 12–13
The Future and Its Enemies (Postrel), 12

G

Galileo, 51, 114
General Motors, 36–37, 243
Gergen, Kenneth, 238
Giddens, Anthony, 237
Gladwell, Malcolm, 23
Globalization, 247–50

Global village, 22
Gore, Al, 44–45
Governance in organizations
 brand and, 204
 bureaucracy and, 193–97
 directors and, 191–92
 employees and, 203
 external forces in, 192
 hierarchy and, 200–202
 internal forces in, 192–93
 overview, 187–93
 performance and, 202–5
 reintegration of labor and expertise, 195–99
 shared paths and, 199–202
 teams and, 200–202
Government action in capital markets, 230–32
Government organizations, 226
 requiring government organizations to report on vision, strategy, and values, 266–67
Graduation Pledge Alliance, 46
Greater good
 defined, 6
 thick we's and, 242–45
Grumbling Hive (Mandeville), 93

H

Handy, Charles, 219–20, 232
Happiness, 207–10
 in organizations, 214–17
 thick we's and, 214–17
Hewlett-Packard, 178
Hierarchy, 200–202, 245–47
Holistic medicine, 108
Human-interest stories, 42–43
Hussein, Saddam, 242–43

I

IBM, 133
Ideas
 advertising and, 117
 censorship and, 112–14
 dissent and, 113–14
 individuals and influence of, 119–23
 networks, 127

organizations, 126–27
orthodoxy, 113–14
overview, 107–12
popular opinion, 113
responses to, 135
shared ideas. *See* shared ideas
Ignorance, 131–32
Individual liberties
civil society, 142–44
family, 142–43
marriage, 142–43
value of individual liberties compared
to value of individual security,
211–12
Individual responsibility and opportunity,
231
Individual rights, 66
Industries, change occurring for, 10
Industry betas, 99
Innovation, 228
The Innovator's Dilemma (Christensen),
228
The Insider (film), 31
Intelligence, moral obligation for, 32–33
Internal forces in governance in organiza-
tions, 192–93
International Chamber of Commerce, 247
In the Age of the Smart Machine (Zuboff),
198
Investor
described, 93
harm to, correction of, 191

J

Jefferson, Thomas, 94, 114, 267
Judicial efficiency, reward of, 272–73
Jury trials of fact inside organizations, 257
"Just Say No" anti-drug campaign, 54–57

K

Kaczynski, Theodore, 135
Katzenbach, Jon, 160, 200
K-Mart, 137
Knowledge
acceleration of, 129–30
surveys of voters for information only,
267–68

L

Labor and expertise, reintegration of, 195–
99
Lane, Robert, 209
Lay, Ken, 209–10
Leaders of organizations, 237–38
Legal values, 11
Lemon laws, 192
Letterman, David, 136
Leveraged buy out firms, 219
Lewinsky, Monica, 53
Liberties, individual. *See* individual liber-
ties
On Liberty (Mill), 113, 120
Lincoln, Abraham, 249
Lindh, John Walker, 13
Lobbyists, establish a third legislative
house with, 264
*The Loss of Happiness in Market Democ-
racies* (Lane), 209

M

Machiavelli, Nicolo, 235–36
Maine, Henry, 165
Mandeville, Bernard, 93–95
Many-to-many phenomena, 29
Margalit, Avishai, 6–7, 8, 12, 239
Market democracies, 176
Market idolatry, 231
Market of one, 125–26
Markets, 7–13
individualism in, 66
individual values in, 88
localized activities now considered, 31
and many-to-many phenomena, 29
market of one, 125–26
mass customization, 125–26
politics as market, 31–32
products and, 125–26
role sets, 82–84
services and, 125–26
for spiritual commitment, 30–31
Marriage, individual liberties and, 142–43
Mass customization, 125–26
McKinsey & Company, 97
Mead, Margaret, 122–23
Media organizations, 248

division in value and values by, 42–45
Medical values, 11
Memetics, 111
Michigan, University of, 143
Microsoft, 29
Mid-level social formations
   defined, 6
   organizations as, 239–40
Mill, John Stuart, 113, 118, 120
Milton, John, 112, 113, 114, 118
Minimum values standards in qualifying
   vendors, 259–60
Minorities, tyranny of, 156–57
Modern Times (film), 198, 202
Moral obligation for intelligence, 32–33
Moral relativism, 211–13
Mortgage-backed securities, 222

N

Natural we's, 161
Negative liberty, 144–46
Networks, 7–13
   ideas and, 127
   individual values in, 88
   and many-to-many phenomena, 29
   products and, 127
   role sets, 83–84
   services and, 127
   six degrees of separation and, 22–23
New media: trusted infomediaries, 274–75
Nike, 133
Nonprofit organizations, 225–33

O

Organizations, 7–13
   buy in, 178–80
   as communities, 162–65
   democratic values essential to perfor-
     mance of, 245–47
   division of labor in, 40–41
   employees in, 180
   fast cycle time, 127
   governing. *See* governance in organiza-
     tions
   happiness in, pursuit of, 214–17
   hierarchy, 245–47
   ideas and, 126–27

leaders of, 237–38
and many-to-many phenomena, 29
as mid-level social formations, 239–40
overview, 86
performance of organization, democratic values essential to, 245–47
products and, 126–27
purposes in, 165–67
reintegration of value and values in, 47
role sets, 83–84
services and, 126–27
shared ideas and, 114–19
shared paths, 175
shared purposes in, 165–67
shared values in, 88
thick we's and, 169–71
Orthodoxy, 113–14

P

Panopticon (Bentham), 199
Paradise Lost (Milton), 112
Past, values from our, 11
Performance
   democratic values essential to, 245–47
   governance in organizations and, 202–5
Pharmaceutical companies, 126, 130–31
Place, 19–22
Plato, 65, 143
Polis, 173–74, 181–85, 190
Political party affiliations for state and
   local judges, abolishing, 272–73
Political values, 11, 39–40
Politics, 31–32, 189–90
Popular opinion, 113
Positive liberty, 145–46
Postrel, Virginia, 12
Poverty, 223–24
The Prince (Machiavelli), 235–36
Private capital leagues for nonprofits, 263–
   64
Problem definition, 188
Problem solving
   overview, 187–89
   problem definition, 188
Proceduralism, 147, 152
Pro-choice advocates, 53
Products and services
   markets, 125–26

networks, 127
organizations, 126–27
scope of, 128
Pro-life advocates, 53
"Proof of concept" grants, 227
Purpose, 27–33
    acting in real world of, 235–39
    blending value and values in world of,
        247–50
    value shaped by, 9
Putnam, Robert, 141–42, 145, 149–51, 153

R

Racial profiling, 60
Reagan, Nancy, 54
Real world, actions having consequence
    in, 235–39
Red Cross, 44
Reengineering the Corporation (Hammer
    & Champy), 37
Relationships. See also families; friends/
    friendships
    shared relationships founded in shared
        fates, 61
    six degrees of integration, 23–27
    six degrees of separation, 22–27
Religious values, 11
The Republic (Plato), 65, 143
Responsibility, 131–32
Retired people, shared paths and, 68
Risk-adjusted cash flow, 97–101
Role sets, 81–84

S

Sandel, Michael J., 142, 143, 144, 145,
    146, 147–51, 153, 154, 250
Sara Lee, 96–97, 101, 102
The Saturated Self (Gergen), 238
Schools, 181
Schumpeter, Joseph, 31
In Search of Excellence (Thomas &
    Peters), 37
SEC, 138
Sennett, Richard, 201–2
September 11th terrorist attacks, 230,
    247–50
Services. See products and services

Shared fates
    civil society and, 150–55
    defined, 5
    shared relationships founded in, 61
Shared ideas, 61–62
    action and how shared ideas influence
        shared values, 110–11
    belief and how shared ideas influence
        shared values, 110–11
    citizen as, 87–88
    comprehension and how shared ideas
        influence shared values, 110
    defined, 5
    exposure and how shared ideas influ-
        ence shared values, 110
    organizations and, 114–19
Shared paths, 239
    choosing, 73–74
    community, 168–69
    defined, 5
    duration of, 74
    enforceability of, 71
    governance in organizations, 199–202
    intergenerational shared paths, 68
    negatives of, 71
    overview, 66–71
    presence in, 73–74
    retired people and, 68
    shared values in, 70–71
    specific aims and objectives in, 73
    values and, 69
Shared purposes, 61–62, 165–67
Shared relationships founded in shared
    fates, 61
Shared resources, 61
Shared roles, 61
    defined, 5
    overview, 77–80
Shared values
    defined, 5
    shared paths and, 70–71
    six degrees of separation and, 23–27
    sources of, 60–63
Shareholders, 229
Shareholder value, 41, 97
    managing, 101–4
    patterns of risks to, 98–99
    risks to, 98–101
Shareholder value

fundamentalism, 219–21
Simpson, O.J., 136
Six degrees of integration, 23–27
Six degrees of separation, 22–27
Skilling, Jeff, 209–10
Small towns, 231–32
Smith, Adam, 93–94, 96, 101, 103–4
Smith, Roger, 36, 243
Social formations, 6
Social values, 11, 39
Societies, 160
Socrates, 65
The Sopranos (television show), 31
The Spirit of Community (Etzioni), 150
Spiritual commitment, market for, 30–31
Stanley Tools, 138
Start-ups, 227
State and local purchasing efforts, 274
Statements of Values, 39–40
Stewart, Martha, 137
Stock options, 222
Suggestions
    abolish political party affiliations for
        state and local judges and reward
        judicial efficiency, 272–73
    annual report to people of enterprise,
        255
    brand values committee of board of
        directors/trustees, 255–56
    census tracking: count organizational
        participation in addition to jobs, 265
    corporate purchasing on behalf of
        employees and their families, 256–
        57
    customer and employee participation
        in board of directors/trustees, 258–
        59
    dynamic deductibility: creating effi-
        cient capital markets for nonprofits,
        263
    employee oversight/review of lobbyists,
        257–58
    employee participation in organization
        charity, 261–62
    establish a third legislative house: lob-
        byists, 264
    ethical scorecard, 251–54
    forward auditing of risks, 260–61
    found a Problem Solvers Party, 265–66

jury trials of fact inside organizations,
    257
knowledge surveys of voters for infor-
    mation only, 267–68
minimum values standards in qualify-
    ing vendors, 259–60
new media: trusted infomediaries, 274–
    75
from organizational newsletter to free
    press, 262
private capital leagues for nonprofits,
    263–64
require government organizations to
    report on vision, strategy, and val-
    ues, 266–67
state and local purchasing efforts, 274
360 degree feedback just in time to
    vote, 273–74
TV/radio show: "Civil Disagreement,"
    270
TV show: "Congress of Organizations,"
    271–72
TV/Webcast show: "Brand Trials," 269–
    70
TV/Webcast show: "Brand Values,"
    268–69
TV/Web show: "What Works," 270–71
SUVs (Sport Utility Vehicle), 89, 117

T

Taliban, 13
Taylor, Robert, 127
Teams and governance in organizations,
    200–202
Technological values, 11
Technology, place and, 21–22
Telecommunications industry, 100
Terrorism, 230, 247–50
Texaco, 138
The Theory of Moral Sentiments (Smith),
    94
Thick we's, 145–46, 148–49, 151–54
    collectivities of I's compared, 239–42
    defined, 5
    greater good of markets, nations, net-
        works, friends, and families; linking
        common good of thick we's with,
        242–45

happiness and, 214–17
Margalit's views on, 7
organizations and, 169–71
Thin we's
defined, 5
Margalit's views on, 7
3M Corporation, 167, 170–71
The Tipping Point (Gladwell), 23
Tonnies, Ferdinand, 160–62, 164–65, 168
Trends, alarming, 42–43
Trilling, Lionel, 32–33
TV/radio show: "Civil Disagreement," 270
TV show: "Congress of Organizations,"
271–72
TV/Web shows
"Brand Trials," 269–70
"Brand Values," 268–69
"What Works," 270–71
Twain, Mark, 134, 135
Two Concepts of Liberty (Berlin), 144–45

U

Unhappiness, singular value leading to,
11–12
Union Vale, New York, 182–85
Utilitarianism, 210–13

V

*Valuation: Measuring and Managing the
Value of Companies* (Copeland), 101
Value
divergence between values and, 2–3
overview, 1–2
types of, 2
Values
conflicts in, 84–85
divergence between value and, 2–3
explanation of, 51–64
from our past, 11
overview, 1–2
shared paths and, 69
as tool to create value, 37–38
types of, 2
Veblen, Thorstein, 116
Volunteers, 85–86
Voting, 57–60, 176–77, 179–80
360 degree feedback just in time to
vote, 273–74

W

Wall Street (film), 35, 101
War protests, 141–42
The Wealth of Nations (Smith), 94, 96,
103–4
Weber, Max, 194, 195, 198
Weight Watchers, 117–18, 120–22
"What's a Business For?" (Handy), 219,
232
Wilson, Charles E., 36
The Wisdom of Teams (Smith & Katzen-
bach), 160, 200
Woods, Tiger, 135–36
World of places, 6
World of purposes, 6

X

Xerox, 125
Xerox Palo Alto Research Center, 127

Z

Zuboff, Shoshana, 198

Brave New Wealthy World

Brave New Wealthy World demonstrates how today's international financial arrangements are spreading prosperity and well-being more widely than ever before—and what it'll take to spread the wealth to virtually every corner of the Earth. John C. Edmunds proposes a new symbiotic relationship between rich and poor countries that offers powerful benefits to both. He demonstrates why "first world" investors will increasingly depend upon growth in emerging economies to achieve the returns they need and offers a blueprint for transforming emerging nations' financial systems into powerful drivers of economic growth. This book cuts through the conventional wisdom and ideologies that hide the true implications of globalization—and reveals a pragmatic path to a hopeful future.

© 2003, 256 pp., ISBN 0130381608, $24.95

Money Changes Everything

While others debate or wring their hands, globalization has triumphed—and it is delivering unprecedented social and economic wealth to billions of people, and it is transforming human needs and values worldwlde. In *Money Changes Everthing,* Peter Marber proves once and for all that globalization is in fact improving life expectancy, literacy and education rates; extending leisure time; and delivering a broad new prosperity that touches most people and most societies. He shows the profound implications to human society, as new material and experiential desires increasingly replace the fight for survival.

© 2003, 272 pp., ISBN 0130654809, $24.95

For more information on our business titles, visit www.ft-ph.com